THE GOOD LIFE . . . or what's left of it

HARPER'S
MAGAZINE
PRESS

Edited by Fred Feldkamp
*Mixture for Men*

the posthumous works of Will Cuppy
*The Decline and Fall of Practically Everybody*
*How to Get from January to December*

# THE GOOD LIFE

# ... or what's left of it

## Phyllis & Fred Feldkamp

———⟨∞⟩———

*being a recounting of the pleasures
of the senses that contribute to the
enjoyment of life in France*

———⟨∞⟩———

HARPER'S MAGAZINE PRESS

Published in Association with Harper & Row

New York

The pieces listed below originally appeared, in slightly different form, in the following:

"Chantilly: Cité du Cheval," by Fred Feldkamp, *The New Yorker,* June 6, 1970; "The World's Most Exclusive Club," by Phyllis Feldkamp, *Horizon,* Autumn, 1965; "Deauville: A Resort for All Eras," by Fred Feldkamp, *The New Yorker,* August 14, 1971; "Paul Poiret—and the Age of Gold Lamé," by Phyllis Feldkamp, *Horizon,* Summer, 1972; "An Evening at the de Gaulles'," by Phyllis Feldkamp, *The Atlantic Monthly,* May, 1967; and "And on the Seventh Day, They Play the Tiercé" (under the title "The Tiercé"), by Fred Feldkamp, *Harper's Magazine,* January, 1972.

FIRST EDITION

STANDARD BOOK NUMBER: 06-122480-4

LIBRARY OF CONGRESS CATALOG CARD NUMBER: 72-79714

*Designed by Gloria Adelson*

*For Phoebe*

# Contents

A section of illustrations follows page 142

# Acknowledgments

The authors wish to thank those who, wittingly or unwittingly, assisted in the preparation of this book. Special thanks are due to William Shawn, editor of *The New Yorker,* Joseph J. Thorndike of *Horizon,* and Miguel Clément; to Robert Shnayerson, editor of *Harper's Magazine,* who provided the initial momentum behind the planning of this book, and to Peter Mollman and to Lesley Krauss, who took it from there.

# *Introduction*

There are a number of ways to collaborate on a book, even for a husband and wife. One is for one person to do all the work, with the second person criticizing the result. This method was ruled out from the start. Another is for both to devote themselves to the same subjects, and then come together and somehow merge the individual efforts. That, too, was discarded as a possible threat to the peace. A third approach is for each person to write every other word. But this would be a time-consuming business, and would require working in close proximity. Besides, one author's follow-up word might well not complement the preceding one.

That left the plan for each author to do half the chapters in the book. This one seemed eminently sensible: an equal division of effort, the possibility of working at arm's length, and the satisfying feeling—for each author—of having written a book while actually having done only half the work. (This introduction, by the way, is writing itself.)

So, on the theory that half a book is just as good as one, each of us went to work on a general subject in which we had jointly become interested during a twelve-year residence: France.

The French have a remarkably varied collection of attributes, which surface in a bewildering array: by turn exasperating, disagreeable, polite to a superlative degree, avaricious, generous, short-tempered, witty, accommodating, serious, gay. A few generalizations are possible: most *fonctionnaires* (those benighted types who work in post-offices or other municipal posts, with a smidgin of authority) tend to be completely negative—before one even poses a question, the *fonctionnaire* is already shaking his or her head from side to side; the package you wish to mail is two *centimètres* too wide, and must be repacked (regulations), or the postcard you have just written is unacceptable because you allowed a word in the message to slip over to the half of the card allotted to the name and address of the recipient. France is the only country we've encountered so far where they charge different postage rates for postcards to the same place, depending on the number of words in the message. Yes, they revel in rules and regulations and expressing their authority, yet the police—unless you are breaking the law or demonstrating without a permit—are among the most polite and helpful anywhere. Some find the French too exasperating: one friend, who had lived in France for some years, summed up his experience with: "France is a great country—too good for the French."

Yet it is the French, with their dazzling variety of qualities, who have made the country what it is—one of the most agreeable and stimulating places to live in, anywhere. After two devastating world wars (and a series of earlier conflicts, including the Franco-Prussian War) fought on their soil, and the debilitating Nazi occupation of their country for four years, it is perhaps understandable that the French feel protective about money and their physical possessions; one rather wealthy Frenchman we know becomes ill when he is forced to write a check, even for such a small item as an electricity bill—a chore he postpones until the very last possible second before the current is cut off. After writing the check, he usually repairs to his bed to recover. Balzac did capture the essential French character.

But in France—in addition to the greatest wines, great cheeses, truffles, talented hairdressers, spectacular horse racing, superb couture creations, incomparable cuisine, magnificent châteaus, gardens, and furniture—there is good conversation, even with shopkeepers, of a sort largely unknown in the United States, where what passes for "conversation" is exclusively concerned with sex, in one form or another, sports, of one kind or another, the weather, and the obsession with making more money. (The French may well be the most money-conscious nation in the world, but they don't talk about it all the time.)

Except for the popularity among a small segment of the population for "snack" bars and *le hot dog*—a relatively recent development pretty much limited to Paris—the French still enjoy leisurely meals; even those *citoyens* with small incomes practice the "art of living." A Frenchman would be shocked at the suggestion of "moonlighting" to increase his income if it meant giving up his accustomed pattern of life.

Though the French students at the lycées still learn by rote, and must memorize just about everything they are told in class, the schools are much tougher and better than the U.S. counterparts; it would be a national scandal if a French student were found unable to read properly.

For the rest, there is a refreshing paucity of crime and dope addiction, even in the large cities (in France, aside from hunters, only the police have guns); the climate is, generally speaking, easier on the system than that on the East Coast of the United States, with no extremes of heat and cold (summer humidity à la New York and Washington is unknown); the French are tidy—they do not litter—and they have taste.

On the other hand, trying to use the telephone in France will send your blood pressure soaring. As a means of communication, it is regarded with mistrust, and with good reason. We found that the chance of completing calls within France itself was minimal. As for calls outside the country, they required persistence and steady nerves. One long-distance operator at Saint-Malo, in Brittany, stubbornly resisted the request to put through a call to a small town in England, and it was only after five days of negotiations that she finally broke down and agreed to connect us with *le numero quatre* at Bishop's Stortford—*"B" comme Bernard, "I" comme Isidore, "S" comme Suzanne, "H" comme Hortense, "O" comme Olivier,* and so on. In time, automatic dialing has brought some progress and now, while you may never get through to a French town or village seventeen miles away, you can reach the principal cities of West Germany, Denmark, Belgium, or England without argument—in fact, almost any country except Spain, where the telephone system may be even more archaic than that in France.

While the workings of the telephone are a source of puzzlement, we found many other aspects of living difficult to understand during our twelve years' residence and in subsequent visits. One hears little of *liberté, égalité,* and *fraternité* these days in France. The Revolution, far from being the kindred struggle for freedom that we, as Americans born and bred—and carefully inoculated with the spirit of '76 and of '89 as well— thought it was, is treated in French schools as a somewhat embarrassingly gory passage in history, not nearly as glorious as the kings who came before and the emperors and the imperial de Gaulle who came afterward.

Thoughts of the Monarchy—or, as some put it, the Father Figure— have never really disappeared in "democratic" France. On television quiz programs, contestants receive ten points for the right answer to a question like: Which king's mistress was Diane de Poitiers? There is no denying that a strong residual respect for the Monarchy lingers on. One can find Frenchmen who cite *la loi Salique,* an ancient barbarian law relating to the succession, and argue that all the Comte de Paris, the pretender to the throne, would have to do to rule France today would be to take his claim to court. What with one thing and another, ancestor worship and *la Gloire* included, one wonders why the French ever bothered to have a revolution in the first place.

But no changes in power seem to affect the French very much. Regardless of who is ruling France, the *fonctionnaires* carry on imperturbably with their tape measures and rulers, and the telephone operators—when they are needed—still give everyone a hard time. The good life, happily, continues in an equally undiminished state as well.

Phyllis and Fred Feldkamp

New York, N.Y.

PHYLLIS FELDKAMP wrote the following pieces: "Rococo Is Relevant, Marquetry Is Meaningful . . ."; "The World's Most Exclusive Club"; "The Great Caréme . . . He Built a Better Cream Puff"; "Paul Poiret—and the Age of Gold Lamê"; "A Nation of Coiffeurs"; "An Evening at the de Gaulles'."

FRED FELDKAMP wrote: "Chantilly: Cité du Cheval"; "Of Curds and Whey"; "À la Vôtre!"; "Deauville: A Resort for All Eras"; "The Heart of the Matter"; "Longchamp, the Bois, and the Arc de Triomphe"; and "And on the Seventh Day, They Play the Tiercé."

# Chantilly: Cité du Cheval

---∞---

In Chantilly, the four-footed thoroughbreds have perpetual priority, with the result that motorists passing through town are obliged to stop, more often than not, to allow a file of nervous race horses to cross the road for their workouts.

---∞---

For eleven and a half months each year, Chantilly which lies in the valley of the river Oise, twenty-five miles north of Paris, and whose name has associations with perfume, lace, and sweet whipped cream, is a somnolent town of some eight thousand inhabitants. Then, on two Sundays in June, with the running of two of the most important races on the European continent, the town assumes the aspect of Lourdes on the anniversary of the miracle, for Chantilly is also the most extensive and best-equipped center in the world for the training of thoroughbred horses. On those Sundays, thousands of the faithful make the pilgrimage, and from early morning the town's streets are choked with all manner of vehicles, its restaurants and hotels are filled up, and even walking space is at a premium. And during the week preceding each of the two racing Sundays a small group of knowledgeable followers of thoroughbreds makes the trip out before dawn to be on hand for the training, which is conducted—as it is all year—on what is known as the Terrain des Aigles, an immense preserve of racing strips, of both turf and sandy soil, surrounded by wooded forest trails that extend for miles.

The two races are the Prix du Jockey Club, or French Derby, for three-year-old colts and fillies, and the Prix de Diane, or French Oaks, for three-year-old fillies. Each of the race days attracts not only hordes of picnickers but some of the most opulently dressed people in Europe, and the legend has arisen that—in terms of outdoor spectacles, at least—Chantilly on these two Sundays is Western Europe's last outpost of true elegance. Whether these chic occasions are truly the last pocket of the sybaritic life in Europe or, as one observer put it, "the last desperate splashing of a sinking society," the fact is that the two Sundays in June have acquired through the years a special significance for lovers of the good life, for enthusiasts of the best horse racing to be found in Europe and perhaps in the world, and for those wistful souls who yearn for a display of nineteenth-century manners to brighten up their lives. It is true that many European members of the horse-racing fraternity, if they were forced to make a choice, would select the Prix de l'Arc de Triomphe—contested at Longchamp, in the Bois de Boulogne, in Paris, on the first Sunday of October—as the outstanding race of the year. But for some discerning followers of the European racing scene the tradition-laden Prix du Jockey Club has a special cachet.

My acquaintance with the Prix du Jockey Club and the Prix de Diane and the festivities surrounding their fortnight goes back only four years, but in that time the attraction that "the Chantilly season" holds for me has become incredibly strong. Last spring, having returned to the United States after a stretch of twelve years in France, I tried to convince myself that it was absurd to travel seven thousand miles to see a couple of horse races, but I failed. I reasoned that it wasn't just the races; spending two weeks in the pleasant country town of Chantilly was easily worth the trip, for a stay in Chantilly gives one an extraordinary feeling of well-being. Accordingly, I arrived in Chantilly on a Sunday, in time to catch the final week of workouts before the Prix du Jockey Club. I had arranged to stay in the Hôtel du Château, a small inn that overlooks the backstretch of the Hippodrome des Condé, where the two classics are run. The inn is similar to many such rural structures in France—three stories, with the first devoted to a restaurant-bar. This restaurant-bar, however, is populated for fifty weeks of the year largely by a dog and twenty-seven birds, including an aging parrot who has mastered the first phrase of the "Colonel Bogey March." Otherwise, except for the presence of a few more small children than usual, endlessly playing ball and shouting, there seemed to me when I arrived to be very little difference between the Hôtel du Château and a thousand other French inns.

The *patron*, a M. Moulin, is an affable gentleman whose motto, he told me on the first day of our acquaintance, is "There's a solution to everything." To have fallen in with such a positive-thinking Frenchman was a stroke of luck, for I foresaw various problems—like waking at four in the morning in order to get to the training grounds at five for the special gallops preceding the big races. M. Moulin suggested that I buy a *réveil* at a *bijouterie* just down the street. The problem of the hotel's front door, which was naturally locked at that hour, was solved by a promise to leave me the hotel's only front-door key. But, for all his good intentions, Moulin forgot, and the next morning it was necessary to wake Madame la Patronne, an imposing figure of a woman; rousing her from a sound sleep at 4:30 A.M. is not something that one would choose to do under normal circumstances. She proved quite gracious, though, even favoring me with a rare smile as I stumbled out into the early dawn.

Up to that point, my knowledge of the accomplishments and the potential of the French three-year-olds had been based solely on the racing results in the airmail edition of *Le Figaro,* which ordinarily goes on sale in New York the morning after the day of its publication in Paris. Unfortunately, the information one can glean from this simple listing—the names of the first, second, and third finishers, of their jockeys, and of the owners of the winners, together with the distance between horses at the finish—is not enough to give one any idea of the condition of the horses that will start in the Jockey Club or how likely they are to make a peak effort in the race. Thus, I was beginning my studies with no preconceived notions.

The town of Chantilly wakes up well before dawn, and at four-forty, sitting in a café drinking strong French coffee, I was already confronted with the business of the day. Resident jockeys and apprentices, and also visitors to town, whether they had taken the precaution of spending the night in Chantilly or had driven out from Paris in the middle of the night, were being offered a choice of *Paris-Turf* or *Sport-Complet,* the French racing papers, with their coffee and croissants.

The Terrain des Aigles, across the Paris-Brussels railroad line from the center of town, is a verdant domain of 220 hectares, or 543.62 acres, on which are a number of racing strips—one strip fine-grained sandy soil and the others of flawlessly conditioned turf. Adjoining this preserve are some eighty kilometers of wooded trails and a succession of well-kept stables, usually attached to the homes of the trainers. Chantilly's normal equine population is three thousand, and it is looked after by about a thousand people—trainers, jockeys, veterinarians, grooms, and exercise boys and girls. The remainder of the town's human population contributes in one way or another to the well-being of horse racing, and so enables the Chantilly Chamber of Commerce to claim that everyone in the community works for the improvement of the breed. Bordering the Aigles is Route Nationale 16, which is the principal road for motorists driving from Paris to Amiens or Dunkerque. In Chantilly, the four-footed thoroughbreds have perpetual priority, with the result that motorists passing through town are obliged to stop, more often than not, to allow a file of nervous race horses to cross the road for their workouts. But not even the most impatient driver seems to resent this wait, the spectacle being agreeable. Besides, all motorists have been warned by a roadside sign at the town limits that this is "Chantilly: Cité du Cheval."

My visit to the training preserve was made in a cloudless dawn, with a temperature slightly higher than average for Chantilly in June, but not high enough, I thought, to interfere with the horses' comfort. There was no hint of fog or mist, such as often gives the Terrain des Aigles an eerie quality in the half-light before dawn. As always, I found it inspiring to walk out into that immaculately kept preserve at daybreak; it has a certain pristine aura, which, combined with the sight of magnificent, carefully groomed thoroughbreds galloping by, and a silence broken only by the sound of hoofs thudding into the turf, produces a feeling of purification and renewal not far removed—at least for the lover of thoroughbreds—from the emotions that a visiting priest might experience upon entering Chartres Cathedral for the first time and gazing at the sunlight that streams through the stained-glass windows and transfers their patterns onto the pews and the ancient stone floor.

It seemed almost sacrilegious to break the silence when I encountered, halfway along the Piste Ronde—a curving swath of perfectly conditioned green turf, with a sandy strip along its border, stretching two and a half miles along the northern periphery of the training ground—a white-haired man named Willy Head, who is the *doyen* of the group of trainers resident in Chantilly. He was seated on his gray hack Grisous, and he looked just as fit and alert as he had the year before. Head is the paterfamilias of one of about a dozen families of English origin that have lived in Chantilly since the days of Lord Henry Seymour, a French-born Englishman who in the eighteen-thirties began the large-scale importation of English thoroughbreds for the improvement of the French breed, quartering them at Chantilly. The descendants of the first lot of British

6

trainers and handlers have continued to live in Chantilly and care for the Chantilly horses, giving the town an English flavor. Today, it is possible to conduct any kind of business transaction, from ordering a ham sandwich to buying a horse, in English. Until the retirement, five and a half years ago, of Percy Carter, there had been Carters training and riding at Chantilly in an unbroken succession since Percy's great-grand-father Richard Carter and his brother Thomas came from England with Lord Seymour's thoroughbred stock. Percy ended his career at the close of the 1964 season, and relinquished his house, Mill Cottage, to Head, who is a relative by marriage. (Percy's grandfather's sister married a British trainer, Tom Jennings, whose daughter married Willy Head. Percy himself, who is a widower, now lives in an apartment near the Aigles.) Just before dawn every day but Sunday, three generations of Heads—Willy, his son Alec, and Alec's son Freddy—customarily report to the Aigles for work, along with some fifty other trainers, several hundred jockeys and exercise boys, and almost the total equine population.

I joined Willy as his charges were returning at a slow walk from their morning exercise, and he ventured a few opinions on training in Chantilly. "This training ground, the Aigles, makes things much easier for the trainer than they are in most places," he said. "Everything is so well organized, for one thing. I have sixty-six horses in training right now, and—like all the other trainers here who have more than just a few horses—I have split my horses into three lots. The rotation of the training time in a particular place is carefully planned. And, of course, the *pistes* are maintained in perfect condition. Also, here at Chantilly I can walk out the back door of my house and I'm at the stables, and the horses can move right out onto the Aigles. In the summer, I can even schedule a special workout for four in the morning if I want, and that's what I did today. I've trained here for only two years—since moving from Maisons-Laffitte—but I lived in this town as a boy. In fact, I was born here, on January 21, 1890. My father, who was also named William Head, was up on the winner in an important hurdles race at Auteuil, in Paris, that day. In my youth, I rode the jumps at Auteuil—until I grew too heavy. My sons Peter and Alec were both jockeys before they became trainers. And now my grandson Freddy is carrying on the family tradition."

Willy's horses, who had been walking slowly in a circle, were now cooled off sufficiently to return to the barns, so I bade him au revoir, but

I carefully abstained from wishing him good luck in the Prix du Jockey Club, for in Chantilly that is regarded as bad luck.

Willy Head, along with some other trainers, sometimes uses a stopwatch to clock two-year-olds, but wouldn't think of clocking classic horses of three years and up. The training of thoroughbreds in France differs from the system in use in the United States, where the horses are usually run singly and their form and speed tested against a stopwatch. The custom at Chantilly and at other French training centers is to match two or three stablemates against one another. In some cases, a candidate for an important race is worked out behind a "leader," whom he is supposed to pass in a burst of speed at the finish of the trial run, and the candidate's fitness is determined by the ease with which he disposes of the leader at the vital moment.

Dawn was beginning to suffuse the Aigles with a golden glow as other trainers—Charles (Mick) Bartholomew, Étienne Pollet, François Mathet—took their turns with their *pensionnaires* on the Piste Ronde. M. Mathet, respectfuly known as the Maître, was studying his horses with close attention as they galloped by. I walked up to him and complimented him on his two-thousandth winner, which the turf papers had reported the previous day.

"The press had it wrong," he replied. "The two-thousandth was last week. The total now is two thousand six or seven—I forget which." As soon as he could shift his gaze from the *piste,* he shook my hand warmly. His string of horses—there were seventy-five in this lot—continued to gallop past, at the rate of one every few seconds, in a seemingly unending file. He told me that he was currently schooling a hundred and eighty horses, sixty-nine of which belonged to the Aga Khan IV, a devoted enthusiast of French racing. I asked Mathet, a twenty-three-year veteran of the Aigles, what he thought of Chantilly's training ground. He gave a mixed verdict. "Obviously, it's the best in the world," he said. "But the turf itself—that is another story. The best ground I have known for training race horses is in England—at Newmarket, for example. It has a *souplesse* that just doesn't exist in the Paris region. In Brittany, yes. From the geological standpoint, the best earth for our purposes is in England and in Brittany. The area near the Alps, in the east of France, is second-best, and the Bassin de l'Ile de France, surrounding Paris and including Chantilly, is third. Of course, over all, training is made much easier here in this preserve."

That day, as on every Monday, the training was being conducted principally on the Piste Ronde. This track is the one that is most often used, for it is the favorite of most trainers. Percy Carter once put the matter succinctly: "That turf is better than it was early in this century, when I was breezing a great horse named Roi Hérode. It's the new watering system that has done it. There's plenty of spring in that turf—the best in the world." Carter's opinion is shared by almost everyone who has worked on the Aigles. The Australian jockey Bill Pyers, then in his sixth year of riding in France, told me that morning, "Working out on the Aigles, we have just about no breakdowns and hardly any leg trouble among three thousand thoroughbreds. We use different turf every day— all of it well watered—and we can pace a horse's training in a way that we couldn't anywhere but on the Aigles. There's just nothing to compare with it in the world."

The Terrain des Aigles slopes gently from south to north, providing effective natural drainage; even after a prolonged rainfall, it is possible to work the horses out within an hour. During the summer, when there is not enough rain, the ground is watered by mobile units and by a system of underground pipes. Whatever the season, the turf never looks parched. For the use of these unmatched facilities, the owners of thoroughbreds kept at Chantilly pay the Société d'Encouragement pour l'Amélioration des Races de Chevaux en France, which operates the hippodrome and training grounds, a basic fee of only a hundred and eighty francs (about thirty-six dollars) a year for each horse, plus seven francs for each gallop and, during the rainy season, three and a half francs for each canter. No charge is made for the use of a grassy area allocated for the training of yearlings. These modest payments cover about a third of the Société's operating expenses, the balance coming from entry fees and a share of the bets made in cities, towns, and villages all over the country, under government control. In brief, a proprietor who elects to keep his horses in training at Chantilly—as about a dozen Americans do—pays in over-all costs about a third of what he would be charged in the United States.

In addition to the Aigles, the racecourse itself is pressed into service on occasion—usually on the Tuesday before a classic race. The directors of the Société zealously stand watch over the condition of the turf, but they have come to agree that the horses competing in an important race deserve a chance to get the feel of the track beforehand.

In the town, excitement rose all week, but in the barns and on the training grounds there was a business-as-usual atmosphere. The horses were given only light exercise during the latter part of the week, but the townsfolk and the visitors, who had begun appearing in increasingly large numbers in midweek, seemed to be working themselves up to a high pitch of excitement. In the bars, discussions about the relative merits of the contenders often turned into shouting matches, accompanied by much waving of arms. And as the tension increased so did racegoers' appetites. In all the restaurants, meals grew larger and longer. The aficionados seemed to be fortifying themselves for the big moment.

On Sunday morning, I had breakfast in my room, dressed at my leisure, and descended to the ground floor at about ten-thirty, to find the restaurant, the terrace on the sidewalk, and the garden at the back of the building crammed shoulder to shoulder with early lunchers. M. Moulin had laid on a *menu gastronomique* at thirty francs, not including wine. It was simply impossible to order a modest lunch; fortunately, having had a late breakfast, I was not yet interested in another meal. As I threaded my way among the devoted horse-lovers who had transformed the town overnight, I noticed that all the other restaurants were also packed and were also insisting that their customers accept a gastronomic menu, at thirty or forty francs; even at that, most of the visitors couldn't have squirmed their way into a restaurant, and those who had not brought elaborate picnic lunches either provisioned themselves at the *charcuteries* and *boulangeries* or headed for the woods flanking the hippodrome, where it was possible to buy any kind of meal, from a hot dog to a six-course lunch with wine, and eat it at a table under the trees. There were also pizza stands in abundance (the French seem lately to have become addicted to pizza), and it was even possible to try to win a large kewpie doll by betting on a number on a turning wheel. By eleven, the infield of the track was filling up with picnickers who were content to have their holiday repast on the grass in the hot sun. (The Prix du Jockey Club, which was scheduled to start at about four-ten, was the fourth race on the card.)

At a bar and restaurant called the Jockey Club, on the Route Nationale, the talk was saturated not only with speculation and expertise on the coming race but also with tidbits on the buying and selling of horses. Sitting at the bar, I could hear an Irishman on my right talking into the bar telephone to someone who must have been hard of hearing. "But, Mr.

10

Frobisher," he was saying, "of course he can't miss in a race of . . ." Mr. Frobisher presumably had other ideas, for my neighbor's voice trailed off. He took a sip of Scotch, and then resumed, saying, "He needs four miles, not two miles, Mr. Frobisher, believe me." After another pause, he made a valiant last attempt. "You mean to tell me, Mr. Frobisher, that he's willing to pay a hundred thousand clams for a filly and he won't go for this horse at a lousy . . ." The heat was almost unbearable, and I left without finding out whether he made the sale.

The course at Chantilly was laid out in 1834, during the period when it was fashionable in France to imitate the British. That year, Lord Seymour and his friends, a group of French dandies who took their inspiration from the fops of Georgian England, founded the French Jockey Club in Paris—which is still one of the world's most exclusive establishments—and decided that the terrain at Chantilly was admirably suited to a hippodrome. Two years later, the course was ready for the first running of the Prix du Jockey Club, and thoroughbred racing in France was on its way. That 1836 running took place before a fashionable crowd, which set the tone for later runnings. Horses owned by Lord Seymour won the first three runnings of the Prix du Jockey Club. The fourth was won by a horse entered by the Comte de Cambis. In the fifth running, Lord Seymour's horse came in second, and Lord Seymour claimed that the winner was not a three-year-old at all but an older animal, bred in England and racing under an alias. When his claim was disallowed by the stewards, he took his case to the courts, and again failed in his efforts to have his horse proclaimed the victor. Thereafter, he participated in only one further running of the Jockey Club, and then—though he won it—he gave up the sport in disgust and repaired to Paris, where he devoted himself to the pleasures of watching cockfights and pursuing beautiful women.

Today, the Jockey Club still turns out in full force for its annual outings at Chantilly. The rules of the club apparently haven't changed much since Lord Seymour's day; the members still sit in masculine splendor in a section of the stands reserved for them, apart from their wives or lady friends, who are seated in a section of their own. There is presumably no rule against members' meeting their ladies under the stands between races for a fast glass of champagne.

If not much else has changed in the past hundred and thirty-four years, the racing itself has improved. The course for the Prix du Jockey Club, which covers nearly a mile and a half, and of which I had a fine view from a section of the stands called the Tribune Réservée, begins far to one's left, virtually out of sight, and crosses over at an angle toward the backstretch, in a teardrop-shaped pattern. The backstretch, just opposite the Tribune Réservée, passes before the eighteenth-century Grandes Écuries, a formidable work of architecture that in its day berthed two hundred and forty horses and their tack, more than four hundred hounds, and living space for grooms and handlers. At the far turn, the course dips down, and in the background is the legendary Château de Chantilly, which houses, among other treasures, the Book of Hours of the Duc de Berry, usually considered the most beautifully illuminated manuscript in existence. Between the far turn and the turn for home, the horses seem to sink almost out of sight; then comes the uphill homestretch, which has proved the undoing of many promising colts and fillies.

The first race was about ready to go now, and though the tables in the restaurant under the stands and on the lawn behind the stands were all occupied, there seemed to be a dearth of top hats and other sartorial reminders of the past. One pearl-gray top-hatted spectator escorted a miniskirted young lady—a sight that elicited many more lifted eyebrows than it would have at Epsom. The racegoers were still filtering in lethargically as the first race went off, and now the tables on the lawn behind the stands were occupied by some gray-toppered gentlemen, probably Jockey Club members, escorting ladies dressed in the handiwork of Cardin, Dior, and Balmain. On the whole, though, I thought the spectacle was not up to former years from the standpoint of *haute couture*.

In addition to the prestige that the Prix du Jockey Club conferred on all connected with it, the race was worth the equivalent of $340,000, which comprised the purses for the first four horses and prizes to the breeders of the first three. The Prix de l'Arc de Triomphe has a still larger purse, but the Jockey Club purse is not bad, it seems to me, compared with American purses. (This year's Kentucky Derby and Preakness both had record purses of considerably less—the first went off at $170,300 and the second at $203,800.)

Before the main event, the horses leave the paddock in single file and walk slowly past the stands, giving their backers a chance to appreciate their fine points through binoculars—though it would now be too late to change one's bet if one wanted to retain one's few inches of space in the stands. In fact, betting at Chantilly is a hopeless proposition for most spectators on either race day; the queues leading up to the ticket windows stretch in winding patterns into the woods bordering the hippodrome.

The Jockey Club race itself was just about perfectly run, at least from the winner's standpoint. Honeyville broke out of the gate in front and set the pace until the turn for home. Goodly was well placed in third position until after the far turn. While racing downhill in front of the Château, he moved into second, and in the stretch he came on strong, along with Beaugency and Djakao, and all three overtook Honeyville, who hadn't enough left for the uphill run to the finish. Goodly won by a short head from Beaugency, and Djakao was third, another half length behind. The race proved to be a personal triumph for the Head family: Goodly was trained by Willy and ridden by his grandson, and Beaugency was trained by Alec.

The traffic out of Chantilly that evening was formidable, and the next morning the streets were empty, except for hoteliers and restaurateurs hurrying to the bank. I awoke to the sound of wine bottles being broken on a rock in the garden by the *patron,* a chore he reserves for himself and performs with enthusiasm. The second week of Chantilly, like the first, began at a slow tempo, but at dawn on Tuesday morning I was faced with the problem of racing back and forth between the Aigles and the hippodrome to view, if possible, the last serious workouts for the Prix de Diane. In the matter of these workouts, the French racing press is kept in the dark about what is going to happen when and where. I was all set to start for the Aigles well before dawn, only to be told by a *Paris-Turf* photographer that the important action would take place at the hippodrome, since it was Tuesday. So, trusting the natives, I went instead to the hippodrome, and found nothing at all happening there. Eventually, a few fillies who were doubtful starters in the Diane worked out in a perfunctory way, and at seven, with the sun well above the horizon and climbing rapidly, the rumor circulated that Saraca, the favorite for the Diane, was going to work a serious mile and a quarter at the Aigles at seven-fifteen. All speed records were broken by aficionados legging it for the Aigles, and I arrived in time to catch a glimpse of Saraca and two stablemates, one of whom, Koblenza, was also scheduled to run in the Diane.

All week, not only the racing papers but the entire French press were trumpeting the invincibility of Saraca, an unimposing bay filly who had won every race she had run. She had won at Saint-Cloud, a suburban track on the Paris circuit, in October, 1968, as a two-year-old, against moderately strong opposition; she had won again at Saint-Cloud in November, over an unimpressive field. As a three-year-old, she had won in her first start, once again at Saint-Cloud, in April, and the bettors were beginning to pass the word that she was strictly a counterclockwise runner, for at Saint-Cloud the horses run with the rail on their left, as in the United States; at most other French tracks, they run in the opposite direction. Then, late in May, she defeated the best fillies of the season at Longchamp (clockwise) in the Prix Saint-Alary, the final important preparatory race for the Diane. Saraca was owned by Arpad Plesch, whose colt Tapalqué, ridden by the eight-time French champion jockey Yves St.-Martin, had won the 1968 Prix du Jockey Club. St.-Martin was scheduled to have the mount on Saraca, who is trained by Maître François Mathet. When everyone touts the same horse, I grow uneasy about the horse's chances. Of thirty-five French papers I checked—including the two principal racing publications; the conscientious *Figaro*; such influential provincial papers as *Ouest-France, République de Tarbes,* and *Nice-Matin;* and even the Communist paper *L'Humanité*—all chose Saraca as the winner of the Diane.

The day before the race, René Bertiglia, a diminutive trainer who had been, like many other trainers, a good jockey in his earlier days, sat down with me at the bar of the Jockey Club restaurant. He had no horse entered in the Diane, but he did have a favorite. "For me, this race is a formality," he said. "There is not a filly in it who can touch Saraca."

This seemed to put the final stamp on the result, but I still had a vaguely uneasy feeling. To a taxi-driver, I said, "But surely Saraca could stumble, or get boxed in, or I don't know what."

He smiled remotely and replied, "No. It's not possible."

Sunday, the day of the Prix de Diane, was clear, hot, and humid. A fresh wave of visitors inundated the town, and the *menus gastronomiques* were posted at the entrances to all the restaurants, but for some reason—possibly the excessive heat and humidity, possibly the run-off election between Georges Pompidou and Alain Poher for the Presidency—the crush of lunchers was not quite as great as it had been on the previous Sunday. One of Chantilly's more expensive restaurants, which had offered a thirty-five-franc *menu gastronomique* on the Sunday of the Prix du Jockey Club, now suggested virtually the same menu for twenty-three francs, and even

14

allowed one to select a more modest meal for eighteen francs. It was also possible to order à la carte, with a pot of caviar going for twenty-five francs, foie gras for twenty, Chateaubriand Henri IV for eighteen francs, and Médaillon de Veau Rôtisserie for nine francs fifty. The pizza stands and the kewpie dolls reappeared in the woods beside the hippodrome, however, and there seemed to be as many picnikers in the infield as there had been on the previous weekend.

The day of the Diane at Chantilly is traditionally dedicated to the ladies, who turn out in their most arresting spring outfits. There were two centers of attraction: the track, where the fillies were to perform, and the Tribune des Dames section of the stands, which this week replaced the all-male Jockey Club area in interest for those who had come to see the people, not the horses. On the lawns surrounding the stands, the fashion show began well before the first race on the card. There were, of course, the creations of Paris's top couturiers, plus some rather far-out numbers. One lady in the enclosure wore a white linen tunic over white linen shorts —and really short they were—that were decorated with embroidered daisies. A well-known female stable owner appeared in a colorful gypsy costume. Another was overheard muttering, "They say if you cross her palm with silver she'll tell your fortune." "Ah, yes," her escort said. "But will she give you the winner of the next race?"

The orgy of gourmandizing in the restaurant under the stands and at the tables behind the stands continued unabated during the early races. The display of the French *mode* also diverted attention from what was happening on the track, and even as the sixteen fillies paraded out of the paddock for the *défilé* preceding the running of the Diane, photographers were still pointing their cameras toward the stands. The Diane is run on the Jockey Club course, but the starting gates are some three hundred meters (a furlong and a half) closer to the finish, so the runners would cover twenty-one hundred meters, instead of the twenty-four hundred covered by the starters in the Jockey Club.

The race was exciting. A horse named Vigia broke on top and set a fast pace, out in front of Mme. Pierre Wertheimer's horse Princesse de Gavarnie, who was entered in the race strictly to set the pace for her owner's other filly, Glaneuse. Vigia, closely trailed by Princesse de Gavarnie, continued to go all out past the Écuries, down the hill in front of the Château, and into the short flat section of the track leading into the uphill stretch. At the head of the stretch, it was still Vigia, Princesse de Gavarnie, and Glaneuse, but between the far turn and the entrance to the stretch the field had closed the long gap that the front-runners had opened up. Mme. Léon Volterra's Djenarelle came on in fourth, with a host of horses bunched behind her and ready to take the lead. St.-Martin had been lying well back on Saraca, and at the head of the stretch he began to make his move, from fifth place. Saraca swung out and began moving in earnest up the stretch, with Glaneuse slightly behind her but matching her stride. Two furlongs from home it looked, finally, like a two-horse race, with Saraca in front and St.-Martin driving furiously. But the crowd suddenly began to roar, for on the outside a filly carrying the orange silks of the textile industrialist Marcel Boussac's stable came on with great speed. Saraca had never really shifted into high, yet she appeared to be tiring. Boussac's Crepellana, with the veteran Roger Poincelet up, passed Glaneuse and then Saraca, about thirty meters from the finish, and won by three-quarters of a length.

Ambassador Sargent Shriver, who, with his wife and three of their five children, was in attendance throughout the afternoon, drank a victory toast with Crepellana's owner. Afterward, Shriver was asked which he preferred—American racing or French. "Well, they're really quite different, and from a racing standpoint I'm not qualified to say which is better," he replied. "But in terms of ambience and spectacle French racing is far ahead. And, as far as my own luck is concerned, I'd have to vote for French racing."

As the racegoers left town, the prices on the menus posted in front of the restaurants began to drop. By eight o'clock, the Jockey Club was suggesting a Victory Dinner at fifteen francs, and the discerning diner could find bargains all over town. By nine-thirty, when it had grown dark, the streets were empty again.

16

# Of Curds and Whey

---∞---

*Today there remains only one* fermier *who produces Camembert in the time-honored tradition, a certain M. Daniel Courtonne, a third-generation maker of Camembert in the small* salle *where his grandfather embarked on the same line of work in the eighteen-eighties.*

---∞---

About a hundred meters from the center of Vimoutiers, a Norman town that was leveled by Allied bombardment in June, 1944, stands a stone statue, decapitated by a bomb blast, of a young lady named Marie Harel, holding a large pitcher. A hundred meters away, in front of the modern building that is the Salle des Fêtes in the town square, is another statue, also stone and life-sized, of Marie Harel. This one is another full figure, but with a head, topped by a native coif. The new statue, unveiled in 1953, was erected by "400 men and women making cheese in Van Wert, Ohio, U.S.A."

And why does Marie Harel merit all this commemoration? It appears she is something of a regional heroine because she is alleged to have discovered, or uncovered, the secret of making Camembert cheese, today the most renowned of all cheeses on the international market. Locally she ranks—on a comparable national plane—with Mme. Curie, and just above St. Joan of Arc.

During one of his more trying days in the office of President of the Republic, General de Gaulle commented on how difficult it was to rule a country that produces more than three hundred and fifty different kinds of fromage. (He was being conservative; the actual figure is more than four hundred.) Fromage is, of course, one of the foundations of

French gastronomy, and of those four hundred–plus varieties Camembert is one of the most memorable.

This most celebrated of all French cheeses, now literally a household word in countries throughout the world, is named after a tiny hamlet a few kilometers from Vimoutiers; driving toward it, one is first greeted by the roadside sign "Camembert"; then follows a stretch of open fields and finally a group of five buildings—a church, a small school, and three private houses. That is Camembert.

The cheese itself is produced in the surrounding countryside, almost all of it by an industrial process which has captured the basic taste and forms of the original but has lost the fine *goût* that has characterized Camembert since, as the legend goes, Marie Harel was passed the secret formula by a grateful priest whom she had hidden during the Revolution. (Even the local residents, who wholeheartedly believe many regional superstitions, no longer put any stock in that story, but Marie is given full marks for having started Camembert cheese on its way to world fame.)

Today there remains only one *fermier* who produces Camembert in the time-honored tradition, a certain M. Daniel Courtonne, a third-generation maker of Camembert in the small *salle* where his grandfather embarked on the same line of work in the eighteen-eighties. Courtonne and his wife, Simone, lovingly create between 250 and 300 flawless examples of their craft by hand six days every week, eleven months of the year.

Courtonne's modest cheese-making establishment is situated in a hilly hamlet just outside Vimoutiers named Saint-Germain-de-Montgommery, a former domain of the original Montgommerys, some of whom later migrated to England, losing, as the local residents like to put it, an "m" in the Channel on the way.

Courtonne's ample house is not only his castle but also his place of business. I visited him there not long ago, and after an apéritif in his comfortably furnished living room, he took me on a tour of inspection. Outside, the fresh milk is heated in an improvised *bain-marie*, in which the *lait* is gently warmed to a temperature of 32 degrees Centigrade (89° F.) by hot water beneath it, which in turn is heated directly by a wood fire in the fireplace below. The warm milk then descends by rubber hose to a series of vats in the basement, where it stands and becomes *lait caillé*, or clotted milk. To help curdle the milk, he adds a small quantity of a liquid called *présure*, an extract created in the stomach of the calf, but first he tests the acidity of the milk to determine how much *présure* to inject. "The more acid in the milk, the less *présure*," he said; watching him at work, one felt that he placed less faith in instruments—except perhaps the thermometer—than in his own intuition.

While skimming the top off the rapidly forming *lait caillé*, Courtonne, a short and stockily built man of fifty-eight who had been born in the house where we were conversing, would interrupt his description of the procedure every now and then to interject some of the pithy extracts of the philosophy by which he lives.

As he prepared to pull the first vats over to the table that bears three hundred *moules*, or cheese forms, he confided: "*On ne bouleverse pas la nature.*" ("One doesn't upset nature.")

Beginning about an hour after the *présure* had been injected into the vats, Simone Courtonne started dipping into the *lait caillé* and ladling it into the forms, which I noted on closer inspection were perforated to allow the *sérum* (whey) to run out after filtering down through the developing cheese. Each of the three hundred *moules* received one large dipperful; then the operation was begun again, and repeated until seven separate *cuillerées* had been administered to all. This application of 2,100 dippers of curdled milk into the *moules* constitutes only one of eighteen separate manipulations that must be performed in the making of a Courtonne Camembert. The filling of the *moules* to the top, a height of about six inches, is performed over a period of three hours.

The *sérum* in the *lait caillé* filters down and eventually out onto the table, which is covered with handmade reed mats, but the calcium and other deposits remain in the *moule*. Courtonne places special emphasis on the mats, which he obtains from an artisan who collects his reeds from a certain marsh, and on the table being of wood rather than metal, as in the industrialized establishments that produce Camembert. "Industrialization and gastronomy don't mix," he said, as if to remind himself and spur himself on.

The dripping and separation of the *sérums* while the *matière* inside the *moules* dries is one of the vital periods in the creation of a good Camembert; within twenty-four hours, the matter inside the *moules* should have shaken down to half its original height, and is then ready to be turned over, preparatory to the first salting. Simone Courtonne, a cheery woman with a warm, outgoing personality who, like her husband, loves her work, does two salting operations, with a *sel très fin*, first on one side and, later, on the other. The young cheeses are also sprayed with a culture of mold and bacteria called *penicillium*, mixed with sterilized water.

The product rests, generally, two nights in the *salle de fabrication*, first on a wooden plateau, then on aluminum wattles, at a temperature of 22 to 25 degrees Centigrade (71-77° F.). In the industrial factories, Courtonne advised, his eyes sparkling impishly, *"on chauffe trop"*— they heat too much—to speed up the process and cut down the time between the arrival of the milk and the cheese being placed on the consumer's plate. The temperature of the industrial *salles de fabrication* is at least 28 or 30 degrees Centigrade (82-86° F.), and the new cheese "sleeps—it is not alive."

*"Ah, l'industrie et gastronomie,"* he added, rolling his eyes toward heaven as he returned to one of his convictions. *"[Vous] ne pouvez pas faire marcher la paire!"* ("Industry and gastronomy don't go together.")

"The Camembert they turn out," he said, in translation, "is less rich, has less taste, and looks like chalk."

Courtonne, who is an enthusiastic exponent of organic farming methods, added that while he realized that progress and the world-wide demand for Camembert called for new techniques, "you can't mix quantity and quality."

The Courtonnes have a herd of almost sixty cows, which produce the 600 to 650 liters of milk used in the daily fabrication of 250 to 300 Camemberts. "It takes two liters ten [2.10 liters] of milk for each cheese," he explained. "In Holland, for example, the cows give a greater quantity of milk than our Norman cows, but not the quality. Just as I was saying a minute ago, you can't mix quantity and quality."

As we walked to the *haloir* or cooler *cave* (temperature: 15° C.=59° F.), he explained that all the milking on his farm was still done by hand, just as it had been in his grandfather's time; he feels that even a milking machine will have its effect on the consistency and taste of the end product.

But something has changed on the farm where the Courtonnes today produce the Camemberts under the same label, "Le Royal Montgommery," that his grandfather used—a lady dressed in red riding on a lion's back. For the past twenty years, in the *haloir* where we were now inspecting the fromages at various stages of their development, the cheeses have acquired a covering of fine hair, colloquially referred to as *poil de chat* (cat fur). "We think it's a kind of *mucor,* a variety of mushroom, but nobody knows how it suddenly formed on the growing cheeses. In any case, we have to brush them off carefully at a certain moment before they're boxed for shipping. It's a manifestation of nature," he said philosophically, "part of bacteriological evolution. It's a rupture of the equilibrium, and it's all tied in with the product's loss of a certain self-defense against certain bacteria."

He turned on a fan, which sucked the cool air out of the room for a minute or so, then clicked it off. "Whatever it is, it makes more work for us."

We left the *cave,* after carefully checking the temperature, and Courtonne offered to drive me about the countryside for a bit before returning for some Camembert and wine. As we drove along, regularly crossing the border separating the *départements* of Orne and Calvados, he rambled on, filling in gaps in my information. "Our cheeses should be eaten about six weeks after they are made. They stay in the box at least twenty days, not the ten days the industrials give them. Our new cheeses stay an extra two hours in the *salle de fabrication,* and it's worth it. You can't hurry nature. . . . The industrial cheeses may be edible, but they lack character. The *haloir* must be humid but not too humid, so that the cheese will dry itself out properly."

"Yes," he said thoughtfully, "now I'm the only *fermier* making Camembert by hand. The artisan is disappearing from this earth." By coincidence, we stopped at that moment at a monument, just outside Camembert itself, in honor of *"Mme. Harel, Marie Fontaine, 1761–18 . . . qui inventa le Camembert."* Unaccountably, the date of birth and married name do not correspond to those on the statues and the date of death is not filled in.

In the cemetery at nearby Champosoult, the inscription on her tomb reads: *"Mme. Paynel née Marie Harel, 1781–1855, Détentrice du Secret de la Fabrication du Camembert."* ("Holder of the secret of the making of Camembert.") The new statue in the center of Vimoutiers carries the same legend, with a plaque stating that it was offered by the Americans.

"Nobody believes that story about the *prêtre réfractaire* [refractory priest] in the Revolution any more," Courtonne told me.

There are even two versions of the first official acknowledgment and naming of Camembert cheese. One gives the distinction to Napoleon I, who allegedly kissed the waitress who served it to him. The second, as recounted by Courtonne, is somewhat different: "Marie Harel was a peasant girl who had been making cheeses in her style and selling them at the market. One day, at the inauguration of the rail line between Paris and Granville, Napoleon III stopped for lunch at the station at Surdon, between Argentan and Granville, had a taste of one of Marie Harel's cheeses, and proclaimed it excellent. When he asked which cheese it was, they told him it had been made near Camembert. '*Donc,*' said the Emperor, '*c'est un Camembert.*' "

Or it may have been a mixture of the two. If the second account were correct, Marie Harel would no longer have been a peasant girl, since the Surdon link of the Paris-Granville rail line was inaugurated in 1858, with Marie already three years in her grave.

We also passed the Champosoult farmhouse in which Marie Harel lived during her childhood and adolescence, completing a tour rivaled only by a formal bus excursion of the Charlotte Corday country. Marie Harel, it seems, was not the only revered personage to inhabit the *pays d'Auge,* the fertile Norman countryside that might be called the spiritual cheese capital of the world. The Corday tour, it is noted in a brochure available to all visitors to Vimoutiers, includes a ceremonial pilgrimage to the house where she was born, Le Ronceray; the church where she was baptized, Les Ligneries; the church where she often attended Mass (Mesnil Imbert); the château of her uncle (Le Renouard); the manor of her grandfather (Manoir de Corday-Mesnil Imbert); and the farm of her father (Ferme des Bois). (No stop at the house where she lived when she cut her first tooth.) The tour lacks several points of interest: the scene of her assassination of Marat in his bath, which was not, of course, accomplished in the area, and the spot where she was guillotined. While Mlle. Corday is regarded as a local heroine, her status does not measure up to that of Marie Harel, perhaps because of the latter's contribution to the region and to the world.

On the trip back, we made a small detour to visit a hilltop—featuring a World War II–model American tank—in Montormel, a vantage point from which one can see a tremendous sweep of Norman countryside, including the site of the famous Falaise pocket of World War II. Like a great many natives of Normandy and Brittany, Courtonne is unabashedly pro-American, and remembers vividly the sacrifices made by the G.I.s who liberated his country. He and his wife often drive, on Sundays, to the cemetery at Omaha Beach to meditate and pay their respects to the Americans who died in the area.

He is equally sad about the deaths of a considerable number of his countrymen and countrywomen in Vimoutiers in the bombardment. "It must have been due to a false tip given the Allies by the French Resistance," he speculated. "There were only two German combat soldiers in

Vimoutiers and they were in the hospital. But the town was destroyed."

Returning to his farm, Courtonne reverted to the subject that occupies all his waking moments. "We have good milk here because of the quality of the *pâturage*. As you know, Norman soil is ideally suited to the raising of livestock. Sometimes in the middle of winter I buy a little *betterave* (sugar beets) to mix into their fodder, but I don't believe, as some farmers do, in having a silo of maize. However, I sometimes buy a bit of corn and wheat from the miller, what is left over from the bread."

We drove through the crossroads that is Saint-Germain-de-Montgommery, with, on one corner, the smallest *mairie* I have yet seen. It is so tiny that when a wedding is conducted there the witnesses must take their positions out in the road.

As we pulled up before his ancestral farmhouse, Courtonne wound up— for the moment, at least—his discourse on cheeses. "Brie and Coulommiers are made in much the same way as Camembert. The form is different— Coulommiers and Brie are flat; the change in form causes a change in the rhythm of fermentation." All are mold-ripened, but because of differences in mixture, time periods, and even slight temperature changes, the characteristic flavor and aroma are not the same.

The delicate piquancy of Camembert is unmatchable by any other French cheese. It should be eaten *à point,* during the two or three days when it is neither underripe nor overripe, its texture a creamy yellow, with a white but nonchalky crust, soft but not limp. A Brie, claimed by some to be a gift from the heavens to the French, is flatter, with a much larger circumference. This moonlike cheese, also a tender white in color on the outside, matches the buttery yellow of the Camembert, and should be runny, at its best, but not to too great an extent. Its taste reminds some connoisseurs of a mixture of mushrooms, cream, cognac, and earth, and experienced turophiles have claimed to detect traces of the taste of Anjou pears, leeks, and even truffles in a great, mature Brie. Its texture has been described as heavy honey, and for an amateur of Brie there is no greater moment of exaltation than when he is about to cut into a perfect, ripe Brie. The Coulommiers is a pocket version of Brie, not larger than a Camembert, usually measuring about one inch high and five or six across, as distinguished from a classic Brie de Meaux (sixteen inches in diameter, and about three-quarters of an inch thick). Coulommiers is not as runny, nor does it have as subtle a *goût* as Brie. Both Brie and Coulommiers are made in the *département* of Seine-et-Marne, near Paris; the real Camembert is made in the *département* of Calvados, just over the border from Orne. (Courtonne's house in Saint-Germain-de-Montgommery is in Calvados; his mailing address in Vimoutiers, a few kilometers away, is in Orne.) Industrialized Camembert is, of course, fabricated in a number of localities, but that need not concern us here. There is a German "Camembert" which bears about as much relation to the real thing as an Algerian red wine made the day before yesterday does to a 1966 Château Mouton-Rothschild or a Château Lafite-Rothschild of almost any year, or as bathtub gin does to a vintage Dom Pérignon champagne.

Back inside Courtonne's cozy farmhouse for a glass of white Porto, his favorite drink, he showed me some of his clippings and a few letters, one from a caterer at Le Mans, where President de Gaulle—in the same manner as Napoleon III in the Marie Harel story—stopped for lunch. As the meal approached its climactic end, the General was offered a selection of cheeses. He chose the Camembert, found it excellent, and asked who had made it. Thus, Daniel Courtonne, like his predecessor Marie Harel, became in effect a *"fromager du roi."*

Today, Courtonne ships most of his cheeses to a very few discriminating *fromagers* in Paris, Marseille, and Bordeaux—none to the United States, since Courtonne, like most farmers in the land of Louis Pasteur, does not approve of pasteurization of the milk; it kills the refined taste of the Camembert, in the opinion of Courtonne and his fellow-*fermiers*, as well as that of most cheese aficionados.

In Paris, authentic handmade Courtonne Camemberts are sold principally in a shop not far from the Madeleine called La Ferme St. Hubert, presided over by a devoted cheese merchant named Hubert, a swarthy, stocky thirty-nine-year-old *affineur* (literally one who purifies and matures a substance) who looks more like a rugby player than a *maître-fromager*. Hubert has been involved with cheeses in one role or another since he was fifteen, when he decided to forgo designing clothes and make cheese his métier; today he stores, cares for, and finally sells between 300 and 400 types of fromage, and has 7,000 to 8,000 cheeses on hand throughout most of the year. In the small *cave* underneath his shop, he stores a small quantity of his total stock, usually the cheeses that are closest to being ready for the customers. All must be handled in their own special ways: most must be turned over regularly; some are tenderly washed with white wine (like Soumaintrain), some with lightly salted water, the Maroilles with beer twice a week during three months, and l'Epoisses with Marc de

26

Bourgogne (the residue) twice a week during two months. Some are simply brushed, like the Saint-Nectaire, three times a week during two months. Others are left pretty much to themselves, like the one-foot-tall Fourme d'Auvergne.

This engaging *maître-fromager* buys and sells a sizable percentage of the Courtonnes' output. "When you deal with a *fermier* like Courtonne," he said recently in his Paris boutique, "you know that the product will not decline in quality; it will be always at its peak of excellence, since it is a product of the same milk, the same cows, and the same savoir-faire on the part of the *fermier*."

Hubert's knowledge of cheese and how each type must mature ("A good Münster takes eleven weeks, a Camembert is ready in six") is appreciated by his customers, who have their own special preferences. Yul Brynner, who recently bought a villa in Normandy, near Deauville, favors a Cabécous d'Aurié, a dry goat cheese from the *département* of Lot, in the Southwest; Marlene Dietrich a Sainte-Maure, a goat cheese from the Touraine, 45 percent greasy; Jean Gabin, another Normandy resident, chooses as his special favorite a Murols (a sturdy, all-year cheese made from the milk of Auvergne cows; Aristotle Onassis is partial to Roquefort. (The late Duke of Windsor's selection was a Brillat-Savarin, a product of Normandy, 75 percent greasy, whose ideal partner is a good champagne.) The Baron Guy de Rothschild, a part-time inhabitant of the province of Normandy, nominates a Saint-Hubert, a greasy-textured cheese made in the *département* of Seine-et-Marne, not far from Paris. Both Zizi Jeanmaire and the Comte Michel d'Ornano, mayor of Deauville and *député* from Calvados in the Assemblée Nationale, vote for Camembert, as does Hubert himself. "It's a classic cheese, and Courtonne is the only one making the *vrai* Camembert," he said spiritedly. (Hubert will have nothing to do with industrialized fromage, except for some soft creamy cheeses like Boursin.)

He also suggests an appropriate wine to be drunk with his cheeses: for Yul Brynner's Cabécous d'Aurié a good Santenay; for Miss Dietrich's Sainte-Maure a Saumur blanc; for Jean Gabin's favorite Murols a Bouzy; for M. Onassis's Roquefort a Sauterne; for the Baron Guy de Rothschild's Saint-Hubert a Clos de Bèze; and for the classic Camembert a Vougeot or, better yet, a Vougeot-Beaune. These nominations of Hubert's are of course in line with the epicurean belief that a good wine of the right texture will underline the special qualities in the taste of a good fromage.

Hubert's customers, many of whom travel a considerable distance to Paris to visit his shop regularly, trust him implicitly; for his part, Hubert says the cheeses he sells must be to his taste. In most cases, he does *not* keep the cheeses that are ready for sale under refrigeration in his shop. His *cave* is kept not too cold but humid: "the humidity is very important, as it is with good wine."

Another of Hubert's best sellers is Pont l'Évêque, also made in Normandy, a province whose three principal products are cheeses, apples (and the resulting hard cider, known as Calvados), and thoroughbred race horses—all three directly or indirectly products of the Norman soil and *pâturage*. These days, most Pont l'Évêque is also produced by an industrialized process, but there is still a handful of *fermiers* making it in the old tradition. M. Hubert buys most of his Pont l'Évêque from a jolly, apple-cheeked woman named Mme. Marcel Pinot, who single-handedly turns out about fifty Pont l'Évêques daily, under a label that bears her husband's name and "*ferme du Beau-Levêque à Canapville*."

In the company of M. Courtonne, who lives and works not many kilometers away, I paid a visit to Mme. Pinot, whose petite *salle de fabrication* was well-stocked with dozens of the familiar square cheeses, segregated in groups. "*Jeudi*," she said, pointing to one group, "*vendredi*," to another, "*samedi*," and "*lundi*." Since we were then *jeudi*, I took these groups to be three to seven days old.

Mme. Pinot makes two batches of twenty-five cheeses each weekday. The process is not unlike that followed in the making of Camembert, but with some major differences: the periods of coagulation, draining, and curing are shorter; the whey passes quickly through the formative matter, usually in an hour. The young cheeses are salted lightly on their fourth day, and are washed while being cured. There is less development of surface mold. As they start their road to maturity, Mme. Pinot gives them a quarter turn each day, right up to the moment of *emballage* (boxing). Mme. Pinot, who has been making Pont l'Évêques for five years, uses three liters of fresh milk in the initial preparation of each of her cheeses, and keeps a herd of twenty-five cows. Like wine, milk has its own growth (*cru*) depending on the pasturage. The milk that goes into a true, nonindustrial Camembert or Pont l'Évêque is just as distinctive in its way as the *grand cru* of a good Bordeaux or Burgundy.

Like M. Courtonne, Mme. Pinot has her own special artisan who makes the reed mats on which the cheeses rest during the early stages of their development. But in her *salle*, these mats—with their cheeses—rest on a plastic, not a wooden, table, a discovery which first shocked, then profoundly fascinated M. Courtonne. The time span of her cheeses, from inception to table, is four weeks, or just under.

I was told that Mme. Pinot learned the technique of making an outstanding Pont l'Évêque from the mother of Mme. Jean Couétil, whose husband operates a neighboring stud farm, the Haras de la Boscraie.

On the way back to Saint-Germain-de-Montgommery, where Mme. Courtonne was preparing lunch, we passed through a village named Livarot, where—according to M. Courtonne—there is today only a single farmer who makes the fromage of that name, a soft round cheese similar in some respects to Camembert, but with a *goût* a bit less refined than Camembert's.

Simone Courtonne's lunch was simple but delicious (a perfect omelette, a tasty veal with a masterly purée de pommes de terre), and topped off, of course, with a Camembert de la maison. It was chosen, as in the case of the cheese for President de Gaulle, by the hand of the master *fermier* himself, and it was obviously exactly the right day to serve that particular specimen.

M. Courtonne expanded on his enthusiasm for natural (that is, organic) farming, and elaborated on his case against pasteurization. I recalled that some years before, while living in Brittany, which was then undergoing an epidemic of hoof-and-mouth disease, I had been told by a local doctor that the milk for my daughter should be *not* pasteurized but simply sterilized.

Ironically, in a Washington newspaper dispatch, which I read on the train back to Paris after taking leave of M. Courtonne, the U.S. Food and Drug Administration warned American consumers in the United States against eating Camembert or Brie cheeses of a brand that had been legally distributed. In all, 143 persons in the United States had suffered gastric disturbances after eating the cheeses, which were found to be contaminated with E. coli bacteria, a common intestinal bacterium. All cheeses bearing that brand name were recalled, and a spokesman at the French Embassy in Washington said that the source of the bacteria was believed to be a worker in the industrial plant in the *département* of Eure. And these were pasteurized cheeses.

But would I be able to pass through customs in New York successfully with M. Courtonne's gift of an almost ready Camembert and Mme. Pinot's Pont l'Évêque, both non-pasteurized?

It developed on my return to the United States, in the pre-Christmas rush, that when I said simply, in answer to a question about food, that I had two cheeses with me, I was waved through quickly, without any examination of the product. Thus, I was able to enjoy an American Christmas dinner featuring two superb, unspoiled examples of the craft of French cheese making, on U.S. soil.

It is not my intention here to examine in detail the four hundred-plus varieties of French cheeses, much less to sample all of them, delightful as that prospect might be. Since the historic, if apocryphal, day when the legendary Arab sat down to refresh himself with milk carried in a skin bottle made from the lining of a calf's stomach, and tasted—according to some—the first cheese curd, a thousand species of cheese have flowered throughout the world, and as many cheese experts have waxed lyrical over tasting an obscure product of some remote mountain hideaway. (Many of these fromage fanciers can trace cheese back to the Greek gods quicker than you can say Holsteiner Gesundheitkäse.)

Nor is it my purpose to challenge the choices of these grand cheese lovers or to repeat or enlarge on their encomiums. Many of these dedicated gentlemen and gentlewomen feel that the supreme moment of ecstasy in life is that devoted to the consummation of a classic cheese at the precise instant that it achieves maturity. Well, why not?

My own philosophical view of the subject is summed up by the French in their useful expression *"Chacun à son goût"*—or, in this particular case, "Each to his own fromage."

# Rococo Is Relevant, Marquetry Is Meaningful . . .

―――――∞―――――

*When King Louis XIV began to construct his palace it was the signal for the formation of a vast army, composed in part of woodworkers, cabinet-makers, founders, sculptors, goldsmiths, silversmiths, lapidaries, weavers, gilders, marble-cutters, makers of mechanical devices, and upholsterers, and their main purpose was to provide furniture and other accoutrements of ravishing grace, beauty, and opulence for the Sun King, his favorites, and for his successors and their favorites.*

―――――∞―――――

One morning late in 1969, the curators of objects of art at the Château de Versailles gathered together for a routine staff meeting. As is their custom, they met in a working area on the upper floors of the gigantic palace, once the playing field of French court intrigue, today a national museum.

The *conservateurs*, whose jobs keep them in daily communication with the luxuriant history of the château, have cause to remember that particular meeting. One of their number arrived rather excitedly waving a copy of the latest issue of the *Bulletin of the Metropolitan Museum of Art of New York*, and his agitation was soon understood and shared by his colleagues. The piece of news carried in the publication would not have made waves anywhere else in the world. But to the curators it was sensational, and they received it with no little anguish—also mystification.

The *Bulletin* contained a color photograph of a lush red desk that had been delivered in the year 1759 to King Louis XV at Versailles. This piece of furniture was from the hand of Gilles Joubert, who was one of the leading royal *ébénistes*, or fine cabinetmakers, of the high period of the eighteenth century (1710–89), a time in France when furniture of a sumptuous, seductive kind was created that was richer and lovelier than any other ever made in the world.

The curators had never seen the desk before. All the same, they recognized it right away as the "*bureau laqué rouge.*" One of a multitude of objects with which it is their business to be on familiar terms, the desk was among the important pieces which are known from detailed records of the eighteenth century to have existed but which, since the upsetting days of the French Revolution, had long ago vanished from sight.

The re-emergence out of nowhere of the Joubert desk (albeit, to the *conservateurs*, in the wrong museum, on the wrong side of the ocean) after years in obscurity was parallel to a discovery by a corps of archaeologists of a lost fragment of the Parthenon. Lovers of French furniture of the *haute époque*, though a relatively limited lot, are as impassioned in their quest after the *commodes, secrétaires*, gaming tables, corner cupboards, and other luxurious paraphernalia ordered during the palmiest days of the French royal court as any seeker after beauties of earlier great worlds.

The desk was flat-topped, of scarlet lacquer of the type called "*vernis Martin*" that required forty-two coats to gain the desired transparency. Painted in gold with scenes in the Chinese manner, of impressive palace size—almost six feet by three feet—with sculptured, gilded bronze mounts and the linear lyricism of the rococo style that was fostered by the King's mistresses Mesdames de Pompadour and Du Barry, it seemed to have survived through more than two hundred years in admirable shape—at least insofar as the curators could tell by its appearance in the photograph. It glowed on the page like a precious gem. As was apparent from another, black-and-white photograph in the *Bulletin*, the desk had become the *pièce de résistance*, the latest fabulous addition, in a room at the Metropolitan filled with rare eighteenth-century French furnishings on loan from the collection of Mr. and Mrs. Charles A. Wrightsman, of Palm Beach and New York.

It seemed improbable to the Versailles staff that the desk would be anything but the genuine article, although forgeries of furniture of the high period are in plentiful supply and their hand manufacture has reached a high level of craftsmanship, especially in France. Excellent nineteenth-century line-for-line copies of celebrated pieces are also floating around on the market.

However, the Joubert desk had been given a thorough going over, or so it would appear. On checking into the matter further, the curators

34

found that the *bureau laqué rouge* had been authenticated by no less an expert than Francis J. B. Watson, with a little help from his friend Pierre Verlet. Watson, an Englishman who is director of the Wallace Collection in London, one of the world's treasure-troves of great French furniture, also serves Elizabeth II as Surveyor of the Queen's Works of Art. In addition, he is consultant to the Wrightsmans and author of the catalogue of their extensive collection. M. Verlet, chief curator of the department of objects of art at the Louvre Museum in Paris, is the world's first authority; he is to French eighteenth-century furniture and decoration what the late Bernard Berenson was to Italian Renaissance painting.

In an article he wrote for the British magazine *Apollo* in September of 1969, Watson seemed to have confirmed the pedigree of the red lacquered desk. He cited all primary and secondary source references to the piece, including those in the books of M. Verlet. He noted that, although it is not marked with Joubert's *estampille* (the signature brand used by the cabinetmakers), the underside of the desk bears the number 2131 painted in black script. As the curators knew, the desk would not necessarily have been signed, because royal *ébénistes* were exempted from the ruling requiring cabinetmakers to stamp each piece. With the aid of M. Verlet, Watson had been able quickly to check out 2131 in the inventory listings of the *Journal du Garde-Meuble de la Couronne* (*Journal of the Store-house of the Crown*), the eighteenth-century record that is preserved in France's National Archives. Watson noted that the entry opposite 2131 in the *Journal* gives a succinct description of the *bureau laqué rouge*. (Later, somewhat to the irritation of his French readers, Watson referred to the desk as 296, the number assigned to it in the Wrightsman Collection.)

As to the provenance and the recent history of the desk, which he characterized as "perhaps the most important single piece of French eighteenth-century furniture ever to have crossed the Atlantic," Watson remained diplomatically vague, apart from disclosing that the desk had appeared "out of the blue on the New York market" early in 1968.

That was all well and good, but pieces of such national value and interest are not supposed to disappear in France and then turn up later in other parts of the world. The French think they have set up a system of controls that prevents this kind of thing from happening. What the curators wanted to know, as they brooded over what looks—for the moment, at least—to be their loss, was how the Joubert desk came to arrive at the door of the Metropolitan rather than at the ornate gates of the Palace of Versailles. Some time will have to elapse before they have all the answers to that question.

The rationale behind their thinking that a piece such as the *bureau laqué rouge* rightfully belongs at Versailles goes back to just after World War I, when restoration of the château, which had long been neglected, began with work largely made possible through the generosity of John D. Rockefeller, Jr. Subsequently the state, assisted by private donors and committees such as the Friends of Versailles and the American Friends of Versailles, has been engaged in a massive scheme to bring back to the château as many of *"Toutes les Gloires de la France"*—as the legend on the façade of the great palace reads in big gold letters—as is conceivably feasible. The refurnishing of the royal rooms, an undertaking close to the heart of the present curator-in-chief, Gerald van der Kemp, has proceeded apace in recent years, speeded along by gifts from such sympathetic Americans as Barbara Hutton and Douglas Dillon and by encouragement from the Duchess of Windsor.

Certain rooms of the palace have been revived to a splendor equal to that of the days when Louis XIV, XV, and XVI lived there. In fact, what bothered the curators most about the defection of the red lacquered desk (and defection it was, for the piece had not too long since departed from the borders of France) was that it was the only major item that is at present missing from the King's private study, the *cabinet intérior* or *cabinet d'angle*.

This room, Louis XV's refuge from the hurly-burly of the court on the first floor of the palace, is nearly completely refurbished, down to the deep red damask curtains at the windows. The staff is partial toward the King's study, for it contains one of the prizes of Versailles: another, but infinitely more famous desk, with a roll top, by two great *ébénistes*, Jean-François Oeben and Jean-Henri Riesener, that is considered to be *the* capital piece of furniture of the *haute époque*. This desk took nine years in the making and is known to aficionados of French furniture everywhere as the *"bureau du roi"* or the *"bureau à cylindre de Louis XV."* By either name, it is easily the world's most fabulous piece of furniture, a peerless specimen of the curvaceous *rocaille*, or rococo, which gets its name from the curious rock gardens first designed by the renowned ceramist Bernard Palissy for Catherine de Medicis in the gardens of the Tuileries in the fifteen hundreds.

As word of the affair of the red lacquered desk spread, its reappearance engaged the interest of the learned personnel of other museums besides Versailles and its story was recounted by clusters of canny *professionnels,* the dealers, and by groups of connoisseurs, *amateurs,* the "men of taste," and collectors in France and elsewhere. They make up a special world of men and women whose hearts all beat faster when they read a catalogue description of a pair of firedogs by the genius bronze-worker Jacques Caffiéri or some other signed piece from the collection of Prince de X, Y, or Z that is coming up on the block. In antiquarian circles as well as along the corridors of the Hôtel Drouot, the Paris auction house, the tale of the red lacquered desk and its voyage out of France went the rounds.

The acknowledged general opinion was that had the *bureau laqué rouge* come up in a public sale, it would never have left the country. It would have been claimed by the government. In France, if a museum curator or a gentleman from the commission of the Beaux-Arts observes that the antique you feel you must own should be considered part of the patrimony of the state, he will exercise the government's right, within the law of June 27, 1951, to buy the object from under your nose at an arbitrated price. The only way you can prevent him from doing this is to agree to keep your antique in France and promise to restore it in the future to a museum or a corner of a national palace such as, say, the King's study at Versailles. Therefore, it was reasoned in the antiquarian world that, whoever had sold the red lacquered desk, the transaction would have been private, *à l'amiable,* "between friends."

Because of the restrictions on exportation, buying antiques of the quality of the Joubert desk can be a parlous business. Then, too, for French people there is the tax inspector. His watchful eye must be taken into account and preferably avoided by means of quiet deals in cash when large sums are involved.

Taking one thing with another, it soon became a matter of public knowledge through the *téléphone arabe,* or grapevine, along the Paris antique circuit that the red lacquered desk had passed from Frenchman to Frenchman but, things being as they were, few cared to divulge from which Frenchman to which Frenchman. Assuredly, neither the owner nor the middleman nor the dealer would have been eager to let the government in on what he was doing—especially if any of them had been positive of the identity and importance of the piece they were handling.

Given these circumstances, sometimes the only way to realize a decent profit on an imposing eighteenth-century piece is to get it out of the country without passing it through customs. The legitimate procedure is to present oneself and one's object at the central customs office in Paris, where every Wednesday afternoon furniture and other art objects over a hundred years old destined for export are examined by a scholarly group of curators of the Museums of France who have the authority to stop any piece that is of interest to the state from leaving France. As the curators of Versailles knew, the *bureau laqué rouge* was never presented at customs.

Plenty of other topflight pieces are, however, and the majority are allowed to pass through each week. Although the treasure of great furniture has diminished since the Revolution closed the curtain on the fabled life of the court, the supply of good *haute époque* antiques is far from depleted. The heavier, often jewel-encrusted furniture of Louis XIV and the bronze, tortoise-shell, or ebony-and-ivory marquetry inlay seventeenth-century pieces by André-Charles Boulle are exceedingly difficult to come by, partly because they were not to the taste of the next king, Louis XV. He took it into his head to auction off a good many of them, which makes it harder to track them down. The solid-silver pieces went to the mint to be melted down to finance some of Louis's impetuous sorties on the battlefields. Yet surprisingly little else of the great crown furniture was destroyed, and as furniture was the status emblem of the century, masses of it was produced.

When King Louis XIV began to construct his palaces and put his chief Minister, Jean-Baptiste Colbert, in over-all control as Superintendent of the King's Buildings and appointed his court painter, Charles Le Brun, as Director of the Manufacture Royale des Meubles de la Couronne at the Gobelins factory, it was the signal for the formation of a vast army. This force was composed in part of woodworkers, cabinetmakers, founders, sculptors, goldsmiths, silversmiths, lapidaries, weavers, gilders, marble-cutters, makers of mechanical devices, and upholsterers, and their main purpose was to provide furniture and other accoutrements of ravishing grace, beauty, and opulence for the Sun King, his favorites, and for his successors and their favorites. When they wearied of an object or became displeased with it and felt that its day was done, as they periodically did, the kings and queens and mistresses and courtiers casually gave the object away—at which point their army of *fournisseurs* was called upon to set to work on still another, newer, more ravishing, graceful, beautiful, and opulent piece. As a matter of fact, this was what had happened to the Joubert red lacquered desk, which one could say was a castoff of Louis XVI. After the demise of Louis XV, the new sovereign took over the King's study and, in time, made some changes. He replaced the *bureau laqué rouge* with a glorious new flat-topped desk by Guillaume Benneman, which is a near replica of the lower part of the wondrous roll-topped *bureau du roi*. Eventually the Benneman desk made its way, through the English branch of the Rothschild family, to Waddeson Manor, in Buckinghamshire, where, as a part of a permanent collection, it is forever beyond the reach of the curators of Versailles.

Louis XVI kept his grandfather's *bureau du roi* in his study, and when its companion piece, the new Benneman desk, was delivered in 1786, he dispatched the old red lacquered Joubert desk to his brother, the Comte de Provence, who was known at the time in the court parlance for younger brothers of the King as "Monsieur" and was, much later, to become Louis XVIII. Monsieur held on to the desk until he took off for England, and it was still among his possessions in 1792, according to an inventory of that year drawn up by the National Convention, when presumably it was seized as émigré property. It then disappeared for nearly a hundred and eighty years until it recently resurfaced in New York.

In the mirror of the aristocracy, the *haute bourgeoisie* of the high period also had a mania for elegant furnishings to the extent that it was not unheard of for a banker or a tax farmer to have four separate changes in furniture to follow the seasons, one for winter, one for summer, one for spring, and one for fall. Thus, hundreds of lush pieces came into being. No one worried much about overspending. The upper classes disposed of unbelievable amounts to keep their châteaus, *hôtels particuliers*, and little *folies* livable with superlative furniture that managed to endure the turmoil and aftermath of the Revolution better than the people who owned it.

"Everything exists. It only rests to find it," says the Louvre's Pierre Verlet.

Such an opinion sustains the collector in keeping alive his hope that one day he will reclaim a rare piece from some dingy *brocanterie* or in the Balzacian recesses of the Hôtel Drouot, or at the chic sales in the Palais Galliéra. Perhaps he will. Says another exceptionally well-versed expert, auctioneer Jean-Louis Picard, whose office, Maîtres Ader Picard Tajan, in the French capital specializes in effects of the *haute époque*: "A mass of royal objects comes up in the sales. There may be a hole of more than a hundred years with no trace. Then a presumably lost article will suddenly reappear on the market."

Just after the Revolution, a voluptuous piece of aristocratic cabinetry by one of the great royal *ébénistes* was about as sought after as an invitation to take a ride down the Rue Saint-Honoré in a tumbril. What pieces had not been whisked out of France or successfully stashed in a country hideaway so that they escaped the pillage of the troupe of marauders called the Black Band were being sold for absurdly low prices. During the Directory, the Princes Potocki carted off twenty coachloads full of magnificent furniture for their castles in Poland. In the time of the First Empire, Louis XV taste was reviled and despised and nobody would profess to want it once it had been replaced in fashion by the dreadnaught shapes recommended by Napoleon's pet painter, Louis David. Those were the days when, among the British, cognizance of French high-period furnishings took hold, a vogue spurred by the pro-Royalist anti-Bonaparte enthusiasms of the English. The Prince of Wales bought as early as 1791 at the Paris sales of the furniture, and the trend continued in the nineteenth century, with Richard Seymour-Conway—Fourth Marquess of Hertford and elder brother of Lord Henry Seymour, the founder of the Jockey Club of Paris—in the purchasing lead from 1840 to 1870. Lord Hertford's acquisitions formed the basis of the present Wallace Collection.

Even as recently as the late nineteen-thirties, one could have picked up first-quality *haute époque* pieces readily, as J. Paul Getty did, for at that time the prices of prime articles were well below their intrinsic worth and, outside of France, were temporarily *démodé*. In the nineteen-sixties, when the sales of Old Master and French Impressionist paintings attained plateaus of far beyond a million dollars, people looked around for other things on which to place their money. For much less than a hundred thousand dollars, a Louis XV piece bearing the stamp of BVRB (Bernard van Ryssen Burghe, considered the greatest artist in marquetry) was an enjoyable investment and as sound as—in the long term, perhaps sounder than—a second-rate Cézanne or Renoir.

In 1970, the market value of Louis XV, the most prized of all Louis furniture, was worth twenty times its 1939 price, an appreciation of 2,000 percent. By that time, the happiest hunting ground for the highest quality pieces had narrowed down to Paris, although prices in London are generally lower, with choice articles often available, and although the real bargains, should one chance on them, are in the smallest of the three major markets, New York. Rare is the occasion when a knowing dealer encounters a find by digging through to the back of a colleague's truck at dawn as the Marché Biron opens in the Paris Flea Market. When that sort of discovery does occur, the piece is sold immediately and resold and sold again in a tortuous climb, ending up at a smart antique shop on the Quai Voltaire or the Rue du Faubourg Saint-Honoré.

If you are the most persevering type of furniture suitor, then when you are traveling in the outskirts of Paris or elsewhere in the country you never pass up a sign that says *"Antiquités."* You cultivate aristocratic acquaintances who might be prodded, for cash, into parting with an old family armoire or two in order to augment their annual income. In the French capital, you haunt the *salles* of the Hôtel Drouot, the atmosphere of which calls up the darkest passages of Zola.

Some 600,000 times a year, the auctioneer snaps, *"Adjugé!"* as he whacks his ivory gavel during one of the 4,000 sales held in Paris annually. In the welter of objects, the provenance of the majority is dreary, even sinister, and only occasionally romantic. Among the names figuring in the old catalogues is that of Marie Duplessis, the original Camille. The bulk of the goods on the first floor of the Drouot has either been carted off for debts by some squint-eyed *huissier*, the bailiff who seals the door on the house of a hapless unfortunate at the order of some infuriated creditor, or is being disposed of to settle an estate. In September, 1878, the painter Claude Monet, who was behind in his taxes, wrote frantically to a friend one night that he needed a hundred and ninety francs before nine the next morning, when all of his household effects, seized by *"les contributions,"* were to be sold at the Hôtel Drouot. Middle-class housewives frequent the *salles* for heavy pure-linen sheets which often have intriguing monograms with crests embroidered above the initials. Odds and ends, rejects of inheritances, are sold by the wicker hamperful for the equivalent of five or ten dollars.

Once, the rumors run, at the bottom of such a basket nestled a grimy little rolled-up canvas. After cleaning and *expertise,* it was certified: a real Manet, so they said, authentic signature and all. Such stuff of dreams keeps the habitué going to the Drouot, day after day.

The first-floor salesrooms are full of Henri II dining-room sets of recent manufacture and of countless nineteenth-century imitations of the Louis XV and XVI furniture made in the days of the Empress Eugénie. These types of copies continue to please the bourgeois French, many of whom have managed to set up housekeeping by bidding carefully at the Drouot, a big building on the corner of the Rues Chauchat and Rossini, in the 9th *arrondissement* not far from the Opéra Comique.

On the second floor, the better items are dispersed—signed pieces of Gallé or Tiffany glass, rare butterflies, porcelains, fine furniture that is reliably *de l'époque,* the terminology for the genuine antique, and not merely *ancien,* a reproduction that has aged fifty to seventy-five years, or *de style,* a modern copy of an old piece. The auctioneers, or *commissaires-priseurs,* charge 16 percent of the sale price up to $300, 11½ percent from there to $4,000, and 10 percent for any sale above that. All purchasers are comfortably covered, however, by a guarantee of authenticity which they do not enjoy anywhere else in the world. In France, if an acquisition fails to live up to the catalogue description, which is customarily quite cautiously written by a well-qualified expert, the buyer may, on demand and after arbitration, have his money refunded.

"This seldom happens," says Jean-Louis Picard. "The expert is not God, to be sure, but perhaps ten times out of hundreds of thousands of transactions in a year the expert will make a mistake."

The detection of fraudulent pieces is seldom a problem to the Drouot's appraisers. They, like nearly all responsible dealers, are versed in the techniques of using old wood for newly made furniture and other tricks of simulating antiquity, down to the last drilled wormhole. A useful source book concerning the legerdemain of furniture forgery, *In the Land of the Antique Dealers—Confidences of a Professional "Make-Up Artist,"* by André Mailfert, has been committed to memory by most French experts.

Mailfert, who started off as a watercolorist, built up a bustling business in Orléans during the early years of this century, doing particularly well in the nineteen-twenties by counterfeiting antiques in his "Ateliers d'Art," located in "an Historic Hotel said to be [the attribution is Mailfert's own] of the period François I." Mailfert's was a glorious career of flimflam, and to cap it, he confessed all to a Paris publisher.

Early on, he said, he discerned a difference in people. There were, he perceived, two kinds in the world; i.e., "Those who roll others, and —the others, that is, those who are rolled," and Mailfert knew which kind he intended to be. The ease with which he put over his first sale, "a crass copy of a Louis XVI barometer" which he had glued together, at a total cost of forty francs for the materials, along the lines of a real barometer entrusted to him for repairs by a certain Baroness de Saint-A——, reinforced the intuitive feeling he had of having hit upon the right business. The old magistrate who picked the fake over the genuine piece when he saw them both side by side insisted he knew better than Mailfert what it was worth, and over Mailfert's protests he paid a thousand francs for it.

From then on, Mailfert grew more scientific about the arts of his trade, studying every useful ploy. Did he need antique dust? He collected it from nooks and crannies in old churches and then inserted it into the cracks of his false ancient furniture. Flyspecks were another specialty, and he found out by experimenting with sprays of nitric acid that he could reproduce specks that were not merely like the hundred-year-old ones but, if viewed without a magnifying glass, would pass for "the real, the true, the 'of the period Louis XV.'"

He fabricated so many overmantel mirrors framed in wood and gilt and decorated with his own paintings of figures in powdered wigs cavorting à la Fragonard that, by the time Mailfert wrote his book, his conscience hurt him and he felt obligated to tip off the public. "A word of advice," he told his readers. "Never buy an old overmantel mirror; the real one is one in a thousand and is in a museum (not every time!), in a château or in its original *boiserie*.

"Consider this, that in Paris alone, there are as many antique and secondhand dealers as there are wine merchants and that there exist in their shops more 'antique' overmantel mirrors than there are ancient chimneys in France and you will see that an authentic mirror is rarer than a dinosaur's egg."

Mailfert could turn one genuine console into two semi-genuine ones and knew all about multiplying a long sofa into triplet chairs by dividing it up into three parts and judiciously adding the missing arms and legs. His highest achievement, though, was his creation of Jean-François Hardy, of the imaginary School of the Loire, who was purportedly made a master *ébéniste* in 1746 in Tours. To shore up the cabinetmaker's identity, Mailfert provided spurious ancient sketches of buffets and *fauteuils* as well as some wash drawings from the hand of Maître Hardy, which fortuitously came to light at a convenient moment. Hardy's "portrait" also miraculously appeared, in a state of stunning preservation, which was understandable if one happened to know the picture's origin: an 1850 painting of a clergyman over which Mailfert had painted a new head topped with a periwig and had also added a quill pen and a note-book.

Of course Hardy was given a brand, his initials, J.-F. H., with which Mailfert could stamp all of Hardy's masterpieces. The famous forger, the descendants of whose partner still carry on the business in his ateliers today, was often called upon by Paris dealers to "authenticate" an old piece of furniture by marking it with the stamp of a celebrated *ébéniste,* and Mailfert was very adept at his work.

Other fakers have not been so skillful. Jacques Helft of the family of noted Paris dealers has told of being telephoned by a forger of Versailles who said he had just received a formidable *commode.* When Helft saw it, he recognized immediately that it was a fraud and said so.

"What?" said the forger, lifting up the marble top. "Why, it is even signed Leleu!"

"Look," said the dealer. "Next time, mark it 'Leleu' and not 'Leuleu.' "

"You hear that, Héloise?" the forger called out to his wife. "I told you plainly it was L-E-L-E-U."

Alert to the trumperies of fakers, the auctioneers and experts are also kept well-advised about stolen antiques. On the bulletin board outside the office of the director of the Compagnie des Commissaires-Priseurs at the Hôtel Drouot are Polaroid color prints of specific descriptions of valuable objects that have recently been taken in burglaries. There is also a list of stolen goods that is circulated by the antique dealers' syndicate and, if a theft is of sufficient international importance, the missing objects may become the subject of an illustrated brochure put out by Interpol. However, the lists and the Drouot's bulletin board are not so crowded these days as they were in the nineteen-sixties when a ring of thieves, masterminded by a scholarly but mentally quirky doctor, Xavier Richier, was operating on a regular basis in cagily planned forays on churches and châteaus in France. The story of the eight-million-dollar haul of *le Gang des Châteaux,* as the ring was known in the newspapers, has been told by David Leitch in his book *The Discriminating Thief.* Richier's pre-raid research was so detailed that the thieves' selectivity was infallible in picking out the authentic pieces from the reproductions. At the Duc de Luynes's Château de Dampierre, for example, the thieves, having crossed a moat to enter a first-floor window, walked off with four genuine chairs by Boulard out of a set of twelve, and of the ones they left behind four were the copies. A special task force set up by the French police finally closed in on the ring and arrested its members but failed to recover all of the gang's loot. Articles that have been "Richiered" are still around on the antique belt and some are long since thought to have been slipped across the Belgian border, which is not far from where Richier lived, in Liévin, and not an unusual exit route for hot antiques from France.

The cloak-and-dagger aspects of antiquing are generally restricted to the worlds of the dealers and the decorators and seldom affect the work-aday lives of the men at the Drouot, according to Jean-Louis Picard. Although he shares an urbanity of manner that seems universal with auctioneers everywhere, Picard, like the seventy others who practice his profession in Paris, differs from his colleagues outside of France. In other countries, anybody can choose to be an auctioneer, but Picard and the rest of the three hundred and fifty *commissaires-priseurs* of France are government appointees. He is a ministerial officer, entitled to be addressed as "Maître," and must obtain a diploma of capacity in law as well as a professional certificate attesting to his juridical and artistic knowledge before being sworn in to his *charge*, or post, which he and his confrères regard most seriously. Theirs is an ancient calling, dating back at least to Imperial Roman times. Wax tablets recording the transactions of one Caecilius Jucundus, *magister* or *auctionnator*, in the year 79 A.D. were recovered in the ruins of a house in Pompeii. Today's French auctioneers count the beginnings of their association, the Compagnie des Commissaires-Priseurs de Paris, from the charter of 1556 created by Henri II, establishing the office of appraiser-seller of furniture, "who must be capable, experienced, and informed."

Three times during the year, in late November, March, and June, the most precious pieces come up for sale. For the big jewels, the Impressionist and modern paintings, the museum-quality porcelains, silver, and bronzes, and the great furniture, the auctioneers need a more elegant setting than the dusty Drouot, so their association rents the spacious marble-walled Palais Galliéra museum near the fashionable Place d'Iéna. Here there are no sensational bargains. "But surely great quality is always a bargain," Maître Picard points out.

The furniture is generally put up in the afternoons at the Galliéra sales, making them a part of the Paris social round for pretty women from the 16th *arrondissement* who want to add a pair of sconces to the salon wall or acquire a Louis XV chair or *commode.* They sit in the front row and criticize the inlay designs of the marquetry, and the way some of the *seizième* ladies bid up scandalizes the dealers.

A chest of drawers is presented, undeniably *de l'époque* but, as is noted in the catalogue description, bearing a signature that is partially effaced and that has been submitted at some time in its long life to, as the auctioneer comments, "*quelques réparations.*" A lissome young woman in a Givenchy suit raises the price from $20,000 to $35,000 in a matter of seconds. Every dealer in the room knows that "some repairs" can mean anything from the replacement of a bit of veneer to a total overhaul and reconstruction, and one of them turns to stare at the young buyer and cluck, "Not worth it."

The ladies are still partial to floral motifs where the marquetry may combine numerous exotic woods, both native to Europe and from the Indies, East and West: violetwood, tulipwood, Amboina, rosewood, thujawood, wild cherry, limewood, and white woods that were tinted with color for the composition. "But on the whole," says Maître Picard, "one appreciates the simple subjects in marquetry nowadays more than the elaborate flowers. Cubes and chessboard patterns appeal to current taste." To illustrate his point, on the same afternoon a superb example in checkerboard-design wood soared quickly from a starting price of $20,000 to $51,000 within two minutes. The fact that the *commode* in question was stamped "M. Criaerd," the brand of a cabinetmaker who was made a master in 1738, and that its ornamentation of ormolu, sculptured in the asymmetrical rococo Louis XV style, was crowned with a coroneted "C" was a help.

Criaerd was of Flemish origin. Beginning with Domenico Cucci, the sculptor and furniture maker who was summoned from his native Italy in the sixteen-sixties to live at the Gobelins where he directed work on grandioso cabinets for Louis XIV, many of the élite artisans of the crown were foreigners, principally Germans. The craftsmen were given special quarters and belonged to a guild of *menuisiers-ébénistes* which was set up, with a minutia of rules, along the lines of the medieval unions. *Menuisiers* were generally chairmakers. *Ébénistes* worked in ebony and other fine woods, hence the name. The number of artisans was limited by decree; they could practice only one trade; and before setting up in business they must serve a long apprenticeship, then prove their worth with a chef-d'oeuvre, and finally pay a considerable sum of money to acquire their title of master. The system still obtains in many trades in Europe to this day.

The guild members could charge whatever they thought they could get for their most elaborate pieces. Most of the time, they needed the money. Many cabinetmakers were themselves passionate collectors of fine furniture and paintings, with highly impractical notions about money. At the age of eighty, André-Charles Boulle saw his Old Masters and great pieces he had made with his own hands sold at auction. The same fate later awaited Charles Cressent, the greatest *ébéniste* of the Regency, who saw his Dürers, Holbeins, Rembrandts, and Rubens go on the block in his declining years. Also, the aristocracy took its time about paying, so that debts were an everyday problem for many artisans. The day Oeben died, his widow had the bailiff at the door clamoring for money.

In the latter part of the eighteenth century came an invasion of German cabinetmakers unaffiliated with the guild who made good furniture and charged less than the masters. The entrance fee to the guild was lowered to let the foreigners in, and by 1785 nearly a third of the thousand *maîtres-menuisiers* were non-French. Even more immigrants poured in to form what Comte François Salverte, the diplomat-historian of art objects, has called "a turbulent colony, easily excitable, where the Revolution would find its best elements of disorder. Out of six to seven hundred 'victors' who stormed the Bastille, sixty were furniture workers, mostly Germans, many of whom did not speak our language, and others were younger than twenty years old. These improvised 'patriots' were nonetheless impelled to avenge France against the horrors of despotism."

They were moving toward the debacle, after which nothing like the high period in furniture-making would again be reached. Miraculously, the apogee of the *haute époque,* Louis XV's roll-top desk, came through the worrisome end of the century unscathed.

In 1738, the King had begun certain renovations in his private quarters to make them an area where he could truly get away from it all. It was in his *cabinet intérieur,* where only servants and trusted cronies such as the Duc de Luynes were allowed to enter, that Louis poured over his intaglios and his medals. The study had, in fact, formerly been identified as the Room of the Medal Cabinet when, after he had altered the room's size to 24 feet by 21 feet, Louis had ordered a splendid chest of drawers, with fittings for storing his treasures. On the top of this chest, by Antoine Gaudreaux, stood the Candelabra of the American Independence, by

Pierre-Philippe Thomire. In the corners of the study were two cabinets that were designed, by Joubert, to contain more medals, and were similar in ornamentation to the Gaudreaux chest. The flat top of Joubert's gorgeous red lacquered desk was a work surface where Louis could spread out his charts. But adequate drawer space in which to store the royal papers was lacking. In 1760, the King commissioned from Oeben the spectacular *bureau à cylindre*.

Jean-François Oeben was German-born (one of his daughters, Victoire, married the lawyer Charles Delacroix de Coutant and became the mother of the painter Eugène Delacroix) and was a specialist in ingenious mechanical constructions. Oeben had delighted Mme. de Pompadour and other clients with secret compartments, chairs with perambulating or elevating devices, and dressing tables with disappearing mirrors. Before he died in 1763, he had shown the King a full-size model of the *bureau à cylindre*, the top and all compartments of which, both within and without, were to open and close at the turn of a key in a single lock. Only the silver inkwells, placed in drawers on the sides, could be opened at will.

The task of completing the desk fell upon Oeben's assistant, Jean-Henri Riesener, who not only succeeded him in his atelier but also married his widow. Born in Gladbeck, near Essen, Riesener was to become the sole cabinetmaker to the crown, the favorite artisan of Marie-Antoinette. Between 1774 and 1784, he turned out nearly seven hundred pieces of great furniture of a refinement that has earned him the title of *"le plus grand ébéniste de son époque."*

A lengthy memorandum presented in 1770 with the bill (for 62,945 livres, more than any piece of furniture had ever cost before) detailed the complexities of executing this "secretary of different woods of the Indies." The marquetry consisted of twenty-two designs representing: " a quantity of trophies, attributes of royalty, dramatic poems, terrestrial and marine war, the terrestrial globe and the attributes of geometry, the celestial globe and the attributes of astronomy, representations of fruits, cornucopias of abundance, the riches of the sea such as coral, pearls, shells, and others, the attribute of penmanship, a quantity of flowers and bouquets attached with ribbons, the cipher of the King, several panels of very intricate mosaics." This description covered only the woodwork. The sweeping gilded bronzes, by Joseph-Sifrède Duplessis and J.-C. Hervieux, were another story and so was Lépine's clock, posed at the center of the desk's top gallery.

In May, 1769, the whole thing, having been demounted and the parts packed in crates, was borne from Paris on litters by "a quantity of men," who were accompanied by four skilled workmen, and transported to Versailles. There, under the direction of Riesener, the workmen cleaned, assembled, and polished the *bureau* and set it in place in the King's study, where it stands once again today.

"It is, quite simply, the most beautiful piece of furniture in the world," says Pierre Verlet, who grew to love and cherish the desk during the many years when it was in his care at the Louvre. Before that, it had been used by Menneval, Napoleon I's secretary, in the Tuileries during the First Empire and by the Empress Eugénie at Saint-Cloud during the Second.

"From the point of view of richness, line, proportion—it is all of a grand perfection." Verlet made no secret of his deep disappointment in 1955 when, through a political maneuver by a Beaux-Arts Minister, the desk was taken from his custody and returned to Versailles.

During the time the desk was at the Louvre, Verlet had discovered that certain alterations had been made by Riesener during the Revolution, when the *ébéniste* was ordered to change the "signs of feudality." The royal monograms on the sides were replaced with Sèvres plaques in the style of Wedgwood; the crown that the bronze statuettes of children on the clock held was removed.

Now the *bureau du roi* will remain in the *cabinet intérieur,* where it began life with Louis XV and where most people think it belongs. The King took a tremendous interest in furniture and followed the stages of the desk's development through nine years of drawings and plans and models of the final creation. If as *"le meuble le plus célèbre du monde"* the roll-top desk has been a bone of contention among Ministers and curators, that would have been due somewhat to the cultural climate in France, where a sense of history is so everyday and innate that it becomes second nature to slip back a few centuries and fall in love with vestiges of the past. When that happens, it no longer seems arguable that what was made for Versailles belongs at Versailles.

It is a heavy desk, weighted further with garlands of ormolu and reclining statuettes of Calliope holding candelabra on the curves of the cylindrical top. Yet so buoyant and harmonious is the composition that it looks as light as air on the room's Savonnerie carpet.

"In the Louvre it was too rich, but here it is seen in all its qualities,"

M. Daniel Meyer, a young curator at the Museum of Versailles and the Trianons, said recently when he was showing the roll-top desk to a visitor. "We live in the midst of all of this," he continued, gesturing toward the balcony outside the window from which Louis XV watched, tears rolling down his cheeks, the passing of the funeral cortège of Mme. de Pompadour. "And we see how this furniture was made for a certain use, in relation to the *boiseries* of the walls, in relation to the draperies, in relation to the other furniture in the room. These pieces were studied for a certain place, and when you put them in their rightful place, they again find all their proportions."

As to the *histoire* of Louis XV's flat-topped red lacquered desk and its rightful place, the complete story is yet to be told. M. Verlet, whose immersion in the past is such that he admits, "I have the impression sometimes that I am in the eighteenth century, a little bit an attendant of Louis XV or Louis XVI," was consulted soon after the Wrightsmans' purchase of the desk in New York. Nevertheless, like other authorities who have been close to the affair, he declines to divulge whatever he may know or guess of its twentieth-century history beyond saying its departure from France entailed *"plusieurs ramifications."* An executive at the New York office of a Paris decorating firm, who wishes to remain anonymous and whose company has worked closely with parties involved in the affair of the Joubert desk, goes so far as to doubt its authenticity, despite the scholarship that was applied to its identification; and he adds, "As a decorator, I never ask a dealer how he acquired an object." At the Metropolitan, the only discreet comment a high functionary wishes to make is "Officially, I know nothing of how the desk came here."

Others, both in New York and Paris, are somewhat freer with information. They say the desk left France *"maquillé"*; that is, with its red japanning and gold decorations of Chinoiserie disguised under a coat of black paint, and with its bronzes *"retirés,"* removed, and packed and shipped separately. The Joubert desk could well have been in that condition for dozens of years. Many elaborate pieces of beautiful old furniture were in the eighteenth, nineteenth, or twentieth centuries covered over by their owners with a camouflage as protection in times of wars and revolutions and occupations.

When, where, and however the paint came to be applied, the red lacquered desk arrived *maquillé* and incognito in New York, having traveled by way of an antique merchant in Brussels who had received it from a French *antiquaire*. First it was stripped of its cover by an expert, who would have experimented by patch-testing a tiny area with various solvents and who left a bit of the black on the inside curve of the knee-hole of the desk—paint that looks quite fresh, but then so does the black used for the numbers on the underside.

The desk was then put on display in the rooms of the firm of dealers who had imported it, one of the most respected on Fifty-seventh Street. The dealers, who appreciated it as the greatest *haute époque* desk that had come into their hands in a lifetime and probably the finest in the entire United States, had no clue whatsoever as to its identity.

Within a few weeks, Mrs. Wrightsman, who is a good client of the house, stopped in. The desk immediately struck her eye. It was, she said, exactly what her husband, who is an oil multimillionaire, needed for his study in Palm Beach. A price in the $160,000 to $170,000 range was agreed upon.

Then several months elapsed after the delivery of the desk during which the New York dealer heard nothing from Mrs. Wrightsman and nothing from any other quarter that would put light on the origins of the piece. She meanwhile had turned to the foremost authorities, Verlet and Watson, who corroborated her intuition that the piece was something out of the ordinary. Their findings fell at a propitious moment, being just in time for the red lacquered desk to be featured on the cover of Volume III of *The Wrightsman Collection*, by Watson and Carl C. Dauterman, published in 1970 as one of a series of expensive art books cataloguing the Wrightsmans' furniture and *objets d'art*. In the course of the authentication of the desk, Mrs. Wrightsman had decided that it should preferably be exhibited in a temperature-controlled room behind a thick glass partition in the Metropolitan Museum rather than in use in her house in Palm Beach—for the time being, at any rate.

The story of the red lacquered desk only goes to prove what M. Verlet and many of his cohorts in the field have been saying all along about the lost treasures of French court furniture: most of them still exist; all we have to do is to find them somehow and, of course, have the money to pay for them. It is a tale to bring hope and gladness to the hearts of antique searchers everywhere—if you except the curators of Versailles.

# The World's Most Exclusive Club

---···---

*The Jockey Club in Paris has been portrayed as "the only place where one can still be treated as a gentleman and can authenticate one's title; where admission is the equivalent of the honors of the court."*

---···---

Most men in the position of François Schneider, an influential power in French business and industry who figures in Georges Simenon's novel *The Bells of Bicêtre*, would feel that they had won all of life's first prizes.

At sixty-five, Schneider is in perfect health. Every morning before he leaves his handsome *hôtel particulier* on the best street in Paris, he is given a treatment in his private exercise room by his yoga professor. Then he is shaved and combed and manicured by his personal barber. When he arrives at the Bourse, he increases his already formidable fortune through stock manipulations; his voice carries heavy weight on several consequential boards of directors; he cuts a mean figure in French racing circles; he is welcomed in the salons of the most clever and beautiful women in Paris.

Yet in spite of his eminent position Schneider is not satisfied. There is only one group that really interests him, and so far it has failed to admit him. Like dozens of others in France who are exceptionally successful, he wants the crowning status symbol: he wants to belong to the Jockey Club of Paris.

Ever since it was founded in 1834, membership in the Jockey Club has been the ultimate stamp of French social approval. A choice museum piece that outsiders rarely see, the Jockey is the last stand of the remnants of the French aristocracy. Behind a deliberately anonymous façade at 2 Rue Rabelais, near the Rond Point des Champs-Élysées, the members—descendants of *"les lions"* and *"les demi-dieux du Jockey"* who fascinated Balzac and Proust—relish their privacy and are united in tireless vigil against any intrusion on what they regard as their hereditary rights, even if most people think these were dispensed with a long time ago.

Parisians like to pin the label of "the world's most exclusive club" on the Jockey, although an Englishman might argue for the Royal Yacht Squadron at Cowes. Even if the club does not hold this distinction, it is unique in another respect. There is surely no other place in the world where President Charles de Gaulle can be disposed of in conversation as "the son of old Talhouët's tutor."

Although noble birth is not necessarily a requirement for eligibility, 85 percent of those who make up the list of twelve hundred members have titles. At least three princes of the blood, two dozen *ducs*, and an array of lesser nobles compose a group whose names sound like a roll call from a French history book—if the book stops at the end of the nineteenth century.

Fame, intellectual brilliance, or distinguished public service are not of stunning significance at the Jockey Club. The Duc de Lévis-Mirepoix and Jacques de Lacretelle, both of the Académie Française, do not belong to the club because of their writing talents, but in spite of them. The Duc de Doudeauville, who was the club's president for forty years until he died in 1963 at the age of ninety-three, summed up the prevailing attitude when someone broached the name of the celebrated novelist and Academician Paul Bourget, and began cataloguing his achievements with a view to proposing him.

"Fortunately," said the Duc, "we are still those few in France for whom these matters are, thank God, of no importance whatsoever." The Duc was of the La Rochefoucauld family whose motto is: *"C'est mon plaisir."*

Provided they meet certain conditions, men such as Simenon's fictional François Schneider, who have simply concentrated on making money more or less honorably, stand a better chance. If Schneider belongs to a family of the *haute bourgeoisie*, if his fortune has been ripening for three generations, and if his relations have been kindly disposed toward the idea of marrying off daughters to insolvent sons of the aristocracy, he may even be on firmer ground than a candidate whose pedigree should make him a shoo-in but whose great-great-grandfather backed the wrong duke a hundred years before. Many of the Jockey's members have long memories.

The tangible rewards of admission are slight: an unobtrusive letter "J" after one's name in the *Bottin Mondain*, the French social register; access to the Jockey Club tribunes at the racecourses of Longchamp, Chantilly, and Deauville; and, at the club, a passable lunch or dinner for a modest fifteen francs.

Still, the warning of a sophisticated Parisian, "It's useless to knock at the door of the Jockey Club. . . . There hasn't been a new name in the yearbook in fifty years," will not restrain the François Schneiders from continuing to try. Ambitious Frenchmen who have reached the top of the material and social heap figure that the gamble is worth taking; and although they know that the entire membership votes on new entrants under a system whereby one "*non*" cancels out six "*oui*"s, they cheerfully risk being blackballed as many as two or three times over. If they fail often enough, they are in good company, and there is even a certain distinction to be gained. The record for blackballs at the Jockey Club is held by Charles Haas, Marcel Proust's model for Swann, who was put down four times before finally being elected.

Men's clubs started in France during the reign of Charles X on the wave of Anglomania that swept in with the *Restauration*. Every fashionable young Frenchman wanted to be a fop à la Buckingham or Beau Brummell. It was very bon ton to wear yellow gloves, lean over balconies smoking cigars, and practice looking detached and bored. *Les dandys* ate plum cake and spiced gingerbread and spoke French with a strong British accent. "Goddam," went a popular song, "*Moi, j'aime les Anglais!*"

The moving spirit behind the formation of the Jockey Club and the man chiefly responsible for the introduction of thoroughbred racing into France was an Englishman, Lord Henry Seymour, a leading eccentric of the day. No one in France had ever cared much about sports, much less horse racing, although today some Frenchmen will argue that it began with a contest organized by Charlemagne and won by the legendary Bayard. However that may be, Godolphin Arabian, one of the three founding stallions of thoroughbred racing, was said to have been sold for next to nothing by Louis XV and was later discovered pulling a dray cart in Paris, whence he was shipped off to England to breed champions that were later eagerly imported into France. Seymour, a small man, was a sports fanatic whose house in Paris was fitted out with a gymnasium and a massage room, and was packed every day with languid dandies who came to watch him and his muscle-conscious cronies box, fence, and work out with punching bags.

*Les dandys* much preferred looking at exercise to actually taking it. They thought the size of Seymour's biceps, which was said to equal the span of a young girl's waist, *"un monstrueux développement."* They were appalled that a man of high birth and great fortune would go in for weight-lifting and would join a crowd of thugs and rowdies to hang over the rails and shout at dogfights.

But Seymour loved racing, and in 1833 he founded, with the help of a number of like-minded and wealthy associates, the Société d'Encouragement for the improvement of horse breeding in France. Among his colleagues were the Russian Count Anatole Demidoff, who owned a bathtub carved from a single piece of malachite; Marshal Ney's son, the Prince de la Moskowa; and a Portuguese nobleman, De Gama Machado, who kept two hundred parakeets at home and never went out without one of them on his shoulder. (Seymour himself is supposed to have been the illegitimate son of the Marchioness of Hertford and the Adonis-like Comte Casimir de Montrond, Talleyrand's right-hand man. His money came from his mother's family, for the Marquess of Hertford, on whom Thackeray modeled the insufferable Lord Steyne in *Vanity Fair*, left Seymour out of his will.) Under the sponsorship of the Duc de Nemours and the Duc d'Orléans, the heir presumptive to the French throne, the aristocratic sportsmen set up the framework for thoroughbred racing in France, following the Newmarket regulations which prevailed in England.

Not every man in Paris was as taken with horses as they were. Few dandies cared to risk their skins as gentlemen jockeys; why expose oneself to useless dangers? To attract more supporters, Lord Seymour and his group organized the Jockey Club the next year, with Seymour as its president. Members were required to sign up in the Société d'Encouragement. Since the events of 1789, the word "club" had had nasty revolutionary political connotations, and clubs were, in fact, prohibited by law. The Jockey was officially known as the Cercle de la Société d'Encouragement until early in the twentieth century.

Among the stated aims of the founders of the Jockey Club was "to make a chain to bind the classes together," but which particular classes was not specified. At least, the club got *les dandys* out of Seymour's house

58

for part of the day. As soon as there were two hundred members, they rented quarters conveniently near their favorite restaurant, the Café de Paris, and the ballet dancers' foyer at the Opéra, and had a wonderful time spending money on decorating the premises. They voted to admit the novelist Eugène Sue, who later became a Socialist deputy and was dropped for nonpayment of dues, but they turned down the poet Alfred de Musset.

Seymour, when not busy strengthening his little finger so that it could sustain a hundred-pound weight, was engrossed in his stables at Neuilly and his breeding farm at Glatigny. After the Prix du Jockey Club was established in 1836—it is the French Derby, run the first Sunday in June at Chantilly—his horses won the race for three years straight.

The horsy types at the Jockey were quickly outnumbered by the non-horsy types, who belonged to two categories: the gastronomes and the whist players. The gastronomes thought that funds for the encouragement of the breed might better be given over to the encouragement of better dining. Their preoccupation with sedentary, sybaritic meals and all-night high-stake gambling sessions infuriated Seymour. He flew into a temper when the board proposed revising the rules to use some racing funds for the club itself, and after less than two years in office he resigned as president.

He was a rotten loser. When, in 1840, one of his horses failed for the first time to win the Prix du Jockey Club, he claimed a foul; and when the charges were dismissed, he sold all his horses and pulled out of racing completely.

Since Seymour's time, the club has maintained its ties with the Société d'Encouragement, which administers three tracks in France and the training grounds at Chantilly. Roughly half of the thirty-two to thirty-eight member chairs of the Société are by statute occupied by owners who are Jockey Club men and who serve on the racing commissions. But most present-day members of the club lack the passion for racing—and the money to keep large stables and breed race horses. Hunting, card playing, and the complex rules of social life concern them more. To the early men of the Jockey, whose idea of interesting gambling was a bet of something like ten thousand dollars on a single throw of the dice, the bridge games of today would seem tame. The members still appreciate the period charm of such exploits as that of Charles Laffitte and the Comte de Châteauvillard, who charged up the stairs on horseback in

1849 and trotted into the billiard room to play a round *à cheval*, but no one has shown any inclination to try anything similar for many years.

The prosperous era of Napoleon III fostered such extravagant gestures, which were epitomized in the Jockey Club set by the Duc de Gramont-Caderousse, who tossed his money around with plenty of panache. His crowning achievement was an Easter present for his mistress: a gigantic artificial egg, which cracked open to reveal a victoria with two horses, a coachman, and a footman. At this time, the *beau idéal* of the Continental upper crust was Albert, Prince of Wales, later King Edward VII. He had only to turn up his trouser cuffs or leave the last button of his ample waistcoat undone to create a fashion among the *élégants* of Paris.

On Bertie's annual sprees across the Channel, he joined his fellow-members of the Jockey Club in paying surprise backstage visits at the theatre and the Opéra. "With wavy whiskers and curly hair, square monocles set in the eye, towering stovepipe hats on their heads, the fast young men of the day drifted along the passages to knock at the little iron door which gave access to the wings of the stage." The members of the corps de ballet were the biggest snobs in Paris. They graded their suitors according to their clubs. The Jockey came first, and after that, the Cercle de la Rue Royale, the Cercle Agricole, and the Cercle de l'Union; the dancers snubbed everyone else.

As an imposing symbol of the good life, Edward VII formed a one-man link between the Second Empire and the gold Belle Époque, which stretched across the eighteen-nineties well into the new century. On his official trip to Paris in May, 1903, when laying the groundwork for the Entente Cordiale (which was to make allies of those two ancient enemies, France and England), Bertie lunched with Jockey Club intimates as a matter of course and attended the races at Longchamp. His favorite companions included two members who were source material for Proust—Charles Haas and General de Galliffet.

An exotic club member at the turn of the century who was welcomed by all of the elect—with the exception of Edward VII—was that decadent bloom, Comte Robert de Montesquiou, another Proust original. He served as the model for the depraved Baron de Charlus and worked hard at the game of aestheticism. Montesquiou also posed for J.-K. Huysmans's hero Des Esseintes, in *Against the Grain*. "His Arrogance," as Montesquiou was called by a society belle, belonged to one of the finest old families in France and was descended from Charles de Baatz, on whom Dumas based the character of D'Artagnan in *The Three Musketeers*. His wit was vicious, his manner supercilious, his hair marceled. Anatole France avoided Montesquiou at parties. "I can't bear that man who is always telling me about his ancestors," he complained.

Kings counted in those days. In 1905, the Jockey Club had among its members the reigning monarchs of five countries: England, Belgium, Holland, Denmark, and Serbia. Keeping up with Edward VII and his peers cost money, and the price of racing stables and social éclat was paid more and more often by great fortunes from across the Atlantic. Such American figures as August Belmont and assorted Wideners, Vanderbilts, and Biddles became familiar on the French turf.

American wives of Jockey Club men helped to strengthen the perverse affection for the United States that has always been shown by the aristocracy in France, despite differences in outlook on the form a proper government ought to take. In the Jockey Club today, there are about twenty American members, among them former Secretary of the Treasury Douglas Dillon and former U.S. Ambassador to France and Great Britain David K. E. Bruce. Parisians who are not in the know blink when they occasionally read in the newspapers that a dinner has been given at the Jockey Club for, of all people, the Sons of the Revolution. These are, of course, sons of the *American* Revolution.

No Nazi goosestepped into the Jockey during World War II, even if some of the nobility did feel that Vichy was the country's legal, albeit temporary, government. A great many members of fighting age earned the Croix de Guerre and several, notably Emmanuel d'Harcourt and Comte Robert de Vogüé, were star performers in the Resistance.

After the Liberation, the club flung its doors open to American officers. Some confusion ensued. One officer, who was looking for a striptease cabaret also called Le Jockey Club, but in Montparnasse, sat down to dinner and asked the maître d'hôtel when the floor show began.

The club's building, like any other of the Baron Haussmann era, is undistinguished. There are no initials on the doormat. The only equestrian motifs within are the club's collection of racing paintings, the horse-head gold buttons on the footmen's blue livery, and the big brass scale for weighing the gentlemen jockeys at the foot of the staircase in the entrance hall. When footmen present a letter on a tray, they take the precaution of first putting the mail in a fresh envelope—a practice they have followed ever since a member recognized his wife's handwriting on a note being delivered to the man sitting in the next chair.

Whenever they meet, members always shake hands, even if it means putting down a magazine or a hand of cards first. The story of the two Jockey Club members who recognized each other at opposite ends of the bathing area at Deauville and swam the length of the beach to shake hands is probably untrue, as no one who is anybody would dream of going into the water at Deauville.

It is considered beyond the pale to ask anyone in the club his name. The beautiful manners of *la vieille France*, which have practically vanished from the rest of the national landscape, remain in an ideal state of preservation at 2 Rue Rabelais; and any non-U speech immediately chills the atmosphere. Woe to the chance visitor who acknowledges an introduction with the telltale bourgeois *"Enchanté."* "To be received at the Jockey Club," says the Marquis de Rochechouart, a member of the committee who sometimes speaks for the inner circle, "is to be considered 'just like us.' "

The Club has been portrayed as "the only place where one can still be treated as a gentleman and can authenticate one's title; where admission is the equivalent of the honors of the court." Small wonder that eyebrows shot up in the *haut monde* a few years ago when an anonymous genealogist using the pseudonym of Charondas printed a little green book, *Un Juge d'armes au Jockey Club,* which was a well-documented tabulation of the number of dubious, and even fake, titles to be found on the membership list. Two weeks after it was published, there was not a copy left for sale.

The Association d'Entr'aide de la Noblesse Française, to which many of the *ducs et pairs de l'ancien régime* at the Jockey belong, bases legitimacy of title on the direct and masculine line only. Many proud *ducs* were unpleasantly surprised to find themselves in the company of self-made *comtes* and *vicomtes,* ennobled only by hyphenation with their grandmothers' names. The news came at a particularly awkward time, since Prince Philip had just joined the club. (The Duke of Windsor was also a member, as was his brother, George VI. The Comte de Paris —pretender to the French throne, a descendant of Louis-Philippe and head of the house of Orléans—does not belong to the club but his distant cousin, the Duc de Nemours, does.)

As a result of exposures in the little green book, more than one carefully arranged betrothal crumbled. *Soi-disant* barons downed brandies at the bar like condemned men. A spurious marquis had a nervous breakdown. Self-appointed aristocrats, confronted with the evidence, were invited to tear up their visiting cards and have new ones engraved with their legitimate names.

"We do not simply admit a man," one of the clubmen has said, in describing the special air of the Rue Rabelais. "He is accepted into a family." If he is a Broglie, a Ganay, a Gramont, a d'Harcourt, a Vogüé, or a La Rochefoucauld, there will be from five to sixteen members of his own family already in the Jockey. As soon as sons have finished their schooling with the Frères Oratoriens at Pontoise or at the Lycée Janson de Sailly in Paris, and have got their degrees from "Sciences-Po" (now the Institut d'Études Politiques) or spent a few years at the Harvard School of Business, they are introduced into the *Cercle*—"before they are old enough to get into any trouble," says a French aristocrat.

This familiar family climate leaves some men lukewarm. "The principal advantage," grumbled one of them recently, "is that it is the only spot on the face of the earth where you can be sure that your neighbor holds his fork the same way you do."

When they are voted in behind the red screens on the landing of the big staircase, young men of the Jockey Club join a group of courtiers who are without a court. Until the day when they are buried with their illustrious ancestors in the private cemetery of Petit-Picpus, a few yards from the common pit into which the decapitated bodies of some thirteen hundred noble victims of the Terror were thrown during the Revolution, men of the Jockey are assured of at least one refuge in this world from all that is ordinary, all that is vulgar. That is more than most men can look forward to, or perhaps want to.

# The Great Carême . . . He Built a Better Cream Puff

---

He may have been the greatest chef of all time. To Carême, the fine arts were five . . . "painting, sculpture, poetry, music, and architecture—which has as its principal branch, pastry." Pastry?

---

Pleasure is a fine piece of French pastry. Most any person who has made the acquaintance of the delectable delicacies that are ranged on the silver trays of the *pâtisseries* of Paris and of the various provinces would happily bear witness to that. The morsels concocted of butter, cream, flour, and sugar that go by the engaging names of Success, Marvelous, Conversation, Saint Honoré (after the patron saint of pastry chefs and bakers), Baba, Nun, Éclair, Finger of Diane, and Paris-Brest, among others, are thought to be the direct descendants of the light little *oublies*, the wafers of medieval times sold on the streets to the cry of *"Régalez-vous, Mesdames! Voilà le plaisir!"*

Centuries later, it is almost universally possible in France to regale oneself each afternoon with one or another of these delicious pastries at the Franglais hour that is called *"le five o'clock,"* and pronounced *"le fife o'clock,"* or to treat oneself after dinner to the smaller varieties, the petits fours or the *friandises*. Yet all these today are as grace notes to the grand arpeggios of the pastry of an earlier day, for the height of this form of pleasure-taking was reached during the first half of the nineteenth century when the great Carême was in his glory and was constructing his towering sugary masterpieces, his *pièces montées*.

*"Mes grands extraordinaires,"* Carême called them—and how he rose

to the splendid occasion and turned out as many as forty-eight of them for a single meal! Coloratura flights of culinary art, they crowned the centers of the tables he prepared for the most exacting palates in the Europe of his day. Primarily, they were devised to bring pleasure to the eye, which is not to say that these spectaculars (breathtaking aspics and entrées, as well as unforgettable wonders of architecture in pastry, monumental, in keeping with the times in which he lived) failed very often to arouse at least three more of the other five senses, because Carême brought scent, taste, and texture into play as well as sight, and the ear of a discriminating eater might well have perked up, too, at the sound the spun-sugar flourish of a Carême extraordinary made at the first crunch in the mouth.

To Marie-Antoine Carême, known sometimes as Antonin, this would have been as it should have been. Judging by the best gastronomic accounts, he is reckoned the father of *haute cuisine*, a title he would surely have taken seriously, for he looked upon his calling as a sacred trust, with himself no higher and no lower on the aesthetic scale than any other major artistic genius whose object is to enthrall his audience.

So Olympian were his standards for the planning, preparation, cooking, and consumption of food that, far from regarding his contemporary Jean Anthelme Brillat-Savarin with the reverential awe that the author of *The Physiology of Taste* is now accorded, Carême considered him just one more *soi-disant* gourmet. The pretensions of another self-proclaimed epicure of the day, Jean-Jacques, Duc de Cambacérès, filled Carême with disgust and despair. Perfection was his aim; at any deviation from it, in his own work or in that of others in his craft, Carême became intensely distressed, and because he tended, as have many cooks before and since his time, to be highly emotional, he would set to moaning, "*O Momus! O Gastronomie!*" and the like, personification being his favored figure of speech.

To Carême, the fine arts were five, a number that accords with most everyone else's way of thinking. But, elevating his own vocation to the level which he believed was its due, he listed the arts with an important appendage, as consisting of "painting, sculpture, poetry, music, and architecture—which has as its principal branch, pastry." Pastry? It took a sublime outlook, befitting a man who was to go down in history as "the cook of kings and the king of cooks," to put *pâtisserie* in such lofty company.

The famous chef at Maxim's in Paris and the humblest pastrymaker whose *tarte aux framboises* is renowned throughout his *quartier* draws pride today from all this, and knows it and more from the voluminous writings that Carême left, wherein he detailed his thoughts on the arts of the table, in addition to setting down menus, recipes, and more than two hundred and fifty fine line drawings of *grandes extraordinaires* of stupefying proportions, on the order of Bach, Beethoven, and Brahms in relation to our modern confectionery.

The *pièce montée* is now nearly extinct (its familiar equivalent in our time is the fussy wedding cake), but it lives on, in a limited way, as the chef-d'oeuvre that the cook who seeks the diploma of master pastryman presents to his professors, or the chef who competes for a prize shows the jury at the great Arpajon Fair on the road to Orléans or at the International Exposition of Ice Cream and Pastry that is held annually in the exhibition halls at the Porte de Versailles in Paris.

Then, too, every once in a while in our times a special moment that calls for an exceptional pastry will come up. Not long ago, Gaston Le Nôtre, who is the head of a family rated as aristocrats among present-day Paris *pâtissiers*, built a *pièce montée* measuring six feet in diameter at the base and twelve feet in height, to celebrate the inauguration of a new branch, the fifth of his family's group of stores, this one located in the shopping mall of Parly II, to the west of Paris. So far as M. Le Nôtre was able to determine, his was the largest *pièce montée* of all time and a form of homage to Carême, who, M. Le Nôtre avers, is never far from his thoughts.

The gargantuan cake was baked nearby at Les Yvelines in the ovens of the family's small pastry, chocolate, and catering plant, which M. Le Nôtre prefers to call a *laboratoire*, perhaps a more appropriate term, since the place is fitted out with immaculate tile floors and the latest in stainless-steel equipment. One wonders what the great Carême, whose working life was plagued with coal gas and cockroaches, would have made of such an establishment, not to speak of the sight, on a recent day, of a full complement of chefs disporting themselves during their lunch hour on the greens surrounding the laboratory, their white toques bobbing in the sunlight as they kicked a soccer ball from one end of the field to the other.

Another modern-day occasion that cried out for something extraordinary was the visit to the French capital of the octogenarian actor Charles

Chaplin—Charlot—for the opening of a festival of his films. To M. Roger Viard, the director of Maxim's, the gala dinner to be given in honor of Charlot at the legendary restaurant on the Rue Royale presented an irresistible opportunity for the making of a tiered *gâteau*, and M. Roger duly dispatched instructions down to the kitchen specifying to Raymond Delizy, the *chef pâtissier*, that the cake ought to be surmounted by a bowler hat and a cane.

"It had not occurred to anyone," M. Roger said a few days afterward, "but at two o'clock on the afternoon of the dinner I remembered that the date was November 3rd, Saint Charles's day. It is not out of the ordinary for us to make such a specialty, for we are always fêting something at Maxim's, above all, *le happy birthday*. In the times, I have ordered other, more elaborate big *gâteaux*. For a party for the film of Sacha Guitry on Napoleon, for example, the pastry chef made five grand cakes to represent events in the life of the Emperor—the coronation, the great battles—but no, since you are asking me, no, not the one of Waterloo."

"We must always be prepared here for the sudden order," Delizy recalled in his quarter of Maxim's crowded basement cooking area. "Who knows, they may call out, 'We need an *omelette surprise*,' and the surprise sometimes is for us. The cake of Charlot we built in a few hours and it was of three stories, garnished with nougatine and terminated at the top with a cupola decorated with roses of almond paste, the bowler of *bisquit* iced with black sugar, and the cane of nougat."

It is on a foundation of such ornamental tours de force that the repertoire of the complete chef should rest, or so Carême believed. His own technical training, which commenced in earnest when at the age of seventeen he became First Pie Crust Man at Bailly, the house that made the cakes for Napoleon's table, had impressed upon Carême the enduring worth of pastrymaking in the formation of an *haut cuisinier*. "One year of *extraordinaires* is worth more, without contradiction, than three years' experience with one chef," he counseled fledgling cooks in *The Paris Pastrymaker*. In his own case, surely, early mastery of puff paste and cream filling had resulted in the flowering of a talent that was all-round and equal to any culinary challenge. He invented a multitude of dishes besides new pastries such as the *mille-feuille* and the *croquembouche*.

Carême may have been the greatest chef of all time. Many authorities

70

think so. However, about this we cannot know for certain, since he stopped cooking in the early eighteen-thirties and, as he discovered through his own researches, one century's meat may be another century's poison. (After a lengthy investigation into ancient manuscripts in the Vatican library, he concluded: "The cuisine so renowned of the splendor of Rome was fundamentally bad and atrociously heavy." He did approve of the Romans' table decorations.) Also, although he gives us excellent directions for each dish and the composition of a meal by himself, we no longer have Carême to prepare it.

His reputation is, however, probably not overrated. Charles-Maurice de Talleyrand-Périgord, Prince de Bénévent; King George IV, when he was Prince Regent; Czar Alexander I; and Baron James de Rothschild all fought at one time or another to keep him in their kitchens. To Talleyrand, whose house was known throughout Europe as the sanctuary of French cuisine, gastronomy was a valuable arm of diplomacy, and a meal at his house on the Rue Saint-Florentin was the sort of event Casimir Delavigne, a nineteenth-century poet, had in mind when he wrote:

*Tout s'arrange en dînant dans le siècle ou nous sommes*
*Et c'est par les dîners qu'on gouverne les hommes.*

Talleyrand, one of the most cynical politicians in history, was so adaptable to dramatic changes that he could nearly always be depended upon to be in a position to give the kind of dinners where one governed men. Regimes—from *Ancien* to the Revolution to the Consulate, the Empire, and the First and Second Restorations—might come and go, but Talleyrand and the quality of his dinner parties went on, it seemed, forever. If you wanted to succeed in out-maneuvering some other minister of state, there was nothing like a superlative meal, in Talleyrand's book. As he put it in his parting words to Louis XVIII before taking off for the Congress of Vienna, "Sire, I will have more need of casseroles than of written instructions."

It was Talleyrand's morning habit to fortify himself with nothing more than three or four cups of camomile tea and immediately afterward, without delay, he would go into conference from eight to nine with his cook, Carême, laying down the strategy for the daily gourmet campaign. The customary sit-down dinner of the day was for eighty or ninety, and state banquets would have twelve hundred—once, even as many as ten thousand—guests. Talleyrand's were placed at large oval tables, each seating ten to twelve persons, all of whom faced up to a formidable array of elaborate, eye-catching dishes.

The opening volley at such parties was a service of soups, followed by *relevés,* fish, entrées, roasts, *entremets,* soufflés, desserts, and concluding with a grand fanfare attack on the *pièces montées.* Each of the courses consisted of a service of numerous dishes brought in by footmen and placed on the tables at the same time. Consequently, a scramble for food ensued, and the guest who succeeded in getting something on his plate was the guest who was the most adroit and nimble and not inhibited in the use of the boarding-house reach.

After having been defeated in one such evening's skirmish at Talleyrand's house, Lady Bessborough, Henrietta Spencer Ponsonby, who was the sister of the Duchess of Devonshire, the mother of the unhappy Caroline Lamb, and an indefatigable letter writer, wrote, "The dinner was, I believe, excellent, but from some awkwardness in the arrangement it was very difficult to get anything to eat."

To be truly well-dressed, each table needed a central display of comestibles of herculean dimensions, the big-gun *extraordinaires.* These, Carême's *pièces montées,* might be ranged in formations of four, six, or eight per table. Some of Carême's masterpieces—his hot-colds and his jellies—were supposed to be consumed on the spot. Others were mostly for show, meant for the ages, and, so long as they were admired, Carême was not entirely displeased when they got through a party without being dismantled. Since they might be the culmination of a meal of anywhere from forty-eight to eighty-six dishes, most diners could manage to pass them up. In any case, whoever saw them should have felt it would be a pity to eat them. Rotundas, windmills, obelisks, fountains, floral offerings, loving cups, wildernesses, military and naval trophies, helmets, lyres and harps, not to omit such grandiose inventions as Turkish mosques, neo-Greek temples in ruins, globes of the world, and his Grand Pavillon Gothique with its forty-four supporting columns—virtually nothing was beyond Carême when it came to the conception of a *pièce montée.* Some of the fanciest ones did escape demolition and he managed to conserve them. He put them under glass bells and kept them for as long as twenty-four years.

"How many sleepless nights!" wrote Carême of the anguish he underwent in their creation. If he had not been born in poverty to parents who could not feed and clothe all of their twenty-five children, much less educate them, he might have become the architect he seemed to long to be. As it was, the waif Carême, born in 1786 on the Rue de Bac in Paris, the son of a pieceworker, was abandoned at the age of ten by his father, who set the boy loose one dark night on the streets of Paris with these parting words which Carême never forgot: "Go, little one, go. In the world there are good careers. Leave us to suffer. Misery is our lot. We must die. These days are ones of great fortunes. All you need are the wits to make one and you have them. Go, little one, and perhaps tonight or tomorrow some good house will open its doors for you. Go with what God has given you."

That night, Carême, who never again saw his father, his mother, or any of his brothers and sisters, knocked at the door of a grubby little eating house. Later, he moved on to a better restaurant and then to Bailly, where his employer allowed him to spend hours in the print room at the Bibliothèque Nationale to pore over the old drawings of the Italian architects Serlio, Palladio, and Vignola to get new ideas for *pâtisseries*. Afterward Carême would stay up until daybreak sketching and calculating weights and measures.

He soon had composed two hundred pastry designs, all of them, he said, *soignés*, and his great cakes, prepared for Napoleon's table, were causing a sensation. "I saw that I had arrived," wrote Carême. "*Alors*, with tears in my eyes I left the good Monsieur Bailly."

He began to free-lance as a grand chef noted for his *pièces montées*, the completion of one of which took most chefs two full days. But Carême could do four in that time. Essential to the construction of a *grande extra-ordinaire* were, so a nineteenth-century cook has said, plenty of "kitchen boys and sharp fingernails and a short haircut." The main elements were *pâte d'office,* an esoteric mixture of gum, flour, and egg white, and also almond paste, spun sugar, and mastic, which contained starch and marble dust.

For some of the special looks, green-tinted *pâte d'amande* and *pâte d'office* could be pressed through a sieve to produce a sweet vermicelli-like substance that gave "*un bel effet*," Carême thought, to a cottage roof or a grotto. A very acceptable palm frond would be made of puff paste, provided the dough was turned twelve times instead of the usual six. The waves under a Venetian gondola or a Chinese junk came out nicely with the application of several coats of silvered *sucre filé*, the second degree of boiled sugar. Employed as adhesives were *gomme adragante* from Asia Minor and fish glue, but the *colle de poisson,* Carême cautioned in *The Picturesque Pastrymaker,* must be used sparingly.

Most of his masterworks he conceived to be edible. All the same, it would have been the better part of wisdom to avoid sinking one's teeth into some of the surface decorations. One could survive a mouthful of gold leaf or powdered bronze, but other ingredients Carême put into his finishing frostings were less digestible: indigo, Armenian clay, ammonia salts, and soap solutions, for examples.

Once a great new *pièce* had been achieved, Carême suffered from anxiety and resorted to security measures against piracy, for there was always some other chef who could steal his creations and, worse, then have the effrontery to publish instructions for making it in the wrong kind of saucepan. At such times, Carême would wail, *"O Vicissitude! O Ignorance! O Détestable Envie!"*

As flattery in the form of a bad imitation nettled Carême, so the poor copy of one of their pastrymen's *gâteaux* or a *glacier's* work in ice cream and cake will today stir up the Le Nôtre family. Any imitation of a *glace Le Nôtre* is likely to provoke the clan into meeting in council where Father Gaston will take up the question of what action can be made against the reproduction of their special version of a pineapple iced *à l'Orientale* or a *délice de Turin.*

"It is with the Japanese that we have difficulty, for they come often now with their cameras and take pictures of the cakes and the ice creams in our windows," said Alain Le Nôtre when he recently escorted a visitor through the family *laboratoire.* "French pastry is as desired in Tokyo today as French couture and we must guard against the theft of our products. Even our name might be taken, for there is already a Pâtisserie Carême in Japan." Alain Le Nôtre is Gaston's twenty-five-year-old son —charged with the administration of the firm, which is described by French gastronomic guidebook experts Henri Gault and Christian Millau as having "a respect of marble for the old bourgeois virtues and a maniacal care for the quality of ancient times."

From the cold room, the hot room, the pastry room, the three chocolate rooms—one for the preparation of the interiors of the chocolates, another for the cooking of the chocolate, and still another for the coating of the candies—go the provisions that stock the family shops in Auteuil and on the Avenue Victor Hugo in Paris, in Boulogne, and at Parly II, as well as in Normandy, where their tiny shop faces the town hall in Deauville.

74

It was in Pont Audemer, a town of 9,000 inhabitants near Deauville, that Gaston Le Nôtre first came to notice. Certain fashionable Parisians with cultivated palates would drive several miles from their houses in the surrounding countryside for his croissants, his ice creams, and, sometimes, specially ordered *pièces montées*.

"All of this *belle société* had a house or an apartment in Paris," Alain Le Nôtre told his visitor, "and many—the Duc de Lévis-Mirepoix and the Duc de Broglie, for example—urged my father to come to the city so that he could do their parties there, too. In 1958, he made the move with a staff of twelve employees. It was an important year for *la France*. Now we have a hundred and fifty on our staff, and in 1971 we catered to five hundred thousand persons in meals and buffets, including serving as the caterer for half of the affairs given by President Pompidou at the Élysée Palace. When we do a reception or a dinner, it is from A to Z, as a rule, with linens, glasses, cutlery, flowers, chairs, and decorations. My father, Gaston, is Président-Directeur-Général; my mother, Madame Colette Le Nôtre, directs our stores; my sister Sylvie is secretary to my father; my younger sister Annie manages our branch on the Avenue Victor Hugo with my wife, Catherine; my cousin Patrick is a pastry cook here at the *labo*; my Aunt Josette is in charge of presentations, shipments, and packing. There are, however, plenty of other Le Nôtres who do not work here." Alain Le Nôtre and his visitor approached a man in the *laboratoire* who was apparently in charge of operations. "And now may I present my uncle, the chief pastryman, Marcel Le Nôtre?" he said, nodding at the rosy-faced chef who, in the fashion of all cooks in French kitchens, offered, in lieu of his dough-covered hand, his floury elbow to shake.

"I have been to the famed Demel's in Vienna," Alain Le Nôtre continued, "where, I regretted to observe, they used margarine in their pastry and seaweed derivatives in the ice cream, but when I worked at Springli and Frey in Zurich I was impressed by the quality. We employ only Normandy butter for the cuisine and Charente butter for the *pâtisserie*. Quality is everything, and as we grow, we must take care to preserve it, for once our business ceases to function on the artisan level, it will be in danger of becoming"—here Alain Le Nôtre hesitated and shuddered lightly—"*un snack bar*."

"*O Profanation de la Gastronomie!*" Carême might well have exclaimed. The thought that the lips of a *bouche fine* would be brought to touch any but the most superior ingredients always disquieted him greatly. Seldom did he permit himself to fall into the hands of an employer who would not set up the most exemplary larder, and Carême knew by heart which of the hosts of his day had the most sensitive gullets.

"The eaters of my time," he stated categorically, "were the Prince de Talleyrand, Murat, Junot, Fontanes, the Emperor Alexander, George IV, Castlereagh, and the Marquis de Cussy," and Carême worked for several on this list, which left out Napoleon I, but that should surprise no one. The Emperor was noted as a bolter of food and is supposed to have said of himself, "If you want to eat like a soldier, dine at my house." Napoleon's chef, Dunand, went campaigning with him, doing his utmost along the route to keep the Emperor's dinners elegant, but once Napoleon tucked into a meal, it was a losing battle.

The two anathemas to Carême in the gustatory circles of his day were the magistrate and author Brillat-Savarin and the archchancellor of the Empire, Cambacérès. "Neither of them ever knew how to eat," said Carême. "Both of them loved strong, vulgar foods. They simply filled their stomachs. Savarin was a big eater. He had a heavy air and he looked like a parish priest. After dinner his digestion absorbed him. I have seen him fall asleep."

As for the archchancellor, the show he put on as a leading Amphitryon, a synonym to the French for host, particularly rankled Carême, who had firsthand knowledge of Cambacérès's parsimonious nature. So tight was the archchancellor's grasp on the purse strings in his household, according to Carême's account, that the life Cambacérès's chef, Grand-Manche, led could not have been much easier than the one Maître Jacques has with the miser Harpagon in Molière's *L'Avare*.

"My work as an *extra* took me into all the great houses of the Empire," Carême wrote to Sidney Owenson, Lady Morgan, an Irish novelist who was widely read in France and who was a friend of Lafayette and of Benjamin Constant. "I had the highest esteem for Monsieur Grand-Manche. This worthy man asked my assistance at several grand culinary solemnities so that I have seen with my own eyes what went on in the archchancellor's kitchen."

Cambacérès hoarded the provisions, and food never appeared on his table until it was "at least stale." His game was hung to high heaven. "The acme of avarice was his order to his staff and those aiding as *extras* at his grand dinners to serve only eight of the sixteen entrées presented. When his guests asked for the reserved dishes, the butler was under instructions to turn a deaf ear. *O Honte!* [O Shame!]"

Throughout the dinner, Cambacérès would be keeping an eye on the tables, watching out for the leftovers which—as everybody knew he would see to with his niggardly concern—would have to be reused sometime later. ("*Quelle Parcimonie!*") Leftovers, in Carême's view, "must be employed only with caution, ability, and, above all—silence."

All the great *pièces montées* at Cambacérès's feasts were there solely for looks, Carême noted. "His grand *pâtisseries de fond* had to last forever without being attacked. This is expressly prohibited by the Amphitryon. Molière has said that the true Amphitryon is the Amphitryon where one dines. One dined badly at the house of the archchancellor of the Empire.

"I finish these miserable details," Carême concluded to Lady Morgan. "My pen refuses the citations I could still make on the villainy of this man who was rich but avaricious to excess and not in the least *sensuel. Quelle Pitié! Quelle Maison!*"

Luckily for Carême, he seldom had to work in a place like that. His twelve glorious years in the service of Talleyrand put him in the pantheon of *grande cuisine*. Thanks to Talleyrand, France's reputation for magnificence and hospitality went around the world once again. Alexandre Dumas *père* tells us in his *Dictionary of Cuisine* that the refinements of cookery had spread from the Princes de Condé and the Soubises to Richelieu, to be eclipsed during the horrendous years of the Revolution and the Terror. During the Directoire, with the creations of his chef Bouché, or Bouche-Sèche, who was trained in the Condé household, Talleyrand's table became the most celebrated one in Europe. When Bouché died and Carême succeeded him, the munificence of Talleyrand's meals continued unabated.

"In 1667, we know from the third satire of Boileau, Paris dined at noon," Eugène Briffault wrote in *Paris à Table,* in 1846. "Under Louis XIV the court dined after mass; under Louis XV, after the theatre; during the Revolution people ate in a hurry. Under the Directory great dining came back." In Empire days, the bourgeoisie had dinner at 4 P.M. and the government people—Talleyrand's set—at five or six in the evening.

"The inevitable name one encounters in the chronicles of the first thirty years of this century," wrote Briffault, "is the name of Monsieur de Talleyrand. One has made of him the first of the men of politics and the last of the grand seigneurs. He obtained the good graces of sovereigns, the favors of women, the adulation of the ambitious, the hatred of honest folk, and the sarcasm of the mob. As if all this were not enough to make him famous, *La Gastronomie* placed him in its highest order."

Here was a host after Carême's heart, an employer who would spare him nothing in the way of fresh seafood, pheasant, butter, and cream. Carême dedicated *The Royal Pastrymaker* to Talleyrand. "It is that Monsieur de Talleyrand understands the genius of the chef," Carême told one of his contemporaries. "It is that he respects it, and that he is the most competent judge of the delicate nuances of cuisine and that his expenditure is wise and grand at the same time."

Nor, when it came to good victuals, was there a stingy bone in the body of England's Prince Regent, later George IV. If eight months at Brighton and Carlton House seemed time enough to Carême, his departure from the service of "Prinny" had nothing to do with any reluctance on the Prince's part about laying in ample supplies. The Prince's stomach, which eventually grew to such proportions that he was in later life to conceal himself, whenever he ventured out, in a closed carriage, ranked among the outstanding of the century, right alongside that of Louis XVIII, for whom Carême also designed *extraordinaires*. ("The gourmet king," as the French sovereign was indulgently called, had a gourmand's limitless capacity, or so it seemed to the Princess Palatine, who recounted, "I have frequently seen the King eat four plates of different kinds of soups, a whole pheasant, a quail, a large plate of salad, mutton in gravy and garlic, two good-sized slices of ham, a plate of pastry, and then various fruits and jams." Louis was fond of spinach, which his doctor, Portal, forbade him to eat. When there was none at the table, Louis would pound his fist and tell his first gentleman of the chamber, the Duc d'Aumale, to go out to the caterer and get some. "What?" Louis would bellow, "I am King of France and I cannot eat spinach?")

Every morning, as Talleyrand had done, "Prinny" conferred for an hour with his chef, plotting the day's menus. "Carême," he said one day, "you will make me die of eating too much; I want everything you set before me, truly." Carême replied that his business was to stimulate the Regent's appetite, not to regulate it. However, the chef took such care with his recipes that while he worked in the royal household the Prince never had a touch of the gout.

Having invented *Le Pouding de Cabinet Anglo-Français,* Carême departed. The Prince Regent's was a *"ménage bourgeois"* Carême told Lady Morgan, but to others he tactfully explained he had suffered from *mal du pays* and could not bear the English climate.

Despite his aversion to the cold, Carême was later induced to go to St.

Petersburg by Czar Alexander I, and at that lavish court none of the necessities was lacking, either. Although Carême was haunted by the memory of his teacher Laguipère—Murat's cook who froze to death at Vilna, one of the fifty French chefs who perished in the retreat from Moscow ("Arise, shade of Laguipère! You should have died in Paris!")— it was unthinkable to turn down the Czar, who had had a taste of Carême's cooking as a guest at Talleyrand's. Carême hated to refuse the call of a truly good provider. At the Congress of Vienna, later, it came from the British Ambassador, Lord Charles Stewart, Lord Castlereagh's half brother. Even in the extravagant company of the Congress, Stewart's prodigality was noticed.

Yet in the midst of all this *gloire* Carême often labored under abominable conditions. His lungs were weakened by constant inhalations of the gases from the coal-heated ovens into which he was forced to place his head for many hours during the day. The cooking arrangements for a fête, such as the military dinner for ten thousand held in a vast tent during the Empire on the Champs-Élysées, were primitive. At the grand ball in the Grand Gallery of the Louvre given by the Garde Royal and the Gardes du Corps on February 5, 1815, to celebrate the return of Louis XVIII to Paris, a kitchen was improvised for a hundred chefs. Although Carême had his own room in which to prepare forty-eight cold entrées and *extraordinaires* of sugar, the oven—fifty feet long and six feet wide—was a communal one.

Many times a strange new kitchen would be inhabited by hordes of "the black beasts," the cockroaches that are the scourge of a chef's life. On one occasion, Carême did away with 1,215 of them, "on my first day at work, by putting little pots half-filled with jam along the wall under the stove."

It was often from such an unlikely environment that Carême's beautiful *pièces montées* would come, but his place in the history of fine cooking has, in the long view, rested not so much on these spectaculars and other culinary masterworks as on his inspiring dedication to the highest standards of quality and on the encyclopedic knowledge he poured into his books about food. These have made him an almost saintly figure to such present-day practitioners of his art as the Le Nôtre family and to such wardens of gastronomic excellence as the members of France's élite eating society, Le Club des Cent, one of whom is forever enshrined in epicurean memory as having, in the heat of a gourmet discussion, arisen and shouted,

"*À bas la gélatine!*" (The use of prepared gelatin is a subject that can arouse strong differences of opinion in the culinary milieu but less violent ones, perhaps, than those over which of the five or six ways of boning a filet of sole is the correct one.)

Carême would have regarded the addition of gelatin as a betrayal of the tradition of starting every dish from scratch with the natural ingredients (his aspics began with the boiling of a calf's foot), on a par with substituting a vegetable fat for pure butter. But some poor cook who had had the misfortune of concocting an unfelicitous mixture could rile Carême even more. If a soup based on anise brought forth from the great chef an outburst of vocatives ("*Quelle Drogue Médicinale! Quel Mauvais Génie!*"), this would only be because Carême saw himself as guardian and arbiter of superlative eating, with every meal an unforgettable experience in pleasure, starting with the soup, which, he said, "must be the *agent provocateur* of a good dinner."

On the day he died, January 13, 1833, after a long and difficult illness, he was still preaching his mission. "Ah, it's you, thank you, good friend," he said to the student who had stopped in to see him. "Tomorrow bring me some fish. Yesterday, the quenelles de sole were very good but your fish was not good. You did not season it well. Listen," said Carême, raising his right hand and moving it back and forth in the air, "you must shake the casserole." Those were his final words.

At a meal prepared by Carême, the soup was respected less as an *agent provocateur* and more as the opening passage of an experience likened to listening to the interpretation of a great symphony by a brilliant conductor, or so Lady Morgan thought. She believed, incidentally, that Carême was a descendant of the noted chef of the Vatican who, under Leo X, invented a thin soup for the Pope for Lent and consequently became known as "Jean du Carême." Lady Morgan left an account of a Carême dinner to which she was invited, one warm summer night, at the Baron James de Rothschild's Château de Boulogne. The company was brilliant (Baron François Gérard, the painter, and Gioacchino Rossini, the composer, were there), and dinner was served in a pavilion separated from the house, an oblong building of marble in the Grecian style set in a grove of orange trees and refreshed by fountains.

"It was not without emotion," Lady Morgan recalled, "that I heard the announcement '*Madame est servie.*' To do justice to such a dinner, one would need to possess knowledge equal to that of its author. It was entirely in the spirit of the century. There was nothing of the *perruque* in its composition."

No one uttered a word until after the soup. Then Lady Morgan, who was seated next to her host, complimented him and said, "I have tasted, for a long time, theoretically, the works of Carême."

"*Eh, bien!* And he, on his part, has tasted your works, and there is the proof," replied the Baron, directing her attention to the *pièce montée* of the evening, which she describes as "a column of the most ingenious architecture on which my name LADY MORGAN was inscribed in candied sugar." After the coffee, she and Carême met in the vestibule and she found him "*Un monsieur*, very correct, perfectly free of all pedantry and affectation."

Did Carême ever wish he could leave the world something a little more permanent? Probably he was an *architecte manqué*, for we know that he hoped the Czar would erect five monuments in St. Petersburg of his design; Carême drew the plans for them and had them printed in a book he dedicated and sent to Alexander I, indicating they should be "of that durable material, granite." Had they ever been constructed, they would by this time most likely have been destroyed. His dreams in butter and sugar and spice, as it has turned out, lasted longer.

# À la Vôtre!

---~∞~---

*The Baron Geoffroy de Luze, who has considerably more than a nodding acquaintance with the celestial fluid, feels there should not really be all that much mystery about wine. Through the centuries, man has learned how best to cultivate and ferment grapes, in the proper proportions and under the best conditions, to arrive at the best result.*

---~∞~---

On the Quai des Chartrons, along the Garonne River in Bordeaux, everything, they say, looks pretty much as it did in the middle of the nineteenth century. The docks themselves are not much different, except for an occasional tall crane. The area where the wine merchants settled, just across the waterfront avenue from the docks, still features the same narrow old buildings, side by side, presenting a common façade.

When the merchants chose their business sites, property prices along the waterfront were extremely high, for the time, since access to the docks and the ships that berthed there was the most important commercial consideration for anyone shipping his goods to the world's markets. The deeper inland one went, the cheaper the land became.

But a wine merchant of the eighteen hundreds, with a narrow foothold along the riverfront, could roll his barrels out his front door and directly onto the ships. Today the headquarters of the wine merchants of Bordeaux, the area in which the most refined, sophisticated French wines originate, still stand shoulder to shoulder along the *quai*, even though their product is no longer shipped from the docks across the way. The buildings still stretch a considerable distance back from the heavily traveled *quai*; the interiors and the *caves*, where the wine ferments, matures, and is bottled, have been altered only minutely over the last century and a half.

Today the ripe grapes are no longer crushed by foot, although most of the merchants on the Quai des Chartrons and the vintners in the châteaus of the Bordeaux region remember when, not too long ago, that was standard procedure. Machines have taken over from tromping feet; otherwise, viticulture is still practiced in the same tradition as it has been for hundreds of years. And the wines today are, if anything, better than ever.

The nest of wine merchants' establishments on the *quai* is only a seven- or eight-minute taxi ride from the center of Bordeaux. The driver stopped before the address I gave him, the *maison* of A. de Luze & Fils, but since I was sitting in the back seat of the cab my door swung open before the entrance to the headquarters of Alexis Lichine.

A few steps and I stood in front of the doorway of the de Luze building, an eighteenth-century structure that showed its age and also its character, even on first view. The smell of fermenting grapes greeted me as I stepped inside onto the tracks that guided the barrels on their trip to the ships across the *quai* a century ago. In addition to the pervasive musty odor, the premises had a comfortable eighteenth-century feeling about them.

As a long-time enthusiast of French wines, both in the United States and during a twelve-year sojourn in France, I had often promised myself that one day I would explore the heartland of vintage civilization. My quest, finally, had brought me to the epicenter of the world's viniculture. It struck me at once that I was in the right place: not only does the de Luze firm handle some of the greatest and most renowned wines in the world, but its heritage stamps it as a serious candidate for the honor of foremost wine merchant in France and therefore in the world.

Even before checking on the family tree of the proprietors of the establishment, I felt intuitively that the first three officers of the firm I met must be the solid, direct descendants of the founders. I turned out to be right. Baron Geoffroy de Luze, thirty-nine-year-old administrator and member of the board of directors—gracious, accommodating, multilingual—is the great-grandson of the founder of the firm: the first Baron in the family, Alfred de Luze, who settled in the same building to begin his Bordeaux operations in 1820. Comte Bertrand du Vivier de Fay-Solignac, cousin of Baron Geoffroy and nephew of Francis de Luze, is the firm's president and chairman of the board—fifty-one, graying, more formal, exuding great personal magnetism, and immediately identifiable as a leader. Baron Yves de Luze, Baron Geoffroy's sixty-eight-year-old uncle, was the third of the company's executives—and the third of the eight-member board—I met at the commencement of my journey, a labor of love, through the Bordeaux wine country.

Unlike most family histories—often dull, unrewarding material—the chronological record of the de Luze dynasty, a notable success in the cultivation, development, and specialized marketing of great wines, seems to match or even outdo the fascinating history of the Rothschild family in the field of world banking.

The de Luze family saga really begins about 1817. It was then that two brothers, Louis-Philippe de Luze, twenty-four, and Alfred, twenty, embarked on a sailing vessel for North America. Both were great-grandsons of French émigrés, were born in Frankfurt, Germany, and raised in Switzerland. (An uncle of theirs, Frédéric de Luze, a colonel in the Swiss Guards of France's Louis XVI, was later—1792—to distinguish himself in the Battle of the Tuileries, for which he received the Great Cross of the Order of Saint Louis from Louis XVIII.)

In those days, French wines were known by reputation in a few corners of the world outside France, but there was very little chance to come upon a bottle of the really great wines without making a trip to the mother country. In New York, the brothers de Luze came to the conclusion that there was an untouched market for goods from the Old World. Without agonizing over their decision, they promptly set up an import business, under the guidance of Louis-Philippe, at 18 South William Street, New York City. The shingle outside said simply "L.-P. de Luze & Co." Its quick success led the brothers to the further decision that Alfred should return to Europe to select the goods and send them on.

After consulting his uncle Maurice de Bethmann, a prominent banker in Frankfurt, young Alfred took his advice—and perhaps some of his capital—and set up in business in the growing port city of Bordeaux, on the Garonne River, with ready access to the Atlantic Ocean.

In 1820, Alfred—already a baron, a title he had received from the Grand Duke of Hesse, whom he served as Consul General—formed a partnership with a gentleman named Dumas and opened for business under the firm name A. de Luze & Dumas. Two years later, it became A. de Luze & Fils, and continued thus until today, with his direct descendants controlling the operation of the firm throughout the intervening century and a half.

"We began our international operations fairly promptly," said Baron Geoffroy de Luze, as he continued to recount—with understandable pride

—his great-grandfather's progress. Four years after the firm's foundation, Alfred decided to deal exclusively in the developing and marketing of choice wines on an international scale—a decision that shaped the lives of all his descendants. In the manner of the Rothschilds, he organized a network of agencies throughout the world: four of Alfred's five sons entered the business—Alfred II, Francis, Charles, and Maurice—and soon agencies were opened, by the traveling Francis, in Russia, Poland, Scandinavia, England, Continental Europe, and India.

Besides founder Alfred's Consul-Generalship for the Grand Duke of Hesse, elder brother Louis-Philippe, in New York, became Consul General of Switzerland there, and Alfred II was made Consul of Bavaria. Through his acquaintance with Prince Metternich, Francis sought the same position for Austria. These consulships helped the firm tremendously in placing its wines and cognacs in the most powerful royal courts of Europe as well as in its most distinguished private wine cellars. The free-trade policies of Emperor Napoleon III favoring exportation of French products made the expansion of the markets of A. de Luze & Fils possible.

Just forty-two years after the firm's foundation on the Quai des Chartrons, Francis, second son of the founder, bought the Château Paveil and its venerable vineyards, in the Margaux region of the Haut-Médoc, and the de Luze establishment acquired a new dimension.

Baron Geoffroy glanced at me questioningly as he held up a diagram of his family tree. When I assured him that I was indeed interested in his family history, he passed me the diagram, bearing the names of twenty-two de Luzes, including his own, and three du Viviers, to enable me to follow the story more easily.

On the death of the founder in 1880, nine years after the death of his son Francis, killed in the battle of Mans in the Franco-Prussian War, the control of the firm passed to his grandson Alfred III; assisted by his cousins Charles, Albert, and Édouard, he advanced the firm's frontiers even further, to include Egypt, the Dutch East Indies, and the Far East, opened warehouses in the Netherlands, and expanded the English and North American distribution facilities.

After World War I, a new quartet took over the management: Alfred's son Francis, Albert's son Olivier, and Charles's sons Roger and Yves, both of whom are currently members of the company's eight-man board of directors.

To a Frenchman, life without wine would be inconceivable, a point of view which is beginning to be understood and shared by nationals in other countries. It is on this ever-broadening foreign market that French wine merchants are today concentrating their attention, particularly for the best quality and most expensive wines.

The Baron Yves de Luze offered to drive me to the Château Haut-Brion for a visit to the seat of one of the most esteemed vineyards in France, but first it was decided that I should have a look at the firm's own cellars in the two-centuries-old building. My guide was the Baron Geoffroy de Luze, who punctuated our stroll through the 1,100-foot-long *cave* with illuminating comments about wine and its development to a state of perfection.

"We now use some glass-lined tanks for the fresh wine, after the grapes have been stemmed by machine and pumped into the vats. New techniques are being used—we have receptacles made of fiber and even stainless steel. But there is just no substitute for wooden barrels—preferably old ones—so that the wine can breathe during the maturing period. Each of the 15,000 aging oak barrels holds 225 liters, or 49.5 Imperial [English] gallons [59.4 U.S. gallons]; the wine benefits tremendously from the tannin content of the oak barrels. Every three months, the wine goes through a process called 'racking,' during which the maturing wine is poured out and transferred to other casks, eliminating the residue, or lees, each time. Generally speaking, the *grands crus* mature for at least two years before making the critical transfer to bottles. The wine is checked —that is, tasted—at regular intervals while it is in the barrels, and the decision on the right moment for the bottling is a very important one.

"Some wines," the Baron continued as we passed row on row of barrels stacked four high, "are subject to bottle illness. The switch from wood to glass upsets them, and many must rest quietly here in their bottles for four to six months before being shipped."

And how many bottles are resting quietly in the seemingly endless *cave* at 88–89 Quai des Chartrons?

"Oh, about a million bottles, plus or minus," he answered. "Including, of course, bottles already packaged for shipment, and that includes wines that we distribute from some of the great châteaus in the Bordeaux area. These wines mature and are bottled at their own châteaus before being sent here for a final period of storage before shipment. That goes for Burgundies, which we also distribute, and cognacs, some of them our own, from the Grande Champagne district of the Cognac region."

We paused for a taste of a maturing *graves rouge*. A barrel was punctured and we solemnly tasted the fragrant but still rough liquid as the attendant bunged the barrel. In the accepted tradition, I spat out the young wine, making a mental note to inquire into the wine-tasting process. Even the brief taste of the wine was stimulating on this extended journey through the cellars, which are kept at a temperature of about 55 degrees Fahrenheit. The constant temperature, Baron Geoffroy told me, is one of the key factors in the maturing wine's progress, just as the tannin in the wood is important, and later the dryness of the corks after bottling.

As we walked past newly packaged boxes of the product of the great Bordeaux vineyards, all neatly stamped with the name and insignia of their particular château, I asked about the widely held notion that some wines "travel" well and others don't. This belief was quickly debunked by the Baron, who—over the course of the next few days—demolished a number of the popular myths held dear by aspiring connoisseurs.

"All wines can travel," he replied flatly. "Usually it's a person who can't travel, and sometimes because he's sick. The wines are healthy. Climate makes a difference and so does temperature," he explained. "A man may have a glass of a certain rosé, for example, while sitting on a terrace on the Riviera on a warm sunny day after a swim. He may try the same rosé at his home in London, on a cold winter day, after having walked several blocks through the slush, with a cold coming on, and he wonders why it doesn't taste the same. Also many wine buyers don't store their wines at the proper temperature. No," he said firmly, "usually it's the person—not the wine—that doesn't travel well. All wines can travel."

Over lunch at a small restaurant frequented by wine merchants, the Baron elaborated with some general comments on wine and its appreciation. Each firm had storage space in the restaurant for a few bottles of its own wine for its own use. We started with a Château Paveil de Luze '66, from one of the vineyards owned and operated by the de Luze establishment.

"These wines from the Médoc are older and more sophisticated than the Burgundies that are so popular," he began. "For the wine drinker who is just beginning to develop his palate, a Burgundy is much easier to understand. It matures and evolves faster; partly because of the type of grapes, the process of vinification moves a lot faster. The result is a wine with less depth than a good Bordeaux.

"We also buy and ship Burgundies—to the United States, among other places. Actually, the vineyards of California are not, as some people seem to think, competition for us. The growing popularity of California wines in your country is really helpful, because it's getting people accustomed to the idea of drinking wine. Many start with California wines, move on to Burgundies, and finally grow to appreciate the classic Bordeaux."

We had progressed through most of the lunch as well as two-thirds of the bottle of Château Paveil, and the atmosphere was ripe for some questions of a more personal nature. After all this time as a Bordeaux vintner, I asked, was he ever stumped at a dinner, for example, when challenged to identify a certain wine?

"Well, of course, this blind-tasting dare comes up from time to time," he replied, "and one must play the game. There's nothing that apparently pleases some persons more than to try to fool someone who supposedly knows something about wines.

"I've been put on the spot that way many times; sometimes it can be a bit unpleasant. Especially when traveling abroad. Once in England, I remember, my host sprang this parlor game on me, asking me to name the district and the year of a certain white wine, which I must say I didn't recognize.

"I did say that it was definitely not a Continental wine, but I couldn't positively identify it. And for a very good reason. It turned out to be from a small patch of land in Nottinghamshire, northwest of London, and of course I'd never tasted it before. But it gave my host pleasure, so everyone was happy."

We started on another bottle of the Paveil, with the cheese. "But the best way to win that game is to bribe the butler," he concluded, with an engaging smile.

During the pauses in our conversation, while we enjoyed the wine's extraordinary bouquet, I grew aware that everyone in the small, cozy barroom of the restaurant was discussing the same subject. If I hadn't known the métier of my fellow-lunchers, I would have sworn they were talking about their wives or mistresses. "Voluptuous," "elegant," "charming," "spirited," "gallant," "tender"—all applied flatteringly to various wines—were some of the words that penetrated the buzz of general conversation.

As Premier Raymond Poincaré once said, in a lyric passage in one of his speeches: "Our French language would be, without the vine and without the wine, impoverished by the loss of a multitude of the most picturesque expressions, for when we say that the wine has *une robe brillante, ou que le vin a du corps* [has body], *qu'il a de la chair* [flesh], *qu'il a de l'étoffe* [fabric], that the wine is fruity, that it has a fine bouquet, we are repeating, in the twentieth century, the words that formerly were gaily bandied about by our ancestors."

And, as Pierre Andrieu has put it, in *Notre Ami le Vin*, in translation: "The *robe* of a woman entices because one knows that it hides a mystery always renewed. The *robe* of a wine also hides a mystery; it is that of a spirit delicate, subtle, capricious, and changeable—entirely that of a woman!"

(The *robe* of a wine is, of course, simply the color, in red wines brought to perfection by the substance called tannin.)

The second bottle of Paveil was almost gone now, and the air was full of other descriptive terms—*"corsé"* (full-bodied), *"velouté"* (velvety), *"généreux"* (strong, invigorating), *"nonchalant,"* and others. As we drained the bottle, Baron Geoffroy suggested, in reply to another question on my part, that I meet with the firm's principal *dégustateur*, or wine taster, for some further expertise on the art of distinguishing a good from a great wine.

Back at the company's headquarters, I was introduced to still another member of the dynasty, serious young Alain du Vivier, elder son of Comte Bertrand du Vivier, the firm's president and board chairman and cousin of Baron Geoffroy de Luze. Though only twenty-eight, Alain has been pursuing the intriguing career of wine taster for six years.

What, I wondered, are the qualifications for the job? And, further, how does he pace himself through his day's work?

The qualities that make a good wine taster, it seems, are God-given, principally a good sense of taste and smell, and the memory of a computer. Since he is obliged to taste wines at various stages of their development, he must be able to judge what a young wine will taste like at full maturity and thus be able to commit the firm to the future purchase of a considerable number of bottles based on his fleeting early acquaintance with the wine.

Alain approaches his work as conscientiously as a good musician addresses himself to the performance of a classic piece of music. He eats lightly before and during working hours and does not use coffee to neutralize his palate after each wine; neither is he affected by its alcoholic content, since he retains the wine, rolling it over his tongue, for only a matter of seconds before spitting it out. Usually he tests about ten samples at a stretch, and works a long French business day.

"I prefer to work on an empty stomach," he said. "If one tastes really critically, it is better without food."

In answer to another question, he said, "Yes, after a full day's tasting, I do enjoy drinking a good wine with dinner. Preferably a good Médoc— light in strength but with depth. Sometimes with meat I like a good Saint-Émilion."

Baron Geoffroy joined the conversation, to describe the qualities that Alain hesitated to mention about himself: "He must not drink too much grain alcohol, he must avoid having late nights before a working day— it's not quite the ideal job it sounds. He must be acutely sensitive, percep- tive, and be able to make allowances for a wood taste, or too much sulphur, depending on the age of the young wine. In sum," the Baron said, "he must be a good buyer, since he must not only taste wine in our own cellars—in the casks, as well as just before and during bottling—but he must also sample the wines in the châteaus we deal with—two or three times monthly. A very demanding, exacting job."

The vineyards of Bordeaux sprawl in a wide semicircular pattern around the city and even put down their roots within the city itself. The Château Haut-Brion, which I visited with Baron Yves de Luze, uncle of Geoffroy, today lies within the expanded city limits of Bordeaux; its prestige as one of the oldest and greatest of the Bordeaux reds, which the British call "clarets," is known in every pocket of the civilized world.

There are several stories about the beginnings of the vineyards of Haut-Brion; in each, its first recorded history dates from the early years of the sixteenth century. One account places it in the hands of Jean de Ségur, in the very early fifteen hundreds, passing—in 1525—under the control of Admiral Philippe de Chabot, who was also mayor of Bordeaux, who in turn yielded the property to the daughter of Mayor de Bellon of Libourne.

Another version credits the initial development of the world-celebrated vineyard to Jean de Pontac, who is said to have acquired the property in 1533 from Jean Duhelde of Bordeaux. In either case, the Pontac family became the owners of large tracts of land in the region, including a number of vineyards. (The daughter of Mayor de Bellon in the first ac- count married a Pontac.)

The vineyard of Haut-Brion—which today covers about 42 hectares (103.782 acres)—has been the fountainhead of a never-ending series of great wines. Through wars, revolution, droughts, and a variety of fungus diseases, and through at least twenty-five changes of ownership (including a span of about four years when Talleyrand was its proprietor), Haut-Brion has survived in impeccable style. After some five centuries, it is still producing incomparable wines of the *premier cru*.

Today the château and its vineyards are owned by American Clarence Dillon, father of Douglas, former Secretary of the Treasury and one-time United States Ambassador to France.

"And a real bargain it was," said Baron Yves de Luze, expertly driving through a muddy by-pass, around a new cellar under construction. "When Mr. Dillon bought the château and vineyards back in 1935, prices were down. Why, today the land alone, without the vines, would be worth more than he paid for the whole place. And the wine, of course, brings a top price in the world's markets."

As we entered the main cellar, he reminisced a bit. "I remember about twenty, twenty-five years ago when they still crushed the grapes by foot. Today they have a machine that stems the grapes, as well as a hydraulic press and stainless-steel vats, and employ fork trucks to move the cases about.

"But, come, let's have a taste of Haut-Brion '70." We repeated the formality, rolling the rough young wine over our tongues, concentrating on the taste, and then spitting it out into a small box of sawdust provided for the purpose. I decided I was not ready to apply for a job as a wine taster after all; I did not really covet Alain du Vivier's position, since I would have been at a loss if I were asked to estimate the eventual quality of the wine at maturity, or even to compare it with the wine I had tasted the day before. My companion, however, was confident the '70 would be a fine year, if not an outstanding one.

Outside at the edge of the vineyard, the vines were bare in the winter sun. "These vines produce an annual crop, each September, for about forty years," Baron Yves related. "Then new vines must be planted, and it usually takes about five years for the first good crop."

How much, I asked, did the vines of Haut-Brion produce each year?

"The year 1971 was a poor one in quantity because of a very wet spring," he replied. "But the usual yield is between a hundred and a hundred and fifty tonneaus." (A tonneau equals four casks, or 237.6 U.S. gallons.) As we drove back toward the center of town, I learned that Haut-Brion grapes are 55 percent Cabernet-Sauvignon, 22 percent Cabernet-Franc, and 23 percent Merlot, and it is of course the mixture, in that proportion, that gives the classic wine its particular *goût*.

Baron Yves had some good things to say about some California wines, and their beneficial effect on the sales of Bordeaux in the U.S. All the members of the de Luze and du Vivier families I met had a fresh, open, and non-pontifical approach with relation to the classic French *crus*.

The subject of aspiring connoisseurs of great wines, especially in the United States, was broached at dinner that evening in the Comte Bertrand du Vivier's stunning Château de Malleret, in the Médoc country. Flanked by the Comtesse and the members of their family, he spoke easily in English about the growing enthusiasm for French classic wines abroad.

"We have been supplying wines to most European countries for many years," he began as we started on a high-spirited Malleret '61. "Of course, we have furnished wines for the Royal Court of Denmark for almost fifty years now. But today America is one of our best customers.

"And it's curious—for a long time we couldn't understand why certain really excellent wines just wouldn't sell in the United States. I don't think you know the reason."

I couldn't guess.

"Well, it seems that in your country when a gentleman who is beginning to appreciate fine French wines wants to order a bottle of a particular kind and finds that he can't pronounce the name of the vineyard, he passes on to one with an easier name. He is embarrassed at not being able to order it without mispronouncing it and without pointing at the *carte*.

"Take a good second-rank wine like Ducru-Beaucaillou, for example. We can't sell it at all in America. Too hard to pronounce. On the other hand, Beychevelle, one of our more admirable wines, sells very well—partly because its name is easily managed."

Reminded by his story, the Comte asked his wine steward for a 1955 Beychevelle, which proved to be a delicate but full-bodied wine with, as they say, a certain elegance. It may even have been *nonchalant*, for all of me. But satisfying to the palate it most certainly was, and that—whatever adjectives are used—is really the whole point.

After a dinner faultlessly prepared and served, we were treated, over coffee in the pleasantly furnished salon on the château's ground floor, to a few glasses of the firm's memorable twenty-year-old cognac. It was agreeable to toy with the idea of what it must be like to devote one's life to fine wines and cognacs, and it is not difficult to understand why wine plays such a major role in the life of the average Frenchman and why its appreciation is approached, throughout the world, with an almost religious reverence.

During a swing with Baron Geoffroy de Luze through the Médoc, the Bordelais region that produces the most superior examples of the *grand cru*, I tried to discover a simple answer to the recurring question of why this particular area, more than any other, should possess the faculty for the production of such a variety of incomparable wines. Baron Geoffroy offered one of his customary pithy replies.

"It's a combination of the sun, the climate with—most years—just the right amount of rainfall and no frost, and—perhaps most important—the miserable soil."

I thought I'd heard correctly, but I asked for a repetition of that statement anyway. "It's true," he said. "You'll notice how stony and poor the soil is here." We were inspecting a vineyard at the Château Cantenac-Brown in Margaux.

"When the soil is rich, the production of grapes is large. So the individual grapes draw less concentration of the good things in the earth and from the sun. You'll find that the most refined wines come from the poorest soil. With fewer fruits and more sun, one arrives at unbelievably good grapes."

We watched, briefly, the workers pruning the vines carefully to the same end—a less prolific but top-quality crop nine months hence. A helicopter passing overhead reminded Baron Geoffroy that new methods—the use of tractors, and helicopters for combating the disease-bearing fungi —were responsible for improving the texture and general health of the grapes, but he was quick to add that pruning, binding, and picking were still done by hand.

"Here at Cantenac-Brown, the composition is 60 percent Cabernet-Franc and Cabernet-Sauvignon—its life, its tannin; 30 percent Merlot—its softness; and 10 percent Petit Verdot—its formidable bouquet. A wine that will be improving each year," he predicted.

As we paused in our drive through the Margaux region for a ritual visit to his own Château Paveil de Luze, before returning to Bordeaux, he summed up his own attitude to wine, from the perspective of one who has spent a young lifetime in the métier.

For centuries, wines have been fussed over, fought over, and analyzed by experts and pseudo-experts, who have accorded their preferred vintages with characteristics, virtues, qualities, and propensities that the average wine drinker has never known to exist. But the Baron Geoffroy de Luze, who has considerably more than a nodding acquaintance with the celestial fluid, feels there should not really be all that much mystery about wine. Through the centuries, man has learned how best to cultivate and ferment grapes, in the proper proportions and under the best conditions, to arrive at the best result.

"The entire operation, after all," he concluded, "has a single, simple purpose: to produce an agreeable-tasting liquid that quenches the thirst."

# Deauville: A Resort for All Eras

---

No one can doubt that Deauville's raison d'être is to provide an agreeable place of diversion for those who seek an escape from the pressing problems of today. . . . Nowhere else, surely, can one find its total disregard for the times in which we live.

---

A good resort is hard to find these days—at least, one that combines elegance, chic, and all the stigmata of an accepted nineteenth- or early-twentieth-century watering place—but Deauville, a circumspect town of about five thousand year-round residents on the coast of Normandy, has survived in far better condition than most fashionable resorts. It has had its periods of gentle decline, but each has always been followed by a rise. Unlike other celebrated resorts of the *haut monde*, which give off only a dim reflection of their former brilliance, Deauville is today essentially the way it was when Raoul Dufy and Kees van Dongen painted it in the nineteen-twenties, at the height of one of its periods of ascendancy.

Although Deauville contains all the elements of an old-time society leader's dream of the perfect resort, no one element predominates: it is the mixture of ingredients, as in a good sauce, that has produced an incomparable result. Its yacht club, though first-rate, is not quite a match for the one at Cowes, on the Isle of Wight; its casino is not as elaborate as the one at Monte Carlo; its beach cannot compare with the beaches at Atlantic resorts like Biarritz or East Hampton; its golf course is a hilly, twenty-seven-hole affair that attracts only a few professionals; its baths are not the equal of those at such European spas as Baden-Baden, in West Germany, and Karlovy Vary (formerly Carlsbad), in Czechoslovakia;

and its horse racing, although Deauville is the August scene of operations for the major Paris circuit, is not to be mentioned along with the racing at Longchamp, Epsom, the Curragh, or Chantilly. Nevertheless, Deauville retains its inimitable flavor. If Dufy were painting today, he could undoubtedly be found during August in the paddock at Deauville's Hippodrome de la Touques; if Colette's Gigi were again to be taken to the seaside for the summer, it would again be to Deauville. "The world changes, but Deauville—never!" an elderly resident of this quiet community pronounced, with a touch of asperity, last year at a fête celebrating this town's hundred-and-tenth season since its founding, on a reclaimed swamp, by the Duc de Morny, an illegitimate half brother of the Emperor Napoleon III. It is still referred to condescendingly as "the Swamp" by inhabitants of Trouville, an adjacent settlement, which had been a moderately fashionable resort before Deauville's creation but which has come to be regarded today as quite tacky.

A few days after the elderly resident's statement was made, a group of vandals burned a Lamborghini sports car parked near the casino and painted the hammer and sickle on two Maseratis, a Ferrari, a Jaguar, and a Chrysler. All this was done a good two weeks before the beginning of the high season and the arrival of the Rolls-Royces, and thus gave the owners of the vehicles—all but the Lamborghini—time to have them repainted. But Alain Geismar, the head of a new movement in France called the Proletarian Left, predicted "a hot summer for the bourgeoisie," which would include, in addition to more redecorating ventures, the installation in casinos of nurseries for workers' children, the tearing down of fences surrounding luxury villas and the inviting in of campers, and—horror of horrors—the organization of soccer games on golf courses. The announcement of this program was shortly followed by Geismar's arrest in Paris on charges of subversion, but the coming season was regarded with more than usual interest and some trepidation. The mayor of Deauville cut short his own vacation, in the South of France, and returned hurriedly to make certain that the high season would begin without further untoward incidents.

He needn't have worried. The high season started—as always—on the morning of August 1st. The season at Deauville coincides exactly with the Frenchman's unshakable belief that the month of August is the only appropriate time for a vacation. Generations of French men, women, and children have left their home cities, towns, and villages either at midnight on July 31st or early in the morning on August 1st, come what might—wars, floods, famines—and regardless of the weather. Paris empties almost completely, creating a series of monster traffic jams on all roads leading out of the city, and causing crowds of riot proportions at airports and railroad stations. (It has been said, with some reason, that a squad of men—perhaps no more than nine—could capture Paris during August. If there are two bakeries in one block, both customarily close during August, despite strong efforts by the government to induce factories and shops to stagger their vacation periods. To find a laundry functioning in August in Paris may well take up the greater part of a day.)

The Deauville season began on a Saturday last year, and promptly at two o'clock that afternoon the horses for the first race filed obediently into the paddock of the Hippodrome de la Touques. The weather was warm and sunny, and the first weekend of racing was well attended. There are seventeen days of racing at the Hippodrome, and, since all thoroughbred races in France are run on carefully manicured grass, activities are transferred every now and again to a provincial track—Clairefontaine, at nearby Tourgéville—to give the turf at Deauville a chance to recover. The Hippodrome's racing calendar is punctuated by feature events on Sundays and on the fifteenth of August, the Feast of the Assumption of the Virgin.

The Prix Kergorlay: In this event, which was held on the first Sunday of the 1970 season, and is regarded in French racing circles as a semiclassic, Lester Piggott, Britain's champion jockey, added credence to the prevailing notion of many of his countrymen that Deauville, for which they all have a warm regard, is a sort of British enclave on the Norman coast. Piggott, on an Irish four-year-old named Reindeer, came from far back in the field, went to the outside, and lunged across the finish line a neck ahead of England's Precipice Wood, who is schooled by Britain's first woman trainer, Mrs. R. A. Lomax. Illa Laudo, another Irish horse, was third, two lengths farther back. The posting of the names of the jockeys who finished one-two-three—Lester Piggott, Jimmy Lindley, and Bill Williamson—had many Frenchmen in the crowd shaking their heads. It was a decidedly inauspicious début of operations for defenders of the supremacy of French bloodstock.

The attraction that Deauville has for the English has been explained in several ways, of which the most logical may be that the weather is so damp that the visitors from across the Channel feel right at home. This time, the weather was most unusual—warm, but not hot, with a gentle breeze always blowing. Except for a few overcast, misty days, it could be classed as exceptional. (In 1969, there were four inches of precipitation, some of it in the form of mist, during August—a little more precipitation than usual—and in former years there were, as I vividly remember, long stretches when I sat rainbound in my room at the Hotel Normandy, gazing out at the soaked, bare beach.) The Channel, too, was sparkling, and those few bathers who ventured in for a swim found it refreshing. At Deauville, it is traditional to rent one of the gaily colored tents on the beach but is considered unthinkable by the regulars to go near the water. This is not to say that they don't take pride in the quality of the sea that washes their beach, compared to, say, the Mediterranean at the Riviera resorts, which the Deauvillais consider a lukewarm bouillabaisse. They simply expect the water they don't go into to be the best there is. It is recorded that in the early years of the century Comte Boni de Castellane, who was then married to Jay Gould's daughter Anna, would occasionally break with tradition to the extent of sending one of his footmen to test the temperature of the water and another to sweep the sand in order to create a pebble-free path to the water's edge. Then, as often as not, even if the conditions were ideal, the Comte would decide not to indulge after all.

If the bulk of the human population does not avail itself of the opportunity to take a dip in the sea, this is not true of the visiting horses, a number of whom arrive in the early morning for an exhilarating walk in the shallow water—a treatment that some trainers swear by as the best medicine possible for their runners' delicate ankles. This unusual sight, familiar to both early-rising and late-retiring members of the August community, has been immortalized locally on postcards, and would no doubt be a favorite subject for visitors with cameras, if there were any. But tourists, as they are known in most European capitals and even in small European way stations, are in very short supply here. Perhaps the reason is a combination of rather high prices and the absence of standard tourist attractions. Whatever it is, the average tourist who wanders into Deauville apparently does not find what he is seeking. Still, the town does attract some specialized types in addition to its regular seasonal visitors: according to the local Chamber of Commerce, its population expands to about fifty thousand on the final weekend, which culminates in the running of the Grand Prix de Deauville on the last Sunday. Many of those who contribute to this expansion are day-trippers who come out from Paris, a hundred and twenty-five miles distant, for an afternoon at the track. Those who arrive for a weekend of racing find little more in the way of accommodation than the benches in the railroad station, since there are only a few hotels in the town and only a sprinkling of inns in the surrounding hamlets. However, it is well established that regular racegoers will suffer any discomfort in order to be present for the first post of the day.

By French standards, Deauville is certainly not inexpensive. In Trouville, one may dine at an excellent restaurant, À la Sole Normande, which has had four crossed spoons and forks bestowed on it by the *Guide Michelin,* but in Deauville itself, outside the major hotels, with their usual major-hotel food, there is a dearth of good places to eat. In Deauville, in fact, one pays three-star prices for unexceptional meals. But *crêpes* and cider are available on all sides, at roadside stands and in every small café, and very good, inexpensive fare they are. The best bargain in town is the Hotel Normandy's six-course dinner for thirty-two francs (about six dollars), with portions that are really ample for two; a canny resident of the hotel, by using room service, may thus dine in his *chambre* with a companion, and a kind word to the coöperative waiter can cause two place settings to appear with the single dinner. If one is a very old friend, or even just an old friend, of the management, *and* if one makes one's arrangements in time, it is possible to find a small single room at eighty francs ($14.55), with Continental breakfast included, and live in comparative luxury. The least expensive double is a hundred and twenty francs ($21); a suite, for two, of two bedrooms and a large salon, runs to five hundred ($91) a night. To accommodate a dachshund or a small poodle, one is charged an extra eighteen francs ($3.25), which does not include food.

But without a confirmed reservation made well in advance there is no chance of obtaining a room, especially during the latter half of the month. Late last August, Lester Piggott was a forlorn figure standing at the reservation desk of the Normandy and pleading for an extension to his original booking. "There are just no rooms available," M. Hubert Mailier, *directeur* of the hotel, said plaintively. "There are at least fifty people waiting for an opening right at this moment." The phone rang; it was the secretary of an international polo star scheduled to play at Deauville, requesting a discount on the room rent for Monsieur, Madame, two children, and a nurse. M. Mailier listened respectfully, then replied with infinite politeness, "I understand. He is polo. She is polo. But the children and the nurse—they are polo?"

The Prix Jacques Le Marois: This event, at sixteen hundred meters, or about a mile, on the straightaway, for three-year-olds and up, was the feature of the card for the second Sunday of the season. Nine three-year-olds and four older horses faced the starter in this spirited test, which would take them from one end of the Hippodrome to the other, starting far to the spectators' right and finishing in front of the stands. Of the thirteen, nine were foreign-bred. Here in the heart of Normandy, a region long esteemed as the most productive on the European continent for the breeding of exceptional thoroughbreds, there is particular regard for the achievements of French-born runners. Unfortunately, this Sunday was not a day to be treasured by the Gallic chauvinists in attendance. A German-bred six-year-old, Priamos, who had been winning stakes events both in France and in his native land, had enough spring left to dominate the field of mostly younger horses. Guided by French jockey Alfred Gibert, who is married to the daughter of a German trainer, this product of the century-old stud of Schlenderhan made off with the victory as though he were a young colt in his first season at the races. (Actually, he missed his three-year-old year at the races, because of illness, but he was making up for it now, having won his last four stakes.) Priamos took over from the early leaders fairly far along in the race and was never headed, successfully fighting off challenges in the final furlong by Faster, a French-bred six-year-old who had been racing in Italy, and Britain's fading Yellow God, who finished second and third, respectively. Yellow God, a three-year-old, was ridden by the redoubtable Lester Piggott, who appeared to be making Deauville his own.

Although most Deauville traditionalists will not bathe in it, the sea— the *presence* of the sea—is important to them. They like to regard it from a narrow boardwalk, on which they promenade at intervals before turning inland to devote themselves to the attractions offered by the branches of Paris establishments such as Au Printemps, the department store; Patou, the couturier; Mauboussin, the jeweler; and Régine, the night-club entrepreneuse. For though those faithful who spend each August in Deauville have displaced themselves from their native habitat, they scrupulously maintain their Parisian life style, adapted somewhat to

106

summer-resort conditions. Tristan Bernard, the French humorist and dramatist, summed up the accepted attitude neatly in a single sentence: "I love Deauville—it's so close to Paris and so far from the sea."

To avoid the kind of seafront typical of most resorts, with villas crowding the beach and encroaching on it almost to the water's edge, the original planners of the town wisely decreed that the expanse a hundred yards wide separating the Boulevard de la Mer, which runs along the sea, just behind the beach and the boardwalk shops, and the Boulevard Eugène Cornuché, which parallels it, should be kept free of private buildings, in order to afford an unobstructed view of the seafront. This preserve now includes two new swimming pools, which few Deauvillais elect to bathe in; a miniature-golf course; a pony ring; a midget-auto track; a pleasant flower-lined park, dominated by a bronze bust of Eugène Cornuché, the entrepreneur who built modern Deauville and who is now regarded as a patron saint; and a tennis club, where, each season, the more versatile jockeys take part in a tennis tournament. (No diminutive loser has yet attempted to leap the net to congratulate his victorious opponent in the traditional manner.)

On some side streets, rarely frequented by visitors, and on various streets and lanes on the inland side of town, the building style is Early Ramshackle. But, over all, the town of Deauville and the area adjoining it present a pleasing appearance. The Hippodrome, its grounds bursting with a variety of blooms, is situated not far from the railroad station and a block from the main route through town, the Avenue de la République, which is six blocks inland from the beach. Here and there, one can find facilities for enjoying almost any kind of sport or game devised by the human mind. There is a soccer stadium, and a *cercle hippique* (a club where jumping competitions on horseback are conducted), and a lawn where *pétanque* enthusiasts practice their bowling on the green. There is the yacht club and basin, which is the terminal point of the annual Cowes-Deauville race; the golf course on the slope of Mont Canisy, which rises behind the Hippodrome (where else can one find a course that includes, just off one fairway, some authentic Louis XIV ruins? These are what is left of the seventeenth-century Château de Lassay, once visited by Mme. Du Barry and her pet canary, Fifi, who flew head-on into a windowpane there, in a sortie that proved to be her last); the polo field, in the infield along the backstretch of the race track, where high-ranking international teams compete in games that usually begin directly after the day's racing program; and the alternate course, Clairefontaine, where the racing addict is offered not only flat racing but steeplechases, hurdles races, and trotting events. There is a bridge club, which sometimes holds world's championship matches; an exhibition hall, where an annual championship dog show is held, preceding the high season; an airfield where one may learn or practice flying; seawater baths, offered as a remedy—which the French refer to as "the marine cure"—for overly tense French businessmen; summer and winter casinos, providing a year-round opportunity to indulge in a wide variety of games of chance, at stakes of one's choosing; and even bistros featuring chessboards, for those who feel the need to compete in some sort of game at any hour of the day or night. For those who occasionally tire of gaming, there are several cinemas, a number of *boîtes* and discothèques, and, adjoining the Ambassadeurs night club in the summer-casino building, a small theatre where variety artists and lecturers appear. No one can doubt that Deauville's raison d'être is to provide an agreeable place of diversion for those who seek an escape from the pressing problems of today. Newspapers are available, of course, but many August residents prefer to cut off all communication with reality the moment they arrive. Deauville is perhaps the complete anachronism; nowhere else, surely, can one find its total disregard for the times in which we live. The most heated discussion I overheard there last season involved the relative merits of the sole caught on the English coast of the Channel and the sole that frequent the Normandy side. Since La Manche is only a hundred and ten miles wide at this point, detecting the difference between any two sole taken in that waterway would tax the powers of the world's most refined taste buds. The discussion finally cooled, inconclusively but agreeably, and dissolved in refilled glasses of Dom Pérignon '65.

Between races one sunny afternoon, an elderly count who prides himself on never having trod any soil other than French remarked, "Deauville is one place on earth where one is not annoyed by thoughts of impending wars, depressions, and other irritating subjects. God has been good to Frenchmen in many ways." He added, reflectively, "Even on a very damp day, I prefer Deauville, in season, to any other place in the world." He was, of course, referring to the world that is France. Those carefree souls who have no worries about tomorrow inhabit one of three hotels, if they do not have a villa of their own: the Normandy, a long, low, Norman structure with attractively furnished rooms and apartments whose walls, like the walls of the small theatre in the casino, are decorated in a single pastoral *toile-de-Jouy* print, pink in one room and blue in the next; the Royal, a traditional, U-shaped building, which attracts many of those whose names are familiar to the readers of gossip columns; and the Hôtel du Golf, a rambling structure fronting the golf course, where the atmosphere, appropriately, is more relaxed. For the careworn, there is the recently reconstructed Castel Normand, which was originally an annex of the Hotel Normandy but now caters to those who wish to take the marine cure; its *pension* plan includes not only specially prepared diets to alleviate any ailment but all the therapeutic props necessary for sagging bodies and minds.

Yachting—perhaps the ultimate escape from thoughts of taxes, inflation, and the Parisian Maoists—is one of the main diversions of the August élite. A new marina, for both sail- and powerboats, is being prepared alongside the basin that opens into the mouth of the stream called the Touques; soon it will be possible to accommodate a much larger number of sailors who prefer to step into the heart of Deauville upon arriving from the south coast of England, the Isle of Wight, or the Thames-side. This is by far the most fashionable way to make an entrance. When the J. R. Mullions, of Hong Kong and County Kildare, are in port aboard the Margot II, a member of the crew (carrying an umbrella, if it is required) escorts Mrs. Mullion across the gangplank and accompanies her to the Mullion Rolls-Royce, which is waiting at dockside to drive her to the Hotel Normandy, several blocks away. Some big yachts still make port in Deauville, but not as many as in the past. Even so, a pleasure craft like the Evdore, 163 tons and 104 feet long, owned by a corporation and under Liberian registry, is a "*petit*" in the eyes of M. Pierre Faure Beaulieu, secretary-general of the Deauville Yacht Club. Before the Second World War, the big ones berthed at Deauville in profusion, according to M. Faure Beaulieu. There were more than a hundred yachts of over five hundred tons listed in *Lloyd's Register of Yachts* then, he said, and now there are only twenty. Recently, he recalled some of them, tamping down tobacco in his pipe: Franklin Singer's Xarifa, of 730 tons; Abbas Hilmi's 991-ton Nimet Allah; Sol Joel's 909-ton Eileen; the Duke of Westminster's 883-ton Cutty Sark; Baron Henri de Rothschild's 915-ton Éros; Gaston Menier's 630-ton Ariane; the 540-ton Gaviota IV, owned by Arturo Lopez-Wilshaw, "*le dernier yachtsman d'avant-guerre*"; and the 880-ton Crusader, owned by the millionaire American sportsman A.

Kingsley Macomber. Sir Thomas Lipton's 1116-ton steam yacht Erin was of a size that had not been taken into account at the time the basin was designed, so when the old yachtsman called at Deauville, he anchored the massive vessel offshore and lightered in.

In the years between the wars, the very rich came for the races and the casino, and used their boats as places to entertain. After the Second World War, that custom changed. "Yachting at Deauville has become more democratic and more *sympathique*," M. Faure Beaulieu said. "Today, the owners are people who love the sea. They navigate for pleasure, and don't think of their boats as places to live. They are sailors—good sailors."

Although more seagoing types put into Deauville each season, the majority of visitors still arrive by the conventional routes: by road, through the village of Touques or along the coast; by rail, from Paris (aboard the Turbotrain) or other points; or by air, aboard commercial planes that fly between Paris or London and the Saint-Gatien airport. Some visitors prefer private planes; the Aga Khan IV, for instance, has made the eight-hundred-and-fifty-mile trip from his vacation development on Sardinia to Saint-Gatien in his fan-jet Mystère 20 to see a single race, in which one of his horses competed, and returned immediately to his island retreat. Less advanced private planes, including many Piper Cubs, bear equally devoted racegoers, who—no matter how busy they are—simply cannot forgo indulging their passion.

The Prix Gontaut-Biron: During the week leading up to the Feast of the Assumption of the Virgin, which marks the midpoint of the Deauville season, the English again scored a victory in an important stakes: the Prix Gontaut-Biron was won by Shoemaker (a horse, not the jockey), of the English stable owned by P. G. Goulandris, a member of the Greek shipping family, who lives in London. The margin of victory was one length, with Britain's Duncan Keith beating out Britain's Piggott, up on Granados. On the Feast of the Assumption itself, which is a French legal holiday, Piggott distinguished himself with two first-place finishes and one second, including a victory on Gold Rod in the Prix de la Côte Normande. Jockey Gibert saved the day from turning into another French embarrassment by coming in on Faux Monnayeur, a long shot from a French stable, in the Grand Handicap de la Manche, the other feature.

Except for some grumbling among the holders of losing tickets, the French maintained their tradition of good sportsmanship in the face of the unusual number of British winners. But there was a good deal of discussion—among the English as well as the French—of the conditions for entry in many French races. To be quite fair, it must be pointed out that the purses in England have traditionally been considerably smaller than the purses in France. This has meant that when a race in France was announced for horses who had not won any races above a certain purse figure, many excellent English horses qualified, since in England the figure applied to only a relatively few top-ranking events. After the 1970 Deauville meeting, and perhaps partly because of it, the Société d'Encouragement pour l'Amélioration des Races de Chevaux en France, which controls thoroughbred racing in the country and operates the key tracks of Longchamp, Chantilly, and Deauville, announced that there would be some changes made. Sportsmanship is one thing, but one-sided races are another, and it was felt that, in view of the record of relatively easy foreign victories in many stakes over the past few years, the time had come to *harmoniser* the conditions of the events in question. Thus, beginning this year, as Jean Romanet, *directeur général* of the Société, explained, "important races in England, Ireland, and France will be divided into three groups so that penalties [extra weight] will depend upon the status of the race won rather than on the monetary value. So, instead of having '*le gagnant d'un Prix de 100,000 Francs portera 2 Kilogrammes*,' we will have '*le gagnant d'une course du Groupe III portera 2 Kilogrammes*.' These three groups will include ninety-six French races, ninety-eight English races, and twenty-two Irish races. This scheme has been adopted in order to iron out anomalies caused by penalties' being allotted according to the amount of prize money won, and to insure the selection of the best horses through top-class international competition."

To put it another way, for the British the honeymoon is over. This year, under the new regulations, a hundred days of French racing had gone by before the British won their first event.

Although certain Americans—they include perhaps a dozen proprietors who train and race in France and a number of breeders who import French stallions, at record prices, for their studs—are fully aware of the fine strain that accounts for the performances of French thoroughbred stock, that knowledge appears to be quite limited on the west side of the Atlantic, where most owners in the market for young horses do their foreign shopping in England or Ireland. One perplexed French breeder said he wondered whether it might be the language, but added quickly that in his experience real connoisseurs of horseflesh spoke the same tongue. There are, of course, some conspicuous examples of American appreciation of French bloodlines. Sea Bird, the French champion of six years ago, was leased for what was estimated by French authorities as a whopping seven and a half million francs (one and a half million dollars) to stand at stud for five years at the Kentucky farm of John W. Galbreath. (Nijinsky has since been syndicated to stand at stud for nearly five and a half million dollars.) Certainly French breeding has shown to great advantage in the nineteen runnings of the Washington, D.C., International, at Laurel, Maryland, which the French have appeared in sixteen times and have won five times, against topflight international competition.

A plentiful number of *haras* (stud farms) are situated, sometimes side by side, in the gently rolling Norman countryside surrounding Deauville. In this province, the belief has long been held that there is something about the year-round dampness, and the consequent dewy condition of the grass in the Norman fields, that gives a thoroughbred born and raised here a special start toward becoming a gifted performer at the races and, later, a valuable sire or dam at the *haras*. And, indeed, enough great stakes winners have come off the fields of Normandy to lend some weight to that opinion. Normandy has approximately two hundred stud farms, on which two-thirds of France's total annual crop of three thousand foals is produced.

During the fortnight between the Feast of the Assumption and the end of the high season, Deauville regularly conducts a much respected sale of yearlings at an auction ring just across the street from the Hippodrome. At the 1970 sale, the bidding was lively on most days, but there was—as usual—an absence of overseas buyers, except from Britain. In the hope of improving this situation, an electronic hookup was arranged to link the auction ring at Deauville with Saratoga, whose yearly August meeting corresponds with Deauville's. Videotapes of twenty yearlings were shown as these animals were being presented in France. Oddly, only one American bid was made—on a chestnut colt named Nikiforos, by Alcide out of Nymphet—but this fine-looking young animal was knocked down not to an American but to John Cunnington, Jr., one of about a dozen French trainers of British descent, on behalf of the actor Omar el Sharif, for 210,000 francs ($38,182). After that single, unsuccessful bid, there was nothing but silence from the American side of the circuit, and for a while the auctioneer and the French breeders thought that the equipment had gone dead. Both the Fasig-Tipton Company, of the United States, which conducted the sale at Saratoga, and the Office du Pur Sang, which conducts the sales in Deauville, were disappointed. The French press summed up the experiment with just a trace of bitterness: *"Rien n'est venu d'Amérique, ni voix ni—évidemment—dollars."*

The top price at the sale was 360,000 francs ($65,000), brought by Sanctus Lass, a filly by Sanctus out of Irish Lass, whose sire was Sayajirao, and even though the electronic link with Saratoga produced no sales, the purchases were by no means inconsiderable: 456 yearlings, including 87 sold privately, away from the ring, brought 20,531,275 francs, and, for the most part, both buyers and sellers left the auction area happy.

The Prix Morny: While the yearlings were being prepared for their entrance into the sale ring, their elders by one year were occupied with the running of the Prix Morny, perhaps the most important race of the year for two-year-olds, and, in the opinion of many, unquestionably the most important race of the Deauville season. The second of the classic French tests for two-year-olds (the first is the Prix Robert Papin, at Maisons-Laffitte, in July), the Prix Morny dates back to 1865, a year after the Hippodrome was inaugurated by the Duc de Morny, and five months after his death. The 1970 edition of the Morny—a six-furlong sprint (1,200 meters) on the straightaway—was won in commanding fashion by David Robinson's My Swallow, another promising British runner. Again it was Lester Piggott on the winner, scoring, with another flawless ride, by a margin of two lengths over a French hopeful, Impertinent. The nation's turf writers devoted their articles in equal measure to Piggott, for whom they expressed grudging but sincere admiration, and, as in *Paris-Turf*, to lamentations over the state of the young French horses and predictions of an apparently gloomy future for French breeders and their products.

This third Sunday of the season was not a complete disaster for the French, however, for Baudelaire, an outsider carrying French colors, took the Grand Handicap de Deauville. But somehow that wasn't enough.

Standing next to the heroic stone figure of the Duc de Morny in the Place Morny, the hub of Deauville, one can look down eight streets, which give off the Place like the spokes of a wheel, and see very nearly every centimeter of what has been described by one of the resort's more florid biographers as a garden of unadulterated pleasures—for this town, created in the mid-nineteenth century, is a compact community, bounded on the west by the English Channel, on the north by the Touques, which separates it from Trouville, on the east by the Hippodrome and the golf course, and on the south by the next municipality, Bénerville. The heart of Deauville, where its August inhabitants spend the entire month— dining, drinking, making love, admiring horseflesh, and gambling with panache far into the night—is only seven blocks square, an area carefully staked out by Morny, who, in conjunction with two associates (a banker named Armand Donon and a self-styled doctor named Joseph Olliffe), bought 300 acres of swampland for 800,000 francs in March, 1860.

The Duc, named—to conceal his true identity—after a "seedy merce-nary in the Prussian Army" called Demorny, was the natural son of Charles-Joseph, Comte de Flahaut, himself a bastard son of Talleyrand, and Hortense de Beauharnais Bonaparte, former Queen of Holland and daughter of the Empress Josephine by her first husband, the Vicomte Alexandre de Beauharnais. Morny adapted quickly to the political and social mores of the time, ultimately engineering the overthrow of the Republic and the accession to the throne of his half brother Louis, who thus became Napoleon III. Naturally, the Duc thereafter occupied a place at the right hand of the Emperor. A close friend of Lord Henry Seymour, the French-born Englishman who provided the impetus for the inaugura-tion of French thoroughbred horse racing, the Duc was himself a devoted horseman, and he customarily raced his thoroughbreds at Baden-Baden in the summers. He cultivated few other enthusiasms, in order to keep from spreading himself too thin. But one was the salons of Paris society, where he cut a formidable figure; some of the most notable ladies of the moment found him irresistible. He advanced the illegitimate line to the third generation when, in a liaison with Fanny Lehon, wife of the Belgian Ambassador to Paris, he fathered a daughter, Louise, but as Morny reached his mid-forties he felt a need to settle down. He missed having legitimate family connections, and, after serving as Ambassador Extraor-dinary at the coronation of Russia's Czar Alexander II, in 1856, he fell in love with Princess Sophie Trubetskoi and married her. In that portion of his busy life devoted to horse racing, he became one of the prime movers in the creation of Longchamp, the luxurious race track that was opened in Paris's Bois de Boulogne in April, 1857. He still felt vaguely dissatisfied with the necessity of going to Baden-Baden every summer for the races, though, so he determined to build a French equivalent. Thus was Deauville conceived.

In October, 1861, a bridge across the Touques, linking Deauville with Trouville and the road to Paris, was completed and opened, and in May, 1863, Morny and his associates made the first use of a new rail line between Deauville and Pont l'Évêque by riding an open-top railway coach along the route. The Deauville railroad station was officially opened on July 1st of that year, when the Bishop of Bayeux blessed the building and the locomotives lined up along the tracks. The Duc was an international personage by this time, but his missions abroad were never allowed to keep him from visiting his domain on the English Channel. On April 3, 1864, accompanied by the *député* from Calvados, the *département* in which Deauville lies, Morny, Donon, and Olliffe made a ceremonial trip by rail from Paris; they were met at the Deauville station by the *gendarmerie* and the *douaniers,* and after suitable greetings a procession formed behind the Duc's carriage and moved triumphantly to the newly finished Grand Hotel, where dinner was served in the salons overlooking the sea. The next morning, there was an inspection of the new Hippodrome that had been constructed to the Duc's specifications, with stalls for forty horses.

The anticipatory excitement of the introduction of racing to Deauville had proved too much to bear, and the first races had been held a full year before the opening of the Hippodrome—on the beach at Trouville, on August 8, 1863. The big day finally arrived on August 14, 1864. The casino orchestra played, the ladies wore crinolines, and the Duc de Morny's stable failed to produce a winner. There were several races the following day, and with them the 1864 season closed. Morny's colors (pink silks) had not once been in evidence in the winner's spot in the *enceinte*. The next season's meeting was scheduled for the sixth and seventh of August, but the Duc did not live to attend it. He died in Paris in March, at the age of fifty-three, after a series of dramatic bedside visits from the cream of Paris society, including the Emperor and the Empress. Some say he died as a direct result of taking too many of Dr. Olliffe's "pearls"—pills concocted by the Duc's associate in the Deauville venture, an Irish-born doctor who had been banished from his profession but had nevertheless collected a considerable clientele of affluent patients, and had also induced the British Embassy in Paris to take him on as its physician. Whether or not Olliffe's patent medicines helped to speed Morny's demise, it was discovered after his death that the trouble lay in his pancreas, not in his liver, as most of the French doctors who attended him in his last days had believed.

Deauville wasn't quite the same after Morny's death, but it went on to become a resort of exactly the quality he had always wanted. The Hippodrome remained the focus of attention; the two- and three-day seasons of its early years were gradually expanded to the present seventeen days. Because some of the thoroughbreds in residence for the month occasionally do their early-morning gallops on the racing strips instead of on the training *pistes* inside the principal track, the blanket of emerald-green turf requires constant and devoted attention during the high season; a squad of *reboucheurs de trous* replacing divots with hoelike instruments keeps it in extraordinarily good condition between races. The leafy bower that is the paddock, and the abundance of geraniums and other blooms, have long provided a compelling background for the succession of artists who have been attracted to the area, including (besides Dufy and van Dongen) the marine painter Eugène Boudin, who was born in the nearby fishing village of Honfleur and lived and painted in Deauville in the last decade of the nineteenth century, and Fernand Léger and Marcel Vertès, who were part-time residents. Gustave Flaubert, too, became a part-time resident in the mid-nineteenth century, when he inherited some property adjoining the Hippodrome.

For a handy rule of thumb, the life and times of Deauville are divisible into five periods: pre-Morny, Morny, Cornuché, André, and post-André. A ten-foot bronze statue of Morny, by Henri-Frédéric Iselin, was originally erected in the Place Morny in 1867, a year after the opening of the port of Deauville, one of the projects to which the founder had dedicated himself. But with the outbreak of the Franco-Prussian War, in 1870, the statue was removed and stored for safekeeping until the hostilities were over, and it was never restored to its old position. In 1942, the Germans melted it down for the metal, and the present statue of Morny was put up in 1955. Bismarck won the war, the Second Empire collapsed, and the Empress Eugénie fled Paris with a party that included an American dentist, a Dr. Evans. She appeared briefly in Deauville, where she boarded a small boat, the Gazelle, for England. Her departure marked the beginning of a decline in Deauville's life which lasted until just before the

116

First World War. In 1895, the casino closed for lack of patrons, and it was torn down seven years later.

But although the glow of Deauville dimmed, and some of its clientele defected to Trouville, the races at the Hippodrome de la Touques remained *le clou* of the August season. Léon Levillain, a Deauvillais of the late nineteenth century, recalled the scene vividly: "The Deauville season reached its height during the big week of the races. The *'retour du Grand Prix'* by the Villers road was a great sight for the poor people who did not have the means to pay twenty sous to enter the racecourse, and they came and sat down on benches along the road to watch the flood of pedestrians and the passing of the *voitures,* Victorias, and *calèches,* bearing the ladies in their *grandes toilettes.* The viewers admired the beautiful trappings of the horses and grew enthusiastic over the passage of the mail coaches, whose coachmen and valets were dressed in red and whose coming was announced by long brass *trompettes.* . . . During this week, the villas were lit up for the receptions their owners gave; in the harbor, the big yachts replaced the little ships loaded with cargoes of wood, and evening parties were given on board the beautiful yachts, resplendent with their brasses polished and their *hublots* illuminated—they were floating palaces."

The renaissance of Deauville began with the arrival, in 1912, of Eugène Cornuché, an extraordinary Boniface and entrepreneur, whose father was a wine merchant in Paris. Eugène had begun his career as a waiter at Weber's, one of the best-known Paris restaurants, and had worked with such diligence and singleness of purpose that within a few years he was able to take over a fading restaurant called Maxime's, drop the "e," and develop it into the celebrated Maxim's with a clientele of what has been called *"le monde, le demi-monde, et le quart de monde de la société parisienne et internationale."* In Deauville, he constructed the Normandy and the Royal hotels, both fronting on the windswept area overlooking the beach, and, on the site of the old casino, a new one, in the style of Louis XVI. It has been called a "Petit Trianon" and described as "the only casino in the world that is not ugly"—though the burghers of Baden-Baden might have something to say about that. Having taken over the operation of Les Ambassadeurs, in Paris, as well as Maxim's, Cornuché was well supplied with just the right clientele to populate his new casino and luxury hotels. The casino opened in 1912, and he engaged Nijinsky and Karsavina to perform *Le Spectre de la Rose* as its first attraction. New restaurants appeared on the *planches* (boardwalk), affording the *flâneurs* a chance to exchange gossip over their before-lunch cocktail. The caricaturist Sem (Georges Goursat) installed himself on the scene, to immortalize Deauville and its world-weary regular visitors. Among the Americans in the group were Mrs. Potter Palmer, Mrs. Rutherford Stuyvesant, Mme. Jacques Balsan (Consuelo Vanderbilt), Joseph Widener, Charles Carroll (of the Carrollton, Maryland, Carrolls), T. P. Thorne, James Hazen Hyde, Anthony Drexel, William K. Vanderbilt, and Cornelius Vanderbilt. Another worthy subject for Sem's talented pen was King Leopold of the Belgians, who customarily arrived for the season in his yacht Alberta and lived in a small villa under the incognito of the Comte de Ravenstein—a disguise he dropped only at the Cercle, his favorite club, and on his boat.

It was in the years just preceding the First World War that Americans began taking a more active part in French racing. The pioneer in the field was William K. Vanderbilt, who left his imprint on French racing as early as 1900. Aided by his victories in the Prix du Jockey Club at Chantilly in 1906, 1908, and 1909, and in the Grand Prix de Deauville in 1904 and 1906, he was the leading money-winner for four years during the first decade of the new century, amassing more than a million francs ($192,000) each of those seasons. He was a familiar figure at Deauville, where he was often seen in the company of his trainer, William Duke. Between Paris and Normandy, his time was well occupied, and he had little left for visits to the United States, especially after he bought the remains of an early-seventeenth-century château, Le Quesnay, which stood in a four-hundred-and-thirty-acre expanse of grounds extending into three communes—Vauville, Glanville, and Saint-Pierre Azif. There he established a stud farm with accommodations for a hundred and sixty horses. (On the chimneypiece of a sitting room in the château is inscribed the motto *"Imbre Cadenta Dulce Calefieri,"* which, I was told on a recent visit, is *"bas Latin"* for *"Lorsque la pluie tombe il est doux de se réchauffer,"* or "When the rain falls, it is sweet to warm oneself up." Apparently, the climate of Normandy has not changed greatly through the centuries.) Mr. Vanderbilt added still another Jockey Club Prix to his list of victories in 1919, and then, in July, 1920, while enjoying the races at Auteuil, in Paris, he suffered a heart attack and died a few months later. He had done more for Franco-American relations than many ambassadors. Maurice de Noisay, a historian of French racing, wrote at the time: "We will always remember that model stable where nothing was missing, not even the soul, and where everything went off like clockwork. We will always remember that serious face, much more like a doctor's or a clergyman's than like a banker's." Le Quesnay was sold to another American—Mr. Macomber, the owner of the yacht Crusader—and the trainer Duke went along to take care of the stable. Mr. Vanderbilt's daughter Consuelo later wrote that Duke had told her at the time, "These horses will never run again as they did for Mr. Vanderbilt." She added, "And they never did." During the Second World War, the German High Command for the area took over Le Quesnay, painted the stone of the château black, and allowed the ivy that covered its walls to die. The Roseraie was destroyed, and the stables were turned into quarters for prisoners. Macomber died in 1955, and today Le Quesnay is owned and operated as a *haras* by Willy Head and his son Alec, who bought the property from Mrs. Macomber in 1958.

Cornuché presided over Deauville in one of its most effulgent periods. The Golden Twenties seemed a shade more golden at Deauville than anywhere else. No soirée was considered worth attending that didn't include a smattering of Americans like Rutherford Stuyvesant, Herbert Pulitzer, Frank Jay Gould, Frederick H. Prince (the first), Ralph Beaver Strassburger, Erskine Gwynne, E. Berry Wall, Mrs. Jimmy Walker, and Macomber, mingling with Gaston Menier (the chocolate king), Paul, André, and Émile Dubonnet (of the apéritif clan), James Hennessy (cognac), the Comte de Villefranche, Viscount Castlerosse, the Maharajas of Kapurthala, Baroda, and Patiala, the King and Queen of Rumania, King Alfonso of Spain, and the Aga Khan III. Perhaps the focal point of the gaiety was La Ferme du Coteau, where large house parties were given by Ralph Beaver Strassburger, whose Haras des Monceaux was one of the largest stud farms in the area. The Strassburger villa was equipped with a resident pianist who had a formidable repertoire, a formidable memory, and formidable stamina. "Just press the button for music any time of the day or night," the hospitable host told his guests. If the button was pressed, say, at 2 A.M. on a slow night, "The Music" would appear, in white tie and tails, if a bit sleepy, to play the latest Broadway hits or anything else desired, until dawn or as long as he was requested to. If a guest pressed the button during breakfast, "The Music" would make his appearance in a Charvet dressing gown. At lunch, he was often dressed in Lanvin shorts; at cocktails, in Bond Street flannels; and at night, always in tails. "The house was filled with English Royalty,"

Caresse Crosby recalled in her memoirs, *The Passionate Years*. "Just as twenty or thirty people were about to sit down to a mammoth lunch . . . someone would suggest prawns at Houlgate or snails at Dives, or maybe a sandwich under an umbrella on the beach, or aboard a yacht in the harbor, and off we'd all go, leaving the groaning tables and grim faces at the villa. 'The Music' told me that on these occasions he had the place all to himself. Mrs. Strassburger never appeared for meals, or at any time. She lived on the other side of the garden."

If Deauville was at its most high-spirited in the twenties, it was also a bit more respectable than it had once been. Before the First World War, mention of Deauville at once brought to mind the notorious cocottes, especially La Belle Otero and Liane de Pougy. In the twenties, attention shifted to Chanel, who had opened her first boutique there, and—in the field of song and dance—the Dolly Sisters and Mistinguett. At the races, *Vogue* noted at the time, every lady carried in her handbag a platinum or gold pencil studded with pearls or diamonds and topped with a cabochon emerald or other precious stones. When there was no racing, the uniform of the day was one *pour le golf*, and the afternoons were spent on *les links* until about five, when gambling began in earnest at the casino. On the dance floor at Les Ambassadeurs, the tango had given way to *le Black Bottom*; today, in a hall of the casino near the New-Brummell, a *boîte* in the casino building, a Sem drawing has preserved for the ages an impression of Elsa Maxwell performing that exhilarating dance. In 1924, the ballet *Le Train Bleu*, created by Darius Milhaud, Bronislava Nijinska, Jean Cocteau, Mlle Gabrielle Chanel, and Pablo Picasso, and set on the beach at Deauville, had its première in Paris, and Cornuché arranged to have the famous Continental Blue Train make a special trip to Deauville so that *le Tout-Paris* could celebrate at the original scene.

In 1926, at the age of sixty-nine, Cornuché died in Paris, while en route from the Riviera to his farm in Normandy, and the task of keeping Deauville in the forefront of the world of *élégance, élan,* and *esprit* was taken on by one of his protégés, François André, who had started his career as a dishwasher, had later been a croupier at the Cercle Haussmann in Paris, and from there had worked his way up to become Cornuché's assistant. André was "blessed with good looks, endless energy, and a genius for providing entertainment," noted E. (for Evander) Berry Wall, an American habitué of Deauville who went through his father's and grandfather's considerable fortunes in eleven years. André took over the direction of

Deauville with a sure hand: he constructed the Hôtel du Golf, added a new golf course, and made the town a center for aviation enthusiasts and automobile-rally devotees. "From gambling to golf, from girls to galas, he knows what we want to do," Wall said at the time. André, who reigned as head of the Société des Hôtels et Casino de Deauville for thirty-six years, and died in 1962, at the age of eighty-three, is enshrined in the heart of Deauville with a stone bust of his own, in the center of a small but strategically situated square bearing his name, which is itself in the center of the casino-boutique area that typifies Deauville's special quality and has caused the town to be described more than once as an exquisite gem in a perfect setting.

Les Prix Quincey et de Pomone: On the fourth of the five racing Sundays in the 1970 Deauville season, two features worth a hundred thousand francs ($18,000) each to the winners brought out a crowd of respectable proportions, in town for the start of the Grande Semaine— the week leading up to the Grand Prix de Deauville. Lester Piggott won them both—the one-mile Prix Quincey on a British-owned Irish horse named Lorenzaccio, and the twenty-six-hundred-meter Prix de Pomone on an Irish-owned filly, Santa Tina, who was trained by a dedicated young English resident of Chantilly named Charles Milbank. With Piggott dominating the season, no one gained much of a stake for the evening's activities at the casino, which was beginning what was traditionally its most lucrative week of the year. Lorenzaccio, who beat out Monticello by a short head, paid two francs twenty centimes for one franc to win, and Santa Tina paid one franc fifty for one. Just betting on the red or the black, or on odd or even, at the roulette table, one got better odds than those on Santa Tina.

The casino and the hotels that André took over are now under the administration of a nephew of his, Lucien Barrière, who also directs casinos in Cannes, Le Touquet, La Baule, and Juan-les-Pins, and under his regime this haven for hedonists is continuing to enjoy a golden age. While the mayor, Comte Michel d'Ornano, who is also député for Calvados, keeps busy trying to attract more industry to the surrounding area, and inviting promising young future P.-D.G.s (Présidents-Directeurs Généraux) to Deauville, Barrière concentrates on luring the right breed of European gambler to the casino and, in particular, on maintaining his uncle's tradition of elegance. At the Deauville casino, even more than at Europe's other gambling establishments, it is important to be able to lose large sums without losing one's sang-froid. The Grande Semaine is especially important. "For eight days," M. Barrière said recently, rolling the words over on his tongue with obvious relish, "this is the most elegant place in the world."

To help maintain the proper tone, Barrière calls on the services of a staff of several hundred polished, knowledgeable assistants, some of them with long memories. These include croupiers, bankers, greeters, waiters, bartenders, bouncers, and a staff of eight physiognomists, led by Adolphe Grillo, an inconspicuous man who scans the casino's incoming customers for undesirables and has been credited with memorizing half a million faces. Although this may be something of an exaggeration, he does keep a file of that number of names, which includes the name of every person who has entered the gaming rooms during the past five or six years. Sometimes he makes sketches of the memorable characteristics, facial or otherwise, of men or women he finds particularly worth watching. More often, he simply recalls the faces—he can recognize them even when they're disguised by mustaches, beards, wigs, or plastic surgery—of those he has observed during fifty years of service in French casinos.

Grillo's blacklist, a sort of Almanach de Gotha in reverse, consists of some ten thousand persons, some of whom—despairing compulsive gamblers—have blacklisted themselves for certain periods. Many of these, after disqualifying themselves for, say, a five-year term, beg to be reinstated ahead of time, but that request is never granted. In M. Grillo's view, women are the biggest gamblers. "A man knows his limits, but a woman won't stop when she is losing," he has explained. "She says to herself that her husband or her lover will pay. If women couldn't gamble, we would do eighty percent less business."

Of all the visitors to the Deauville casino, perhaps the greatest gambling wizard was Nicolas Zographos, a Greek-born mathematical marvel who in the nineteen-twenties and thirties was the keystone of "the Syndicate," an association of gamblers who worked together and financed their star *joueurs*. His background was as mysterious as that of the late Sir Basil Zaharoff. Zographos' favorite game was not roulette, boule, *vingt-et-un*, or *chemin de fer*, but the big one, baccarat in its most rarefied form —*banque à tout va* (the sky's the limit)—played in the privacy of the "*salle privée*," a special room with its own set of alert guards. Experts have

122

called Zographos the greatest cardplayer who ever lived. "I decided to perfect myself at them," he once told a Deauville visitor in the thirties, and he added that he had worked hard at his chosen career and amassed a number of fortunes. "Perhaps you do not realize it, but there is as big a difference between a good baccarat player and a poor one as there is between a scratch golfer and a man with an eighteen handicap," he went on. "People think, because at baccarat or *chemin de fer* you have to play with the cards dealt to you, that there is little opportunity for skill, except, of course, when it is *à volonté* to draw. But I assure you they are wrong, and I should know." In those days, he kept himself in perfect shape by playing not six-pack bezique but *eight*-pack bezique and remembering the whereabouts of every card in the eight packs.

Zographos' largest loss at a single session of baccarat was thirty-six million francs, at a time when that amounted to nearly a million and a half dollars. "The largest number of times I have ever won consecutively on both sides of the table is twelve, and on one side of the table nineteen," he has said. "The banker, in drawing his second card after the player's, has a tiny but definite advantage. But the main difference is that the players double up their bets when they are losing and hedge when they are winning. It is only human nature, but there you are. I will put it another way. The bank plays baccarat as though it were contract bridge, weighing up every chance mathematically. And let me tell you it needs the brain of a very good accountant to assess immediately the amount of money being staked on either side of the table and then to work out mentally whether it is worth drawing a third card. . . . There is no such thing as good luck or bad luck." Another member of the Syndicate, a Greek shipowner named Athanasios Vagliano, was often the banker of baccarat games in which two and a half million dollars changed hands in one night.

Today, although the baccarat table in the *salle privée* still has its adherents, the favorite game of chance at the Deauville casino is—as it has been since it was first legalized in France, after the First World War—roulette; unlike roulette in the United States, where the wheel includes a zero and a double zero, the French wheel has only one zero, thereby giving the individual player a bit more of a chance. Even so, one should not feel sorry for the state, which collects a whacking 55 percent of the gross receipts, and thus is certain of always winning. Two supervisors are in constant attendance at the Deauville casino to insure that everything is in order—one from the police and the other from the Ministry of Economy and Finance. But, in contrast to the way things are done in the United States, where the track is required to identify to the Internal Revenue Service the winners of six hundred dollars or more on two-dollar Daily Double or Exacta tickets, for future double-checking against the winners' tax returns, the French fiscal outriders are not concerned with those who win, even if they win staggering amounts. It is the players who lose heavily and continue to lose that interest them. "And where, Monsieur, are you getting the money to lose like that?" It epitomizes a basic difference in the American and the Gallic approaches to life.

M. Barrière considered 1970 a good year for the casino, but then every year is a good year. By the end of the Grande Semaine, however, on the final Sunday of the month, a slight fatigue had set in, even among the most volatile of the visitors. Large sums had been won and lost, friendships and liaisons had been cemented and broken, and great quantities of excellent champagne had been consumed. There remained nothing else to do except observe the high point of Deauville's high season—the annual running of the climactic horse race.

The Grand Prix de Deauville: This race, at twenty-six hundred meters, or a mile and five-eighths, was first run in 1871, and, with six omissions caused by the world wars, it had been run ninety-three times before the 1970 edition. The *grand seigneur* of the area, banker Baron Guy de Rothschild—his Haras de Meautry, at Touques, just over the line from Trouville on the road to Paris, is the largest *haras* in Normandy—had won this elusive *prix* three times, most recently in 1969, with Djakao, thanks to a stylish ride by Jean Deforge. For the '70 running, the Rothschild stable entered a promising three-year-old colt named High Moon—a product of Meautry—coupled as an entry with a three-year-old colt named Ossian and owned by Baronne de Rothschild's brother the Baron Thierry de Zuylen de Nyevelt. Both horses came into the stretch in a three-way battle with another French colt, Mme. Léon Volterra's Experio, who held a slight advantage at that point. But out of the pack following the leaders emerged art dealer Daniel Wildenstein's German-bred four-year-old mare Schönbrunn, under an energetic ride by Australian Bill Pyers. (Lester Piggott on favored Meadowville was already beaten.) Schönbrunn came on down the stretch like something possessed, with Pyers driving all the way. She won by half a length from Experio, with Ossian third, another half length back. Mr. Wildenstein and his son Alec thought so little of their mare's chances that they had gone off to the South of France for a vacation. Another son, Guy, was preparing for the final polo match of the season on the field just inside the backstretch, and Schönbrunn's trainer, Zilber, was *grippé*. So Pyers guided his mount into the winner's circle, dismounted, and posed for photographers alone with his horse.

Of the 465,000-franc purse, Schönbrunn, capping a month of stakes victories by foreign horses, won 260,000 francs for her owner, plus 25,000 for her breeder. The natives consoled themselves with the fact that at least the winner's stable and colors were French.

The high season was officially concluded the next evening, with the Mayor's Ball at Les Ambassadeurs. Once again, Rolls-Royces and Bentleys were lined up in front of the Royal and the Normandy, and men in dinner jackets and women wearing *des rivières de diamants* paused briefly after walking the few steps from the hotel entrances to their cars in order to be driven the few yards to the casino. The atmosphere of make-believe started to take hold just across the narrow street from the Normandy entrance, on the inland side of the hotel, where, in the Square François André, a stand of carefully pruned, identical apple trees, individually lighted from below, gave the whole scene a fairyland glow. At Les Ambassadeurs, the Comte and Comtesse d'Ornano received such assorted guests as the international playboy Gunther Sachs, Mme. Volterra, and Mme. Maurice Schumann, the wife of the French Minister of Foreign Affairs, along with many unpublicized Deauvillais, at a party that seemed to belong to another era.

As the vintage champagne flowed and the expensively gowned ladies danced with their escorts, one observer, looking about him, offered the opinion that only the diamonds were real. All the pieces of the Deauville season had fallen into place; Alain Geismar's earlier threat of "a hot summer for the bourgeoisie" had not been carried out. As the last guests straggled out into the September morning that heralded a return to reality, one had the impression that if, indeed, there should ever be another French revolution, Deauville would be the last to know.

# Paul Poiret . . . and the Age of Gold Lamé

---

*Poiret elevated high fashion to the status of an art. A French authority has written: "A dress by Poiret is recognizable at a glance, like a painting by Renoir."*

---

When Paul Poiret is remembered, it should be as someone who merits a niche in the hall of fame of women's liberation, for he was the fashion revolutionary who, at the beginning of this century, led women out of the corsets that had imprisoned them for so long. Yet only recently newspaper accounts cited Gabrielle Chanel as the Paris dressmaker who, in the nineteen-twenties, is thought to have freed women from stays and tight lacings. If Poiret has not been getting the credit he deserves, that may be because the notoriety he gained later both as a designer of exotic Neo-Oriental costumes and as the inventor of the crippling hobble skirt obscured his most eventful contribution to feminine progress.

When he came on the scene, revolution had been in the air for decades. In European politics, it was the era of the bomb thrower. In Poiret's field—fashion—attempts had been made to stir things up as far back as the eighteen-fifties. There had been the manifestoes of the dress-reform ladies, with Amelia Jenks Bloomer in the forefront, and there had been the British Aesthetes, with their anti-whalebone doctrine and their unfettered Grecian draperies. Vociferous as these groups were, they had attracted serious notice among only a small percentage of women.

Then along came Poiret, who had a natural advantage over the earlier reformers. In addition to the usual equipment of the deep-dyed radical

—sense of mission, full measure of ego—he had an innate aptitude for drawing the widest possible attention.

His instinct for showmanship served him nicely, for it carried him along to power as the first King of Fashion, to reign from 1907 for nearly a quarter of a century. During this time, he left an imprint of his personal taste on dress, art, and decoration that was to last long after his influence paled. Traces linger with us still, in fact, in relaxed, unconstructed clothing that reveals the figure and in the revival of the style of Art Deco, of which he was in large part a creator.

Without Poiret's groundwork in sweeping away the underbrush in women's attire, the route would not have been cleared for later fashion pioneering: Coco Chanel's poor-look jersey dresses of the nineteen-twenties and André Courrèges's ultramodern architectural clothes of the nineteen-sixties, for instance.

Poiret's immediate predecessor, Charles Frederick Worth, known in the annals of fashion as the father of *haute couture*, had in the late nineteenth century made a small dent in the solid armor of female attire by eliminating the cumbersome crinoline skirt. Worth's reform was a moderate one, however, and left much to be done. The timing for Poiret's entrance into fashion was ideal.

"I declared war on the corset," Poiret wrote later on in life, when, after having overthrown the fashion Establishment, he was ruling the world of dressmaking. "Like all great revolutions," he recalled, "mine was carried out in the name of Liberty, to give free play to the stomach, which could dilate without restriction."

The son of a draper who had a small store on the Rue des Deux-Écus in Paris, Poiret worked his way up from relatively lowly surroundings. His talent for dressmaking showed itself early. He never played much with other children. His sisters used some of their savings to buy him a miniature mannequin, which he clothed with scraps of silk he found in the shop of the umbrella maker to whom he was apprenticed. Another of his talents—the prodigality that was to lead to his downfall—exhibited itself early, too. With the first sizable bonus he received when he was working for couturier Jacques Doucet, Poiret went out and bought himself a pair of expensive opal cuff links.

Overweight, in his own eyes "imperious and Venetian," looking to Jean Cocteau like "a pale sultan, a bearded chestnut," he had an impressive appearance. Once he took over fashion, he had no trouble exerting a one-man rule, with a range of activities that extended from the designing of theatre costumes to the breaking down of social barriers by giving extraordinary parties that no duchess, however haughty she may have been, could bear to miss attending. He expanded the scope of the *haute couture* by branching out into allied fields, such as fabric design and interior decoration, and broadened the base of the business to include the production of perfume and accessories, thus paving the way for future far-flung enterprises of the mode like the present-day operations of Dior, Cardin, and Yves Saint Laurent.

Above all, Poiret elevated high fashion to the status of an art. He persuaded many bright young painters of his day—Dufy, van Dongen, Vlaminck, Dunoyer de Segonzac, Fauconnet, among others—to work with him. They shared his ebullient enjoyment in breaking new trails and re-garded him as one of them.

"He was one of the very great creators in the history of fashion," a French authority has written. "A dress by Poiret is recognizable at a glance, like a painting by Renoir."

Poiret became lord of the Age of Gold Lamé. In his heyday, on the eve of World War I, he put women—uncorseted women—into pearl chin straps and sent them off to the races wearing satin turbans spiked with tufts of aigrette feathers, trouser skirts, and gold Chinese embroidered cloaks. Women were perfectly delighted to appear in that sort of regalia, because it was all a part of the thrilling new vogue for Neo-Orientalism, a movement sparked by Poiret and Diaghilev's Ballet Russe, a vogue that made the generous Edwardian S-shaped figure, with its layers of lacy, complicated underclothes, seem hopelessly *démodé*.

"Yes," wrote Poiret afterward, "I advocated the fall of the corset. I liberated the bust. When I declared war on the corset, women's bodies were divided into two distinct masses and the upper lobe appeared to be pulling the whole derrière section along behind it, like a trailer."

Some ladies of the period longed to throw off their corsets, and took vacations in the country just to be able to remove them for a few weeks. Others felt dependent on them. Colette mentions the well-corseted actress Germaine Gallois, who would never accept a part that required her to sit down. Arriving at the theatre "supporting an edifice that was lashed together with six yards of lacing, she stood up every night from eight o'clock until half past midnight, intermissions included."

The elegant corset, of heavy colored silk or satin trimmed with real lace and ribbon bows, consisted of from ten to fifteen curved pieces, not counting the gussets, and was traversed from end to end by dozens of whalebones and steel stays. Under it, a lady wore a garment called a chemise that looked like a long nightshirt. Over it, she—or, more likely, her maid—hoisted voluminous linen *pantalons*. On top of all that went a corset cover, a decorous bodice that concealed her stays. Finally, before being buttonhooked into her dress, she got into one, two, or three elaborate petticoats, which were coyly known as "frillies." The deployment of frillies was a tactic every flirt had to master. "As I knew my frillies were all right," said Elinor Glyn's Elizabeth, in *The Visits of Elizabeth,* "I hammocked—and it was lovely."

The height of the corset-and-frillies era was the Belle Époque when Frou-Frou was having her moment at Maxim's and when the standard-bearers of the mode were the flamboyant demimondaines. These imposing creatures held up their vast and snowy bosoms with stiff boardlike constructions that ironed out their plump stomachs and pinched their waists in sharply at the back.

Then, overnight, they disappeared. The picture of their *grandes toilettes* and jeweled dog collars in the gilded frames of the theatre loges vanished in what Jean Cocteau has described as a sort of lap dissolve. The hard lines of the great cocottes gave way to the fluid ones of the new ideal: the glittering, slouching Poiret girl in her flowing high-waisted dress, with splendid eyes, a headache band, curly hair dressed like a poodle's, and a cruel mouth like a carp's.

The Poiret revolution was to make girls conscious of their bodies and of calorie-counting for the first time in a full century. Extra fat could be covered up by petticoats and leg-o'-mutton sleeves, but not by the slinky Poiret line.

"Anxious to wear the 'sheath gown,'" *Punch* reported, "many stout ladies in San Francisco, we are told, are undergoing a regime which includes an hour's rolling on the floor."

Poiret, years ahead of designer Rudi Gernreich's topless clothes and Saint Laurent's see-throughs, shocked the conventionally minded by recommending that his customers wear nothing at all under the transparent tops of his dresses, advice that was taken eagerly by a fearless but not always shapely vanguard. The bra, as we know it, had yet to be invented by Caresse Crosby in the nineteen-twenties. Breasts à la Poiret were breasts as nature made them, without benefit of modern sports and exercises, left to rise or to droop at will, lifted only by the grosgrain cummerbund he sewed on the inside around the rib cage of his Empire-style dresses.

Pre-Poiret, ladies who were overendowed had worn "correctors" or "flatteners" to trim themselves down; if underendowed, they filled themselves out with the contemporary version of falsies: flounced linen "amplifiers." Such rectifications were regarded as improvements over the cotton wadding that was stuffed into the tops of nineteenth-century corsets or over the padded "bust improvers" introduced in the eighteen-eighties by Charles Frederick Worth, the doughty fighter of the long, lone battle against the crinoline.

When Poiret started out in high fashion, Paris was its undisputed center. A handful of designers, led by the powerful conservative house of Worth, dictated the styles, which were then worn by a few choice ladies. Sooner or later, the rest of the world followed them. The Maison Worth, which had been pre-eminent since Charles Frederick had made his international reputation under Napoleon III as couturier to the Empress Eugénie, was being directed by his sons M. Jean and M. Gaston. Jean had inherited the father's artistic bent; Gaston had the knack for business matters. Each of them could tell a crowned head when he saw one coming, and their clients included almost every royal in Europe.

While Worth dressed the aristocracy, the rival house of Doucet produced flashier clothes for the noted actresses and demimondaines. On Saturday night at Doucet, the staff expected to have to work late during the racing seasons in order to finish the new dresses the *grandes cocottes* would display at Longchamp or Auteuil the next day.

The brothers Worth knew of Poiret as an up-and-coming designer who free-lanced by selling sketches to the various couture houses and as the assistant designer at Doucet who, besides creating costumes for Réjane and for Sarah Bernhardt, had turned out as his first model a deceptively plain little wrap of red coachman's cloth that customers had ordered four hundred times.

Poiret was summoned to the presence of Gaston Worth.

"Young man," said M. Gaston, "you are familiar with the house of Worth, which, from its very outset, has dressed the courts of the entire world. It has the highest and the richest of clienteles, but today that clientele does not dress exclusively in gowns of state. Princesses sometimes take buses. They even walk on foot in the street. My brother Jean has always refused to make a certain type of dress, a simple and practical dress. And yet we are being asked for them. We are in the situation of a great restaurant which is only accustomed to serving truffles. But we are obliged to create a department of fried potatoes."

Hired as the *pommes frites* specialist, Poiret was appalled by *"les exubérances de père Worth"* still influencing the house. The taste of Charles Frederick had run to dresses festooned with telegraph wires on which flocks of swallows were impaled or to embroideries of large snails. M. Jean, for his part, was unsettled by Poiret's novel interpretations of elegance. "You call that a dress?" he would ask, looking at one of Poiret's tailored models. "I call it a piece of trash."

Nor were all the princesses who dressed at Worth ready for Poiret's versions of the simple and practical. *"Quelle horreur!"* gasped a Russian one when she had a look at an austere black kimono coat by Poiret.

Deciding the time had come to strike out on his own, Poiret set himself up in 1904, with his mother's backing, in a modest boutique on the Rue Auber. One month later, he was a smash hit and *le Tout-Paris* was driving up to his door.

There and at the *hôtel particulier* on the Rue Pasquier where he installed himself two years later, he put on fashion *défilés,* the first shows of their kind, which were little theatrical productions and fabulous novelties to Parisian high-society women who, by invitation only, packed the house every afternoon from five to seven. He had his revenge against the Russian princess who had sneered at his Chinese coat by designing a Confucius cloak, the first of his Oriental inspirations, which sold again and again to his clientele.

According to one observer of the daily parade Chez Poiret, mannequins undulated "in lighting knowingly lowered, with steps in voluptuous rhythm and in hieratic poses, women turbaned in red, in blue, or in multicolored madras, measuring their slow tread in girdles of silken velvet." A talented young photographer named Edward Steichen took soft-focus pictures of them. Their stance developed into the round-shouldered, hipbones-forward gait that lasted through the twenties and that Cocteau recorded as "the praying-mantis walk."

Poiret set the traditionalists back on their heels with his startling use of color. Until then under the influence of the Empress Eugénie, taste-mistress of the Second Empire, the couture was mired in a muggy fog of beiges, grays, and insipid blues, watery greens and washed-out pinks, that

134

the Empress had found *"raffiné"* and other women had been induced into thinking distinguished.

"I hunted down the morbid mauves, the neurasthenic pastels," said Poiret, "and into this sheepcote I threw a few rough wolves—the reds, the greens, the violets and royal blues that made the pale and neutral colors sing."

He chucked the corset but he set a new snare. "I shackled the legs," said Poiret. "I remember the tears, the cries, the grindings of the teeth this decree brought forth in the world of the mode. Women complained that they could not walk any more, they could not get into a carriage. And yet everybody wore the narrow skirt."

The harem skirt, said a critic of the day, would go nicely with the "scarum" hat. But such comments failed to hold chic women back in their rush to wear the new Poiret clothes. Elsewhere women of the time were dramatizing their need for emancipation by chaining themselves to lampposts or leaping into the path of sprinting race horses, while the *jolies dames* of Paris were letting themselves be trapped into hobble skirts that forced them to take mincing steps like concubines.

With the hobble skirt went the other Poiret trade marks: the soft clinging bodice, the loose harem pants, the classical Grecian draperies, and the lampshade tunic. The draperies suited his friend Isadora Duncan, whom he introduced to Paris at one of his gaudy parties, and were also appropriated by England's answer to Isadora, Maud Allen, who popularized an early see-through style of dress the British sometimes referred to as "Le Vague"—at other times, "Le Nude."

Impropriety in dress could not make much headway in England, at least not in the opinion of fashion scholar E. Willett Cunnington. "When the French dress designers, with their depraved minds, tried to bifurcate the hobble skirt into Turkish trousers," he has written, "the English conscience rebelled." The French took a practical viewpoint. Hobble skirts slit to the knee or divided into harem pants were, they found, the solution to what to wear while doing the tango, the new dance craze.

Nautch dancing would have been more to the point, for the opulent, mysterious East had become the rage. If not the Far East, then the Middle East, and, to some, even the Balkans seemed Oriental enough. Poiret, who had never been closer to the Asian continent than the course in Tamil at the School of Oriental Languages at the University of Paris, was largely responsible for the uncertain mélange of East and Near East in the fashions and decoration of the period. He shifted his inspirational sights from Hellenic Greece to Persia to ancient Egypt to China and back again before the public could catch up with him.

In 1909, the initial performance in Paris of Diaghilev's Ballet Russe, with splashy costumes by Léon Bakst and Alexandre Benois, gave a further boost to the Neo-Oriental boom. Poiret has been accused of having aped Bakst in his designs. In fact, Poiret was well on the road to the East before the Ballet Russe set Paris agog.

The Poiret costumes for *Minaret,* a verse play by Jean Richepin, had caused a sensation—in particular the bright-green outfit he devised for the eunuch in the third act. Even more prophetic was the silk turban he made for his beautiful young wife, Denise Poiret, for opening night. "The first turban worn by a Parisienne since Madame de Staël," Poiret noted; it was surmounted by aigrette feathers a foot high. Copies of it were to stay in circulation for years, some versions ending up on the heads of Pola Negri and Gloria Swanson.

The intellectually inclined had been reading Dr. Joseph Charles-Victor Mardrus's highly colored new translation into French of *The Thousand and One Nights.* The popular reading was Elinor Glyn's *Three Weeks.* In it, the heroine, a passionate Balkan queen, spent the major part of her time lolling about on a tiger-skin rug.

"The Turkish corner," a nook that *Vogue* had spotted at the turn of the century as "a dream of comfort and elegance" was already a feature in fashionable houses. So was smoking hashish—at any rate, if one did not actually smoke it, one was considered smart only if it at least appeared that one smoked it. Hookahs and foot-long cigarette holders were the chic accessories when one leaned languorously back on stacks of pillows under one of the new electric lamps.

When in 1908 Poiret took over a dilapidated eighteenth-century *hôtel particulier,* with a large courtyard where chickens were running about loose, and resolved to do it over in high-seraglio style, he set off a flood of Oriental-decorations buying. Dealers at the Flea Market experienced a run on items such as peacock feathers and bits of lacquer as débutantes with hazy notions about the East went on the hunt for Oriental bric-à-brac. "Do you have any Coromandel?" asked one young thing. Replied the second young thing: "I should say I do. Why, I even have some signed by him."

In decorating his new house, Poiret had the collaboration of Suë et Mare. Louis Suë was an architect, furniture designer, and decorator who, with André Mare, organized an atelier which eventually employed La Fresnaye, Dunoyer de Segonzac, Maillol, and Despiau. Suë et Mare's furnishings for Poiret—lush metallic curtains, lacquered panels, and thick Persian rugs—led the fashion vanguard of duchesses and actresses Poiret dressed into redoing their own interiors. They followed the couturier's dicta by using a wealth of wrought-iron grilles, plenty of Lalique glass, and lampshades with dangling silk fringes. To the distress of their husbands, they also heaped floors and sofas with masses of cushions. For years to come, men on both sides of the Channel—and the ocean, for that matter—would grumble about pillows. "I say, Monica," complains the man sprawled across the floor in a 1924 *Punch* cartoon, "do let's leave Chelsea and sit on chairs again."

The part of pasha that Poiret enjoyed playing was a case of typecasting. Plump, gregarious, egoistic, and epicurean, he was also an inveterate womanizer from the moment his early employer, Doucet, suggested he take a *petite amie* to be a truly worldly Parisian, on through to his string of liaisons with divers willing actresses who seldom, in consequence, had to pay for their clothes. With mannequins and other young women on his staff, however, his attitude was less sultanic than schoolmasterish, although he did once advise a virtuous *première* in his workroom that she would better understand the sensual charm of his creations if she had a lover.

Poiret's finest hour as sultan of the fashion community came one night in May, 1911, when he was host in his Faubourg Saint-Honoré house at an historic fête, the ball of La Mille et Deuxième Nuit. After the idea for the party had occurred to him, it took him just fourteen days to attend to all the details of an evening that was to electrify the swell and set off a chain reaction of similar galas and balls.

Raoul Dufy made the invitations. Every guest was asked to come in Persian garb, and those who arrived in ordinary dinner or evening clothes were instantly ordered upstairs by a manservant to consult a folio of authentic engravings and miniatures, then to choose appropriate costumes from a wardrobe Poiret had provided for such emergencies.

Poiret's artist friends relied on ingenuity for the occasion. Guy-Pierre Fauconnet, who was out of funds, wrapped himself artfully in several lengths of white sheeting with a result so effectively Middle Eastern that many declared him the best-dressed man in the crowd. Steichen remembers getting by the door check in an African burnoose.

Snobs such as the elderly lady in pink satin harem pants and strands of jewels spooled about her head, accompanied by a gentleman clad as a janissary, claimed to have come merely out of curiosity. But, noting the presence of Princesse Lucien Murat and the Comtesse de Chabrillan, among other members of *le gratin,* the lady concluded that society must be turning topsy-turvy, for *"grandes dames* now accept invitations from their tradespeople."

A torch-bearing flunky, stripped to the waist and draped below in cloth of gold, escorted guests across eight yards of carpet which Dunoyer de Segonzac had painted especially for the party, on through a sanded, canopied forecourt filled with spouting fountains to a blue-and-gold entrance portal which led to a series of divertissements. One of these was Mme. Poiret, the sultan's favorite, in gold lamé, imprisoned in a huge gilded cage filled with rare birds and a covey of dancing girls who hummed Persian airs as they fed their goldfish, admired themselves in mirrors, or ate water ices.

Poiret himself, rigged out as a caliph in a caftan of silver brocade with a gigantic cabochon emerald at his waist and a large turban on his head, received the salaams of his guests from a throne atop a tier of steps which were covered with writhing, supine nymphs. The nymphs were clothed mostly in beads and wore frightened expressions. Glowering through spectacles perched on his false nose, the couturier abandoned himself wholeheartedly to his role, and as the evening progressed, he flicked his tiny ivory whip at passing houris.

Among the night's other entertainments were a python-tamer with diamond-encrusted teeth; a *souk* with a fortune-teller, a potter's wheel, and Turkish delight; and a merchant of slavegirls who would take no offer less than a thousand gold dinars for the poorest of his wares. Recitals of tales from the *Thousand and One Nights* were delivered by the great tragedian Édouard de Max, the stage partner of Sarah Bernhardt. De Max, his eyes ringed with kohl, crouched on the summit of a mountain of cushions and wore a fortune in pearls he had borrowed for the party from an American lady admirer.

A South American tourist who got into the party stumbled over several of the nude odalisques that Poiret had arranged here and there in the garden, under gauze, in the shrubbery. The tourist met these encounters by coming up with suitable quotations from Omar Khayyám. As dinner was served, forty blackamoors burned myrrh and incense. (Poiret had not yet concocted the pungent perfume he was later to market under the name of Night of China.)

138

The Arabic dances outdoors were illuminated by swarms of phosphorescent insects that Poiret had positioned in the trees. When it came time, in the hours after midnight, to ignite the cataract of fireworks, the sparks nearly finished off the Bokhara carpets on the lawn. The insects released with the *feu d'artifice* did not upset the peacock or the flamingos, which were indoors. But they did unnerve the monkeys and the *perroquets* that were attached to branches in the trees. Many of them got loose and were found the next morning shrieking up and down the Champs-Élysées.

Even the famous partygiver Comte Boni de Castellane, the free-spending husband of American heiress Anna Gould, had to admit he had never in his life witnessed an evening like that one. In the months following, every hostess of any importance in Paris tried to top Poiret with her own imitation of La Mille et Deuxième Nuit. The Persian fête of the Comtesse de Chabrillan, who did herself up as Scheherazade, preceded that of Comtesse Blanche de Clermont-Tonnerre, who had the edge, as she had actually visited Persia.

Society's ideas on geography were often sketchy, and Mrs. Harry Payne Whitney came as a South Indian maharani, a sunburst of aigrettes, diamonds, and pearls pinned to her turban. Grand dukes disguised as viziers, Aladdins, and Harun al-Rashids listened to their dinner partners discourse on the poetry of Hafiz, Saadi, or Firdousi—who were everybody's favorite bedside reading. Nor was there any getting away from Araby at the theatre, with its flute solos, saber dancers, nude slaves, and sensational abductions of captive princesses.

The magazine *L'Illustration* showed Paris fashionables leaving mass at the Madeleine, a Roman Catholic Church, their faces veiled with Muslim-style yashmaks. A return gesture was made by the Shah Nasser-ed-Din. Smitten on a visit to Paris with the ballerinas at the Opéra, he ordered a crate of stiffly starched tutus sent back to Teheran for the inmates of his harem.

Poiret gave other parties after that. None equaled La Mille et Deuxième Nuit—not even the one he threw at Butard, the hunting lodge built by Ange-Jacques Gabriel for Louis XV that Poiret acquired, although nine hundred bottles of champagne flowed and Poiret received his three hundred guests done up as Jupiter, his hair and beard painted with gold.

No matter how much money he spent, his subsequent triumphs never measured up to his spectacular performance as caliph of all he surveyed, but he never stopped trying. He bought a yacht and took dozens of friends on leisurely Mediterranean cruises. When he summered at Deauville, he did not take just one villa for himself but rented a whole string of houses for friends, to be sure of having congenial neighbors.

His black Hispano-Suiza leading the way for a fleet of cars, Poiret toured Europe with his mannequins who wore glazed linen hats marked with the monogram "PP," matching the initials embroidered on the shoes he himself sported. He started a decorating firm and introduced the sunken bathtub. He joined forces with Dufy to experiment with fabric dyes while Dufy created a group of uncommon silk fabrics that have become collectors' items. Poiret also went into the perfume business, mixing up, among other scents, one called Mea Culpa.

One of his most influential enterprises, the École Martine, a school he started for the daughters of factory workers, was the genesis of the Art Deco style. The girls were taken out to look at nature and then asked to paint the birds, trees, and flowers they had seen. Their fresh, naïve, stylized pictures were used as basic designs for the production of pottery, fabrics, and wallpapers.

The interruption of World War I, in which Poiret's Army duties included the creation of new uniforms, altered his fortunes in the couture. Afterward he opened a new salon on the Rond Point des Champs-Élysées but ran into financial difficulties. His night club, L'Oasis, had but a relatively brief success. The money and effort he put into decorating and furnishing three houseboats on the Seine for the 1925 Exposition des Arts-Décoratifs were largely wasted. Dufy painted fourteen wall hangings for the barges and the furnishings were equally delightful, but because the exposition opened at a time of year when all the rich had left for their country places, the houseboats were not seen by the clientele that would have been interested in them.

As Poiret's power declined in the twenties—Vionnet and Chanel were getting the attention—he went on the lecture circuit in the United States, where he was billed as "the King of Fashion." He was flattered by the title, he told his audiences, but he did not want to be a despot or a dictator. "I am not your master," he said. "I am your slave, hoping to divine your secret desires. Women are perpetually falling in love with change, perishing with thirst for something new."

His perception of what those desires would be waned. By the mid-thirties, his prodigality and disdain for the practical side of business (he refused all offers to sell his name) had done him in. He left his family and retired to the South of France to paint. There were stories that he was living like a *clochard*. During World War II, he was observed sauntering along the jetty of a Mediterranean port, in an admiral's hat and a suit he had cut from a terry-cloth bathrobe, a pair of scissors stuck in the breast pocket.

When his family located him at the end of the war, Poiret, once a rosy, rotund *bon vivant,* was unrecognizable. He had lost seventy pounds and was suffering from Parkinson's disease. He returned to Paris to die of a heart attack in a private clinic.

During the days of his modish revolution, Poiret bore in mind that "there has never been a truly new fashion which has not caused, at the outset, as Beaumarchais said, a general hue and cry, a universal chorus of hatred and proscription." Yet, when Chanel took over the controls as the revolutionary figure early in the Jazz Age, Poiret behaved like a middle-aged conservative who does not want to be reminded of his own youthful indiscretions, and he seemed to have misgivings about what he had started. Had he, after all, made a dreadful mistake by stirring up a rebellion?

"Women were beautiful and architectural like ship's figureheads," he said. "Now they look like undernourished telegraph operators."

But by 1927 his regrets had disappeared and he had recovered his visionary sense of prophecy. In "Will Skirts Disappear?" an article for the *Forum,* Poiret was looking well ahead toward our time, making this eerily accurate prediction of a synthetic, plastic future:

"I see hats of spun glass, pants of natural palm fiber, fichus of incandescent vegetable silk. The Rodiers of the day will be supplied by their chemist with cellulosahs in acidulated tints, sulfurated glucosinahs which shimmer. Women will wear tunics of scintillating silver, apple-green gandurahs, trousers of paprika satin, pale-blue shocks of hair. . . ."

He was right.

*P. Bertrand & Fils*

In the early-morning fog, some of Chantilly's three thousand resident thorough-breds prepare for their daily workouts on the Aigles, an incomparable training preserve and the hub of that community's existence.

Top-hatted Jockey Club members Comte Michel d'Ornano, Mayor of Deauville, and his father, Comte Guillaume d'Ornano, discuss the strategy for their horses with their jockeys in the coming race.

*Jacques Verroust—Atlas Pho.*

Segregated in their all-male sanctuary, Jockey Club members focus on the field in the Prix du Jockey Club (the French Derby) at the Chantilly course.

*Jacques Verroust—Atlas Pho.*

In August, Deauville becomes the capital of the European thoroughbred racing
world and a Mecca for exponents of the good life. Here the horses are eased up
by their jockeys after a closely contested race.

*P. Bertrand & F₂*

At Deauville, on any pleasant racing day in August, the most rarefied circle of French social life is concentrated under the umbrellas at the luncheon tables behind the stands at the Hippodrome de la Touques.

*Phyllis Feldkan*

It's never too early to acquire a taste for racing at Deauville.

The placid waters of the English Channel, on Deauville's beach, serve as a tonic for the fragile ankles of these regular August visitors.

*Marcel Pevs*

Following in the tradition of the great Carême, chefs of the *maison* Le Nôtre artfully concoct fine pastry and other gala fare. The president of the company, M. Gaston Le Nôtre (far left), admires their handiwork.

Carême drew architectural plans for masterpieces in sugar, such as this of a Chinese windmill.

Carême invented the grand *pièce montée* but Le Nôtre chefs took it to new, soaring heights with a 12-foot cake for shop opening.

# LE COLLIER NOUVEAU

## Robe du soir de Paul Poiret

*Collection René Dazy*

Luxury ruled in the world of Paul Poiret, the couturier who freed women from the corset and sent them off to the races in harem trousers. A dapper womanizer, he toured Europe with his mannequins in a sportive Hispano-Suiza. Well before World War I, he introduced innovative fashions in see-through tops (upper left) and in fluid sack dresses (lower left). His most characteristic style, the lampshade tunic gown (above), is unmistakable as a Poiret creation, as a Renoir painting is instantly recognizable.

Drawings from *Gazette du Bon Ton*

Every three months the developing *grand cru* wines of Bordeaux undergo a process called "racking"—which facilitates the elimination of the residue.

In a small *cave* beneath his Paris shop, M. Hubert, the *maître fromager,* tests the consistency of some maturing Reblochons from the Haute-Savoie.

A happy Périgourdin with the local treasure—the lumpy black fungus with the tantalizing odor called the *truffe* (truffle). Longevity, virility, and good health are attributed to the regular consumption of this expensive comestible.

In the fields of Périgord, a *truie* (sow) performs her valuable detective work in the age-old search for the elusive, esteemed truffle.

The French line of succession of great hairdressers from the 18th century on leads directly to Alexandre, today's kingpin.

Simple elegance of Alexandre's sleek contemporary "Elf" hairdo contrasts with huge coiffures of Paris hairdressing in past.

A yardstick of chic in the era of Marie-Antoinette was a tall hair style. At bedtime and at the coffee hour the lady *à la mode* had to be a tower of strength, prepared to sleep in a large paper-cone nightcap (right) and ready to be extinguished in case her giant coiffure caught fire from the coffee-house chandelier (below).

*Bibliothèque Nationale*

*Bibliothèque Nationale*

AU CAFFÉ ROYAL D'ALEXANDRE

The summit of fine furniture-making in the world was reached in 1769 when the rococo roll-top desk of Louis XV was delivered to the king at Versailles.

The majestic calm of the Bois de Boulogne affords Parisians an oasis free of the pressures and problems of life in the twentieth century.

*Paris-Match/Le Tac*

Contemporary France in Profile. The late President Charles de Gaulle and the nation's official guest of the day, the late King Mahendra Bir Bikram Shah Deva, of Nepal, stand at attention in the forecourt of the Élysée Palace for the playing of the national anthems. A few paces behind the General, standing in his footsteps, is his successor as President of the Republic of France, then Premier Georges Pompidou.

# The Heart of the Matter

---

*What is life really but a comfortable existence in a picturesque town, in an attractive countryside, with delicious food in abundance, to be washed down with superior wines? And at the center of it all rests that ugly fungus with the delicate scent, the mysterious* truffe.

---

Enjoyment of life has many facets, takes many forms. To a Frenchman, the greatest joy life affords is the opportunity to savor and enjoy good food, imaginatively prepared. This takes precedence over the appreciation of vintage wines, the enjoyment of driving his car at maximum speed, the joys of doing the tax collector out of some money, and the pleasures of *l'amour*—in roughly that order.

Gastronomy has long ago achieved the status of a fine art in France. In terms of attracting visitors to the country, it has become one of France's greatest assets. How often have I heard European-bound friends say, "We're staying at an inexpensive hotel in Paris so that we can use most of our budget for France on great meals."

But well stocked as Paris is with marvelous restaurants dispensing dinners that stick in the memory, the French capital is not really the location where one can dine most munificently in this gourmet's paradise of a land. Partisans of the cuisine of all corners of France can be found among the French and foreigners alike, even—unaccountably—for the heavy, Teutonic *choucroute* of Alsace (sauerkraut usually served with chunks of salted or smoked fatty meats). But the preponderance of expert opinion among resident epicures centers on a region in the southwestern part of the country called Périgord.

This cornucopia of France (its treasures include foie gras, truffles, and walnuts) has its roots in earliest prehistoric times, hundreds of thousands of years ago, in the formative period of the Paleolithic era. The caves which abound in the area featuring prehistoric wall drawings, including the famous *grottes* at Lascaux and at Les Eyzies, support that estimate. Perhaps because of its ancient heritage, and in the context of that time span, the natives of Périgord today speak of the Hundred Years' War with the English, in the fourteenth and fifteenth centuries, the way Parisians talk about World War II—as though it had just ended yesterday or the day before.

In Sarlat, a small town in the *département* of Dordogne, which is a microcosm of Périgourdine culture, history, and cuisine, I had the impression, on a recent visit, that the townspeople with whom I spoke remembered the Guerre de Cent Ans vividly, from personal experience. (Indeed, the English are still remembered with some misgivings by many Sarladais. One inhabitant asked another, in English, in my presence: "Who was that Englishman who assassinated us last year? The one who wrote a book saying that French cuisine was no good, and couldn't compare with the English. Ha! Those bloody English." He continued, reverting to French, *"Ils sont nés sans queues, comme tout le monde, mais aussi sans palais."* ["They are born without tails, like the rest of us, but also without palates."])

For a change, the local Chamber of Commerce (Syndicat d'Initiative) in this case cannot be accused of exaggeration when it describes Périgord as *"Berceau de préhistoire, terre d'histoire, refuge de la douceur de vivre, paradis du bien-manger"* ("Cradle of prehistory, land of history, shelter of the soft sweet life, paradise of good eating").

One of the recipients of all these superlatives, Sarlat, a town of 12,000 inhabitants, traces its "modern" history back to the fifth century, in the time of Clovis. Today it has a carefully preserved medieval appearance, most of its buildings dating from the twelfth through the eighteenth centuries, but with a composite look of a town arrested in time and preserved for the ages.

Before sampling its culinary treasures, I decided to go on a personal tour of inspection, starting—perhaps logically—at the *hôtel de ville* (town hall), in the heart of Sarlat. The current building, dedicated in 1900, is in the style of its predecessors, with various reminders of the town's origin and past glories. In the foyer of the structure, there are plaques proclaiming, among other facts, the forming of the Commune in 1204, under the consulship of Magnanat, Castanet, Vigneras, and La Boëtie, succeeded four years later by a slate composed of Delpech, Aymat, Castanet, and Deschamp; another states than on *"28 Janvier 1298 une transaction entre l'abbé et les consuls ratifiée par le roi Philippe le Bel en 1299 constitue définitivement la Commune."* The meetings of the first consuls were held in the tower of the Bouquerie until, in 1250, the first town hall was put into service.

Returning to the square, down the worn stone steps of the town hall, I found myself completely under the spell of the antiquity of the town; like most Americans, who tend to regard any landmark a hundred years old as ancient, I pondered on what the town must have looked and felt like in the twelfth or thirteenth centuries. Not vastly different, I thought, except for the costumes of the inhabitants, and even there many of the workmen and merchants probably dressed in fairly similar fashion to those of today. I was shaken out of my reverie by the sight of two posters, on a nearby fourteenth-century building, advertising a new film, *Sacco & Vanzetti, en couleur,* at a local theatre, and another announcing that the *"Ciné-Club de Sarlat présente Les Marx Brothers dans 'Plumes de Cheval'"* (*Horsefeathers*).

But these were the only jarring notes in my tour of the town, which even bore the odor of antiquity. After a brief visit, a few doors away, to the *cathédrale,* which has been restored several times but has a belfry dating from the twelfth century, I stopped before a small perfect jewel of a house, with Italian windows facing the street; its plaque, on the façade one floor up, proclaimed that this was the birthplace of Étienne de la Boëtie, writer and translator, but principally the celebrated friend of Michel Eyquem, Seigneur de Montaigne, who called La Boëtie "the greatest man of the age." (Indeed, there is some speculation that if La Boëtie had not died at the age of thirty-three, Montaigne's esteemed *Essays* might never have been written.) The building, I learned, was relatively new at the time of La Boëtie's birth, in 1530, but the Italian windows were a later addition—an idea of its new resident's.

Although I found no confirmation, I am reasonably certain that the essayist's friend was a descendant of one of the first four consuls to serve the Commune of Sarlat, of the same family name. During my stay in the town, it became clear that a considerable number of Sarlat's native population of about 10,000 can trace their ancestry back some generations without going beyond Périgord, and in many cases even Sarlat. (Twelve hundred Portuguese and eight hundred North African Arabs complete the population of the town.)

Any drastic increase in its population would surely destroy the character of Sarlat, but here—as in all of France—special inducements, in the form of bonuses, are still given to those who produce children, a reminder that France is even today an underpopulated country in this age of population explosions. Perhaps that is a primary reason for the retention of its charm.

And charm Sarlat has in abundance. In the square, the Saturday-morning market is as good a place as any to mingle with the working-class Sarladais and also to learn what ingredients compose the cuisine Périgourdine. On the temporary wooden counters set up in the square, there were geese in profusion, ducks, turkeys, hare, cuts of beef, a variety of vegetables, and, on each of two small tables, a handful of truffles. At this open-air market, where prices are of course lower than in the shops, geese were selling at 1,500 old francs by the kilogram (about $3 for 2.2 pounds); thus a smallish goose, at 4½ kilos, would bring 6,750 ($13.50), but including the liver inside. Lettuces were priced at from 80 (new) centimes to 1 (new) franc 50 (16¢ to 30¢), tomatoes at 2 francs 50 the kilo (50¢ for 2.2 pounds), and carrots at 1 franc 30 the kilo. (For some reason, meat and game were marked in old francs—roughly, 500 old francs to the dollar before January 1, 1960; vegetables in new francs—about 5 to the dollar.)

When I finally reached the adjoining counters bearing the miniature displays of truffles, I was still thinking in old francs, so when I looked at the chalked price of *"250 fr. par kilo"* the cash register in my mind automatically rang up 50¢. A few seconds later, I was astonished to learn that the rare *truffes*, looking like pieces of lumpy charcoal but with the consistency of damp tar, were being offered for sale at 250 *new* francs for a kilo, or $50. (In Paris shops, I was told, the price would be 50 to 100 percent more.)

The cost of living in Sarlat, it seemed after my tour of the market, is not exactly low; still a six-course lunch—excellent—at the modern hotel where I was staying cost 15 francs without wine ($3), a seven-course dinner 20 francs. In addition, there is almost full employment. But if no one is going hungry, earning a living is not exactly easy. The work week, in the plant I visited, is sixty hours a week: ten hours of actual work (lunch period not included) on six days (7 A.M. to 7 P.M.; lunch from

148

twelve to two o'clock). In some places, the schedule is even longer. An ordinary worker in this plant—Sarlat's No. 1 industry, which turns out food products in jars and cans, and some spirits in bottles—earns a net salary of 800 francs a month ($160). A specialist or subexecutive is paid between 1,500 and 1,800 francs ($300 to $360) monthly.

But one must balance these figures with the government benefits. Figures are flexible, since conditions vary in different parts of the country, occasioning changes in the cost of living, and family situations are not identical—in some, for example, there is just one wage-earner, in others more than one.

A middle-income employee at the plant told me that a family living in Sarlat might receive a government *allocation familiale* of 850 francs monthly for his family of five children; an *allocation logement* (160 to 230 francs); an allowance during illness or incapacitation—half salary after the first three days; 80 percent of all doctors' and pharmacy bills paid at all times; and a retirement plan for those who achieve age sixty-five (a reduction to age sixty is now being discussed) at 80 percent of normal salary. For all these benefits, my informant advised, the employee pays a social security tax of 9 percent of his salary, the balance of payments being provided by the employer and the state. A suitable lodging for a specialist or subexecutive can be found for 200 to 400 francs a month (about $40 to $80); consequently there is little unrest among the salaried class in Sarlat.

Of course, like all Frenchmen, the Sardalais must pay income, property, car, gasoline, sales taxes, and the new value-added tax—even a yearly tax on ownership and use of a radio or TV set. So life is not an unmixed blessing.

My informant then took me on a visit to the establishment where he works.

The spotless plant that specializes in the production of goose liver, shelled walnuts, and truffles in various combinations—the Maison Delpeyrat—is located close to the center of town, only a few blocks from its retail outlet near the cathedral and the La Boëtie building. In addition, the firm produces a wide variety of other products, appetizingly packaged: pâté en croûte, roulade de foie gras, poulet aux champignons; various kinds of viande, moule, terrine, saucisses; roulade de dinde au foie gras truffé, roulade d'oie, terrine de lièvre aux cerneaux (walnut kernels), foie de porc, terrine de foie gras, terrine au foie de canard truffé, galantine de dinde, cassoulet, sauce Périgueux, tripes du Périgord, mushrooms, snails, vegetables, and many more. Its spirits, distilled on the premises, include framboise (raspberry liqueur), cerise (cherry), l'eau de vie de prune (plum), pruneaux (prune), abricot (apricot), and a local specialty, la crème de noix (walnut). (So extensive is its output of packaged meats that hare must be imported from the Argentine from time to time to supplement the local supply, and pork from Chicago.) It is impossible to tour this precision-operated plant without developing an appetite and a thirst of a proportion that cannot long be ignored.

At dinner that evening in the attractive, twentieth-century-modern home of Mme. Albert Carrier, the daughter of the late founder of Delpeyrat (the supplier of these delicacies to all of France and many countries abroad), the guests were served some of the specialties of the firm, starting with foie gras aux truffes, great round slices more than three inches in diameter and three-quarters of an inch thick. After a second serving of foie gras, we addressed ourselves to an omelette aux truffes, again featuring the coal-black segments of truffle, each *morceau* being not quite as large as a standard-sized checker.

The third course consisted of slices of beef with truffles, accompanied by a flavorful Château Boutet, from the southwestern region known as Entre-deux-Mers—between the Dordogne and Garonne rivers. The cheese was the only course served without the "black diamonds."

It was not difficult, I reflected to myself over an excellent Mirabelle liqueur, to fathom the reason for that typically French ailment known as *crise de foie* (liver crisis). The dinner just finished had been far from a snack, and neither was it an extraordinary feast, yet I felt that I would be unable to face the prospect of any more meals for a good day or so.

Here in Périgord, the conviction that food is one of the principal joys of life is especially strong. With Alsace, Périgord shares the honor of being the foie-gras headquarters of France, but in the field of truffles Périgord is the undisputed capital. In this historic province of France—and in this province alone—the prime variety of the mysterious fungus is found. Ranging in size from that of a walnut to, in exceptional cases, an orange, the lumpy delicacy is at its best coal-black with, just under the outer surface, a fine-veined, marbled appearance; it imparts a piquant, aromatic quality to whichever foods it is mated with. This most desirable variety is called by the Sarladais the *vraie truffe,* to distinguish it from the types found in England, Spain, northern Italy, and even Yugoslavia—

which are gray, white, or sometimes reddish, known in Sarlat as the *fausses truffes*.

To try to separate the facts from the fantasies, I sought out, first, the specialist in the field at the Delpeyrat plant—M. Jacques Meffre, an amiable conversationalist who takes his calling seriously. As I arrived, he was occupied completing a lecture on the subject to a group of twenty schoolgirls who were studying, at a nearby specialized *école*, the various aspects of running a household.

A grandson and son of *truffe* merchants, M. Meffre, now forty-two, has been absorbed in his subject since he was a small boy in the *département* of Vaucluse, in the South of France, and is a storehouse of information for anyone, like me, interested in learning a bit more about this exotic edible fungus.

"First, the *truffe* itself," he said in his Midi-accented French as we sat down to lunch in my hotel on a hill overlooking Sarlat. "The best *truffe* you can tell by looking at it, and feeling it, and then smelling it. It must have a certain solidity, and be as round and as black as possible. But if you scratch it with your fingernail it should have tiny white veins running through the black of the interior. If the inside is gray or whitish, you do not have a good *truffe*. The false *truffes* have no odor. In Périgord, you will find the best; farther down in the Southwest they still have a good odor, and in the Southeast they are supple. In Carpentras and Montségur [in south central France], the earth is red—giving the *truffes* there, still moderately good, a reddish cast. Sometimes *truffes* are found as far north as Auxerre, but in Périgord they are really superb."

M. Meffre didn't think much of the varieties uncovered from time to time in Spain and northern Italy. The English type he did not consider worth discussing. (How much of this attitude was due to the truffles themselves and how much was a result of the feelings engendered by the Guerre de Cent Ans it was difficult to estimate.)

The burning issue for a *maître de truffes,* or for anyone who can't abide the thought of goose liver *without* truffles, is the accelerating rarity of the fungus. In 1945, Meffre told me, spearing a liberal cut of foie gras aux truffes with his fork, 1,800 tons of truffles were uncovered and sold in France or exported; in 1970, 120 tons.

"The problem is there is no way of raising the truffle with any degree of predictability. An area can be prepared in a manner that might be said to be ideal for a truffle to grow in. But you can't be sure. The ideal place to find the tuber wild is in the mountains, under the surface near the roots of oak trees and others in an area where the earth looks devastated. The best time to find them is from mid-November to March— actually beginning in mid-December for the best type. And of course we use dogs and female pigs to search them out."

Why female pigs?

"Well, they're usually looking for food for themselves and their young. We use them on fairly level ground; if the terrain is hilly or if there are low fences to be got over, we use dogs—mongrels. To train an ordinary dog to be a good truffle hound takes about a month. First you let them go two days without food or water, then take them on a leash to a likely area. When they find a truffle, we just pull them off it and reward them with a piece of bread, cheese, or meat. After this pattern is repeated several times, they get the idea."

Truffles grow under the surface of the earth, usually in a somewhat moist area near the roots of oak trees, and have long been noted for their health-giving qualities.

"The Greeks and Romans ate truffles—the Romans right here in Sarlat. The husband of Messalina was especially fond of them. And you know, of course, it is considered to be an aphrodisiac," M. Meffre added with a twinkle. *"Les truffes sont bonnes pour la santé,"* he intoned, in a teacher's singsong. *"Elles rendent les hommes plus forts, et les femmes plus aimables."*

A young waitress passed our table, and my luncheon companion paused in mid-paragraph to follow her course admiringly. The Maître-Truffier, who spends most of his work-day immersed in the scent of the esteemed fungus and who samples his product from time to time, is a living example of the revitalizing qualities attributed to the *truffe*. A family man, he is overflowing with life and a feeling of well-being, and has an appreciative eye for every woman and girl who comes within his line of vision.

After lunch we repaired to his base of operations, where several hundred truffles of all sizes were in the process of being washed and graded. One specimen, the size of a grapefruit, was a particular prize—coal black, and with the marbled look of thin white subsurface veins against a black interior.

"This one is a gem," said M. Meffre, beaming as though he had just found an emerald or a diamond. "Four hundred grams at least." The room was humid, and the intriguing odor of the individual truffle was

152

magnified a hundred times over. A truffle hound wandering into this enclosure would, I imagined, go berserk.

"The *truffe*," M. Meffre concluded after inspecting still another shipment and shaking his head over it, "is a veritable mystery of nature. One searches for the reason for their existence."

Still pondering on this unusual tuberous comestible, and with the tantalizing scent of the *vraie truffe* still strong in my nostrils, I sought out a retired professor residing in Sarlat, a M. Henri Cabanel, who is the acknowledged truffle expert in the region. He is also the Secretary-General of the Syndicate of Périgourdine Production for the Truffle and counsels the regional museum as well.

"Yes, the *truffe* is a true mystery," M. Cabanel said. "It's one of only three organisms I know that cannot be reproduced in the usual way—the orchid and the mistletoe being the others.

"As for its having aphrodisiacal qualities, well, we know that Louis XIV ate a pound a day, and Mme. de Pompadour consumed them regularly. And Napoleon I was partial to them. Whether you believe all the stories or not, the fact is that *truffes* help keep you in an excellent state of health and tone up the system.

"The *truffe*, you know, has antibiotic qualities," he continued, warming to his favorite subject, "and contains *hormones de croissance*" (hormones of growth).

"The starlings, blackbirds, and thrushes, the migratory birds of the region [*étourneaux, merles, et grives,* in his meticulous French] eat the grain of the *truffe,* and fertilize it by passing it through their digestive tract. The *vraie truffe,* you understand, has tiny spores, with hidden sacs containing the organs that produce the fruit."

Growing more enthusiastic by the minute, he plunged on without pause: "In the area surrounding Sarlat and to the south, near the fortress town of Domme, dogs are used, since the ground is hilly. Near Salignac, the *truie* [female pig] is employed to better advantage, on the flat terrain.

"You can find *truffes* in a number of regions in southern Europe—thirty or forty varieties," the professor concluded with conviction, "but in Périgord you find *Tuber melanosporum—la vraie!*"

Amateurs of the lore of the *truffe,* though not as numerous as wine tasters, have elevated their cult to a higher plane of philosophical contemplation of the secrets of life itself. La Fontaine, the immortal *fabuliste,* was an acolyte of the sect.

His successors, like Professor Cabanel, and the people of Sarlat generally take the *truffe* and its place in a consideration of the mysteries of the universe just as seriously as moon worshipers or dedicated astrologers regard their own deities. And living in a region of startling cliffs and prehistoric caves, many of them adorned with wall paintings celebrating the birth of art on this planet, the natives of Sarlat and its environs have a keenly developed awareness of man's oneness with the universe.

In this heartland of France and cradle of prehistory, one need not be an archaeologist to perceive the layers of successive epochs which have contributed to the present highly civilized stratum, combining the strongest and best elements of past levels.

The ancient town of Sarlat, which has retained its oval shape through the centuries, can be said to have commenced its "modern" incarnation—following the legends relating to the time of Clovis, Pépin le Bref, and Charlemagne—in the period about 820 to 840, when the Benedictine monastery was founded, perhaps by Pépin of Aquitaine; shortly after, during the time of the Norman invasion, visiting monks brought the relics of their patron saint, Sacerdos. The monks in Sarlat obtained the double protection of the King and the Pope, and thus succeeded in conserving their autonomy.

During those early years, Sarlat was often a battlefield—of the monks versus the bourgeois, of the town against the large landowner. The *abbaye* remained the real seat of power until the rule of the consuls began in 1204, when the influence of the religious declined for a time. But in 1317 the diocese of Périgueux was divided in half, and Sarlat became the seat of one of the two districts, with its own bishop.

In the fourteenth century, in a period of advances in architecture and the arts, an age of anxiety commenced for the Sarladais. The English took the bastion of Domme, thirteen kilometers to the south, and installed themselves in the surrounding countryside as well.

To one standing on the heights of Domme in the bright sunlight of the late twentieth century, gazing down into the fog-shrouded valley below, with just a few protuberances of earth visible above the thick blanket of fog, it is immediately apparent how an army that controlled Domme would dominate the entire area stretching out from that ancient town.

The forces of England's Edward III took the fortress with the vital assistance of some traitors to the French cause, and the internal calm of Sarlat, following on a century of unrest, was once again punctured. The Sarladais took up arms against the enemy and continued to resist; after the defeat at Poitiers the French sank into a state of anarchy, a condition that did not penetrate Sarlat. Eventually, the Sarladais were forced to accede to the authority of the English King, who ruled the town for a decade, until the arrival of the troops of Charles V.

In the latter years of the fifteenth century, the ruins of this tidy town were replaced and its damaged buildings repaired. But in the sixteenth century Sarlat was again besieged, this time by the Vicomte de Turenne, and a continuing series of religious wars ensued; it was not until the middle of the seventeenth that the new century of almost constant turmoil abated. An anti-Catholic movement had gained considerable momentum, but finally Sarlat remained faithful to the Pope, who secularized the monastery which had spawned Sarlat originally.

A period of peace followed, and Sarlat's military history seemed to be at an end. The control of the province of Périgord, once a countship (beginning in the ninth century) and then a fiefdom of the Duc of Aquitaine, passed—after the expulsion of the English—under the control of the house of Bourbon and became part of the royal domain in 1589 when Henry of Navarre became King of France.

During the Revolution, whose shock waves were felt later in Sarlat than in other parts of the country, the diocesan bishop of Sarlat, acting as mayor, was finally succeeded by a procurer-trustee, J.-B. Gueyraud, an ardent revolutionary and terrorist. Like Périgueux, Sarlat was ruled by a popular front. Catholicism waned before the advances of the advocates of reason.

Under Napoleon, Sarlat sent soldiers to fight his battles and celebrated his feast day. But when he was sent into exile on Elba the town acclaimed the ascendancy of Louis XVIII; then, when Napoleon returned to metropolitan France, he was hailed as a savior.

Concerned with its own economic stability, Sarlat lived through many changes of rule—the July Monarchy, the Second Republic, the Empire, the Third Republic, and so on—with little alteration of its own life style. In their fashion, the Sarladais were loyal to each succeeding national government, but mostly they were interested in their own area, their own town, and themselves. After all, they reason, what is life really but a comfortable existence in a picturesque town, in an attractive countryside, with delicious food in abundance to be washed down with superior wines?

And at the center of it all rests that ugly fungus with the delicate scent, the mysterious *truffe,* whose piquant seasoning faculties contribute immeasurably to the well-being and good spirits of Périgourdins.

An outsider from Tours and Paris, Honoré de Balzac, once observed:

"If one *truffe* falls on my plate, that would suffice; it is the egg which suddenly hatches ten characters in my *Comédie Humaine.*" Since the personages in that series of masterworks reflect the essential French character, perhaps it is the lowly but eminent *truffe* that is, after all, the touchstone of the French mystique.

# A Nation of Coiffeurs

---

*Many a Frenchwoman would sooner go without food, drink, clothing, or shelter than give up what to her is one of life's primary necessities—that is, having her hair done. The average Frenchwoman really considers her crowning glory a major asset and nothing to fool around with in an amateur way. She would rather be tortured in the Iron Maiden than be caught in curlers.*

---

Discoursing on love, Stendhal wrote that "the national passion is Vanity." What a crushing comment this is. It seems to break up one of the attractive illusions we all like to maintain about France as a hotbed of jolly amorous frolics—not a place where everyone is basking continuously in front of a mirror. It is a view that is, nevertheless, open to debate.

Someone else has rather unkindly characterized the French as "a nation of hairdressers," an epithet not wholly without justification. If you look about you as you wander along the streets of Paris, you cannot help but notice that for every two cafés there seems to be a sign that says "Coiffeur."

Statistics are not available on how often Frenchwomen make love, at least no figures that are reliable, possibly for the reason that any Gallic equivalents of Drs. Kinsey or Reuben would be laughed off hilariously should they appear on the scene in France. It is, however, a recorded fact that in the Paris region and on the Côte d'Azur one hairdresser exists for every two hundred women in what is considered the "coiffable" age bracket (from fifteen to sixty-five), and the national ratio, which includes the unsophisticated rural areas, is one hairdresser to every 470. In even the smallest hamlet, you will find at least one presentable *salon de coiffure* that caters to the local hierarchy, from the lady of the château to the wives of the mayor, the doctor, the lawyer, the veterinary, the notary, the innkeeper, the druggist, on down to the spouses of the wine and the cheese merchants, the baker, the pastryman, the grocer, the butcher, and the fish dealer.

Many a Frenchwoman would sooner go without food, drink, clothing, or shelter than give up what to her is one of life's primary necessities; i.e., having her hair done. Seventeen percent of the coiffables visit their hairdressers two to three times a week. An additional 17 percent have their hair dressed professionally twice a month. You would certainly never find that level of beauty-salon frequentation in the United States, where up to the age of forty the majority of women are convinced that they do not need the regular ministrations of a *coiffeur* and are sold on the principle of do-it-yourself shampoos, sets, and home permanents.

The average Frenchwoman, on the other hand, really considers her crowning glory a major asset and nothing to fool around with in an amateur way. She would rather be tortured in the Iron Maiden than be caught in curlers. She recoils from the thought of shampooing her hair herself, and if she cannot afford to go to the hairdresser as often as she needs to, she simply leaves her hair unwashed and tucks it out of sight under a becoming hat until she does have the money for the *coiffeur*. So, all in all, the assumption that *vanité* is as preoccupying as *l'amour* may be perfectly reasonable.

In their Latin way, the French do put great stock in appearances. Although they have no expression like the Italian *"bella figura,"* French people have a high regard for their own looks and for each other's, too. Why else would the *citoyens* spend hours out of each day doing nothing but sitting at a sidewalk café nursing a cup of coffee or an apéritif if it were not for the enjoyment to be gained from appraising the rest of the citizenry—especially the aesthetically pleasing rest?

To be *"en beauté"* is to let the world know what a good opinion one has of oneself, and no matter what nature has handed a Frenchwoman, she is in there making the best of it. The habits of coquetry are instilled at an early age and take precedence over daily routines of cleanliness, as we know from the dearth of toothbrushes and bathtubs found in the nation at large in even the most recent surveys. Women who would not dream of missing a monthly trip to the hairdresser will wash only as far down on their necks as the depth of their décolletages, and in country areas the family toothbrush is seldom put to use except at New Year's and Easter. But the homeliest female will usually strive to be beautiful. It may only

160

be worth while for her to do so in France, for there she will be rewarded by becoming *"une jolie laide"*—in other words, a very attractive ugly woman.

As in other countries, all hairdressers are not alike. There are two general categories: *commercial,* the type to be found in the little town or in the neighborhood *quartier* of the large metropolis; and *artiste,* who holds forth only in the most recherché enclaves of Paris or the fashionable resorts. The difference separating the two is as immense as that between the ready-to-wear manufacturer who makes clothing adapted from the ideas of *hauts couturiers* and the creative high-fashion designers themselves. Although many a *coiffeur* of the commercial type can give a haircut that is comparable in shape to the work of an artist *haut coiffeur,* the rest of his performance—the set, the comb-out, and so forth—will not be likely to measure up to the top standards. The profession is as strictly controlled as any other in the land, with examinations to be passed and *brevets* to be granted before any hairdresser is in business. Then the state, which keeps an eye on 70,000 hairdressers and 40,000 apprentices in 55,000 shops for both men and women in all *départements* of France, will class his establishment as one of the following: *haute coiffure luxe,* with no restrictions as to how much he may charge; *salon de coiffure* of A, B, or C quality, with prices regulated accordingly.

"You have only one head and you have to live with it," is the way Alexandre rationalizes the hold that hairdos and makeups have over the Frenchwoman's psyche. As the kingpin of *haute coiffure luxe* Paris hairdressers, Alexandre is conceded to be the world's greatest. The internationally famed *coiffeur* of queens, Kennedys, film stars, and couturiers' mannequins, he epitomizes French hairdressing, and nobody knows as much about it and its history as he does. He has the entire tradition in his scissors' tips.

"Champagne," he will say, snipping away at a client's locks in his glossy salon on the Rue du Faubourg Saint-Honoré, "was the founder of our profession for he was the first artist hairdresser, but he had a wicked temperament. I suppose you have read what Tallement des Réaux, the seventeenth-century writer, has said about Champagne, yes? That he was very clever at dressing the hair but that he was also very *amoureux* with his clients and would finish one side of their hair and would make them pay with a kiss before completing the other; that he would tell one lady what he had received from another lady. He deserved to die, as he did, at the hands of brigands. He was what the *grand coiffeur* must never, never be—*très indiscret.*"

Without his having to imply it himself, everybody knows that Alexandre, on the contrary, is in absolute control of his career, his business affairs, his talent, his poise, not to speak of his tongue.

"Some of them will tell you things they shouldn't," one of his many famous customers, Mme. Hervé Alphand, has said while on the subject of the loquacity of *coiffeurs.* "But Alexandre is the perfect hairdresser. He is always amusing, always gay, but he is also always circumspect." Married to the former French Foreign Office Secretary-General, Nicole Alphand is at present *directrice* for Pierre Cardin, whose high-fashion house is right next door to Alexandre's salon, and her job keeps her in steady touch with comings and goings in the international world of couture and coiffure. When her husband was France's Ambassador at Washington during the Kennedy years, Mme. Alphand caused a flurry by flying Alexandre and some of his staff over to the Embassy residence, where she treated a group of her American friends to the experience of great Paris hair styling.

It was not the first journey of its kind for Alexandre, or the last. Earlier in life, when he was on the Riviera, the Duchess of Windsor became his most energetic advocate and patroness. She sent him by plane across the Atlantic to America to do her hair for a single ball. Since then, Alexandre has seemed always to be flying somewhere, and indeed, from the moment he darts into his salon early in the morning and breezily greets his staff with a melodious *"Bonjour, mes enfants,"* he appears to be in perpetual motion, his hands and his body never still, a creature of mercurial movement and speech.

He is on the phone. *"Oui, Princesse. Non, Princesse. Oui, Princesse,"* he carols, calming the fretful caller, chain smoking, and gesticulating to one of his seventy employees, all at the same time. Until a year ago, when his salon was completely renovated because, as he said, "We must modernize ourselves," he held court before a large triple looking glass placed between two of the tall windows that overlook the street, beckoning to a bevy of hovering helpers in tight black suits in an ambience that was totally Second Empire. The portraits of ladies (vintage Empress Eugénie), the autographed letters and sketches, and the locks of noted customers' hair framed in gilt ovals on the pale silk-covered walls have all been swept away. Now his virtuoso performances of styling and arranging with

162

scissors, comb, and brush (Alexandre never, never sets hair unless it is very, very famous hair) take place before a dressing table much like the other clinical white ones in the salon, with the new burnt-orange walls, where his twenty-four assistant *coiffeurs* and their ten aides work in a honeycomb of activity. The artwork is confined to a solitary, impressive decoration which his clients may contemplate while their sudsy heads are in the shampoo basins: a wall-sized tapestry of brilliant color portraying a sphinx with the name "Alexandre" woven strikingly into the design and signed with the star and handwriting of the late French jack-of-all-arts Jean Cocteau. He was one of the hairdresser's great friends and perhaps the only person for whom Alexandre had sphinxlike attributes.

To most people, Alexandre, with his quick grace, small stature, fin de siècle mustache, and shoulder-length hair, dressed in whatever may be the most with-it chains, medallions, body shirts, and hip-hugging pants of the minute, is the very model of the modern Paris hairdresser. If he advises his customers to "regard the mirror, which speaks, which tells the truth," he obviously does not shun the looking glass himself. Tanned, tuned in ahead of time to all the turns of *la mode* in the looks of the face and hair as well as clothes, he is quite capable of decking himself out from head to heels in apple-green suède, as he once did for an appearance in America. "I was bitten in my youth by the virus of fashion," he explains.

"Madame," Alexandre will say to a lady of fading looks and sad face who is reluctant to be dyed, "gray hair is *distingué* but gray hair is *triste*. We must have the will to be happy, must we not?" And the lady obediently departs for the room of the hair colorists and emerges, smiling, with highlights in her hair three hours later.

Such a knack for persuasion is, of course, vital to keeping one's perch at the pinnacle of the heap as the world's best hairdresser. The French really have no competition in the field of *haute coiffure,* being the acknowledged masters. Any misgivings as to the merits of other countries' professionals—the *Damenfriseurs* of Austria, for example—are resolved at once if you compare the soignée women of Paris with the not so soignée women of Vienna, or any other fashionable capital. From the days of Champagne in the reign of Louis XIII onward, there has always been a hairdresser in France who was unquestionably *the* hairdresser.

Today it is Alexandre. His ascendancy began just before World War II, when, aged fifteen, he showed his mettle as King of the Egg Shampoos while working in the Antoine salon at Cannes. Born Alexandre Raimondi not far away from there in Saint-Tropez, where his Italian parents kept a restaurant, he was discovered to be something out of the ordinary in hairdressers by Mlle. Yvette Labrousse, a long-stemmed dark-haired beauty. As Miss France, she had come to the notice of the Aga Khan III. In time, he married her. When she became the Begum, she presented Alexandre to the Duchess of Windsor, who was impressed.

Once the Duchess believes in someone, she really takes that person over. She not only gave Alexandre her patronage, she taught him how to handle the people in the society in which she moves. "She made me a gentleman," says Alexandre, and he has the taste to add, "a gentleman *coiffeur*." She persuaded him to go to Paris and establish himself there in the salon of the Carita sisters—a stormy relationship that was short-lived, although all three hairdressers still manage to maintain a tenuous friendship. The Duchess introduced Alexandre to all her friends. "It is to her," he says, "I owe my entire career."

In American eyes, Alexandre may well have peaked during the visit of President and Mrs. John F. Kennedy to Paris in May, 1961, when, before doing the Frst Lady's hair in an astonishing brioche style for a state dinner with Charles de Gaulle, the *coiffeur* sold Jacqueline Kennedy on the hairdo by telling her, "We must make an effort, Madame. You are going to see Louis XV."

Alexandre knew best, as usual, and President Kennedy admired his handiwork enough to present the hairdresser to friends. "Meet Alexandre the Great," said the President. The *coiffeur*, who loves titles, could not have been more pleased.

He does not often let the opportunity to drop an aristocratic name slip by, Alexandre. To the biography that has been compiled by his *attaché de presse* is appended a list of his celebrated clients, commencing with four queens, H.M. Queen Sirikit of Thailand through H.M. Queen of Afghanistan, then, with a stop for H.R.H. Crown Grand Duchess Josephine Charlotte of Luxembourg, continuing on through forty princesses, from H.S.H. Princess Grace of Monaco to their R.H.s the Princesses of Bourbon-Parme, and concluding with a passel of movie queens, ending up with La Divine Greta Garbo, who, the press release notes, never fails to lunch with Alexandre when she comes to Paris.

But Alexandre is not a snob. "He is a romantic," says one of his most understanding clients. "He truly feels he is the reincarnation of the *maître-coiffeurs* of the royal court and that he carries in his veins the lifeblood of every great French hairdresser of the past."

164

Only yesterday, it was Antoine, an exotic Pole, who was world famous as the leading Paris hair stylist and who dressed the hair of Europe's crowned heads. For fifteen years, Alexandre worked for him and watched him. But although he says "Antoine was my master and a father to me," it is not so much to the nineteen-thirties era of lacquered caps of hair and Schiaparelli that Alexandre harks back as to the *grands siècles* of the sixteen hundreds and seventeen hundreds.

The pageant of hairdressers in French history begins with Champagne and goes on to Dagé, who dressed the heads of the mistresses of Louis XV, starting off with the Duchesse de Châteauroux. When she went out and the Marquise de Pompadour came in, Dagé did the new favorite's hair— at least he did until the day his tongue slipped.

"Tell me, Dagé," La Pompadour asked, "how have you acquired your immense reputation?"

"*Madame la marquise*," the hairdresser replied, "that is not astonishing. I coiffed the other one."

Needless to say, he was sacked straight off but not in time to keep the story from circulating throughout the court, where, for a while, La Pompadour was "*Mme. Celle-ci*" and the Duchesse de Châteauroux, "*L'Autre.*"

Next in line in attendance on Mme. de Pompadour came Legros de Rumigny, who had a good head for business but who also suffered from the fault of "*la langue trop longue*," or the too long tongue. Legros would chatter along as he worked, naming those of his noble clients who were not overly fastidious and who only had their chignons combed out every fifteen days. When word of this got around, he lost his place, too, but Legros continued as a power and could refer to himself pretentiously as an academician because he had founded an Académie de Coiffure. He charged steep fees to students, who learned how to execute the thirty-eight designs he published in a best-selling book in 1766. His classes tried out their skills on young girls known as *prêteuses de têtes* (head-lenders) who paraded around publicly afterward showing off Legros's styles. At graduation, the honor students were awarded a star, a crescent, or—if they were of magna cum laude caliber—a sunburst. Legros thought the way to cultivate the growth of hair was by cutting the ends at every new moon, a superstition to which Antoine subscribed and which persists today, for Alexandre believes in it, too.

"Quick! When does the full moon rise?" Alexandre will call out, his scissors poised in midair, as he sends his assistants scurrying to consult the almanac. "When the moon is new, I cut the hair. It is the system of the Incas and I practice it on the princesses of France. Pull out the hair when the moon is on the descent; cut the hair when the moon is on the rise. That makes the hair strong."

After Legros was trampled to death in a stampede that occurred during the celebrations following the marriage of Louis XVI to Marie-Antoinette, Frédéric supplanted him and then came Larseneur, both of them to be deposed in their turn by the legendary Léonard Autié, who played a decisive part in French history. He is the figure in the coiffure hall of fame with whom Alexandre has the greatest affinity. Alexandre has, on occasion, attended presentations of his own hair styles costumed as Léonard, in silken hose, satin breeches, and powdered wig. However, the attraction Alexandre has for the eighteenth-century *coiffeur* is not because he finds Léonard himself, from what is known of him, all that *sympathique*.

"He thought he was *beau*," and Alexandre will sniff as he says this, brushing away at a client's hair with light staccato strokes. "But he was not *beau*. I have seen his portrait in the National Archives. If you ask me, he looked like Robespierre—a *croque-mort*, Madame, an undertaker."

Léonard's great appeal is that he was the ultimate in royal hairdressers, having been indispensable to the queen of French queens, Marie-Antoinette. To Alexandre, a fervid collector of antique appurtenances of his trade and all objects made of hair, who possesses one of her curling irons and a lock of her hair set into a brooch, she is *la Reine*—perhaps the only true queen, one sometimes thinks, he so loves to talk about her.

"Every morning in the little private apartments of *la Reine* at Versailles, her attendants would bring out the books with the sketches of her dresses in them and the samples of the fabric attached next to each *robe*, and the Queen would place a pin next to every dress she wanted to wear that day. Rose Bertin, her dressmaker, who was called 'the minister of *la mode*' by the Comte d'Artois, *la Reine*'s companion in all *her* escapades, would be there to advise her as she sat at her dressing table next to her blue, white, and gold sitting room. And Léonard, whom they called the '*physionomiste*,' the '*ministre de la coiffure*,' or the Marquis Léonard, would create her hair style. Then the baskets lined with blue silk taffeta and heaped with her dresses would be lowered by cable from the upstairs closet.

"He was the only person *la Reine* could trust, you know, and maybe that was why Jeanne-Louise Campan, her secretary, hated Léonard. Whom could the Queen use as a go-between for herself and her lover—and we all know Comte Axel de Fersen, the Swedish courtier, was her lover—whom but her *coiffeur*? Léonard was the *boîte aux lettres*, the mailbox, for her and Fersen. Whom could she send ahead, before the flight to Varennes, with the jewels of the crown but Léonard? You are familiar with his memoirs, of course."

The "*Souvenirs de Léonard*," of which Alexandre speaks, were among a spate of post-mortem reminiscences of high life under the *ancien régime* that appeared during the French Restoration. Many of these writings are considered to be either semi-apocryphal or entirely so. Ghostwritten by Baron E.-L. Lamothe-Langon and published in 1838, eighteen years after the hairdresser is thought to have died in poverty in Paris, the memoirs tell a *rocambolesque* tale of Léonard's gymnastics in the bedrooms of various ladies of the theatre and the court, and give a picture of the ineptitude of Louis XVI as well as the desperate frivolity of Marie-Antoinette.

If we are to believe the "*Souvenirs*," Léonard, who was one of two (some say three) brothers, all hairdressers, from Gascony, set forth to make his fortune in Paris with the money for two weeks' rent, a handsome comb of tortoise shell, and ample confidence in himself. In addition, to his advantage, he had legs with a turn of the calf that he pronounced "eloquent," and a jacket and breeches of gray broadcloth fine enough so that, as his story goes, "I could be taken, in the castles in Spain of my vanity, for an accomplished cavalier."

He soon became a part of the world of *galanterie* that centered about the quarter of the Boulevard du Temple. The atmosphere of the quarter is familiar to art-film fans of today as the setting for "*Les Enfants du Paradis*," the historic motion picture made in France during World War II, starring Arletty as the beautiful woman of the demimonde and Jean-Louis Barrault as the mime who performed for the crowds on an outdoor stage. Léonard's first professional triumph was the fairylike hair style he created for his mistress Julie, a dancer at the Théâtre Nicolet on the boulevard, a coiffure described as a macédoine of mock emeralds, pearls, flowers, and curls, crowned with an aureole of glittering stars attached to the top of the hairdress by means of a thin circle of wire. Léonard's work was talked about and he was soon appropriated by a certain marquise, who received him, the very first time he called, in her bedroom. Before long, he attracted the attention of Mme. Du Barry, who summoned him to her pavilion at Louveciennes, where her maid conducted him to her mistress, who was in the bath. None of this was considered at all out of the way at the time, we are assured, *chez les dames de qualité*. Julie, meanwhile, took up with an acrobat by the name of Le Petit Diable, whose jumps were *extraordinaires*, and this *saltimbanque* later gave the Comte d'Artois tightrope-walking lessons—all of which may or may not be true.

On the factual side, it is more reliably recorded elsewhere that Léonard did gain the distinction of becoming hairdresser to the Queen, and Marie-Antoinette gave him permission to keep other clients and maintain his own Paris apartments in addition to his quarters at Versailles. The styles he created for her hair at the beginning of their relationship were no more monstrous than the other bizarre structures that first came into fashion in 1680. In that year, Louis XIV's favorite, the Duchesse de Fontanges, lost her hat while out hunting with the King and tied up her curls into a top-knot with a garter. Thus, the high Fontanges was launched and, supported by wire frames, it later attained towering proportions, bumping into chandeliers and causing the roofs of sedan chairs to be raised.

In 1714, the simple coiffure of the British Ambassador's wife, Lady Sandwich, started a brief vogue for lower hairdos. An English girl is also reputed to have begun the mode for white hair, which men took up first, by accidentally powdering her coiffure as well as her face when hastily preparing for a court ball. The fashion for powder, a fine starch mixed with sweet-pea, violet, and chypre perfumes, lasted for eighty years, during which it was impossible to tell an old person from a young one at first glance. In much earlier times, the Gauls had powdered their hair with well-washed and dried ashes.

Although the era of the most fantastic monstrosities commenced with the "opera loge" and the "sky climber" in 1772, two years before Marie-Antoinette reached the throne, she is thought to have been the perpetrator of the excesses. In France, when anything goes too far wrong, the tendency is to blame the foreigner. So, in their late-nineteenth-century *History of the Coiffure of Women in France*, Èze and Marcel charge their Queen Isabelle of Bavaria with the conical headdresses of the Middle Ages; King Henri II's wife, Catherine de Medicis of Italy, with the whalebones and hoopskirts of the fifteen hundreds; and their Empress Eugénie-Marie de Montijo de Guzman of Spain with the crinoline skirt, Marie-Antoinette of Austria being given the responsibility for the giant hairdos of the eighteenth century.

168

Assuredly, in her reign hair styles did attain heights never known before or since. In 1777, Léonard is supposed to have devised for her the triple-plumed "Qu'esaco" we see the Queen wearing in one of the paintings of her by Mme. Vigée-Lebrun, although some sources give Mlle. Bertin the credit for first having used ostrich feathers in this manner. Later on, Léonard increased the number of plumes to ten for the "Minerva" coiffure, which was, in addition, embellished with peacock feathers.

Before Louis XVI mounted the throne in 1774, women's hair styles had already reached a volume of such enormity that the weight on their necks was oftentimes insupportable. There were cases where the mouth of a lady in *grande toilette* would be at a point equidistant between the top of her coiffure and her feet. "The head was transformed alternatively into mountain, forest, or garden," wrote Èze and Marcel, summing up the extravagances of the period of Mme. Du Barry. "It was an orgy of butterflies, birds, tree branches, cardboard cupids. The hair was teased, crimped, loaded with feathers, gauze, ribbons, garlands, pearls, and diamonds. One went so far as to ornament one's coiffure with vegetables."

One went further than that and carried a whole tableau on one's head. According to a contemporary witness, Louis Petit de Bachaumont, the Duchesse de Chartres wore an eye-catching scene, the central figure of which was a seated female wet-nursing an infant who was said by the Duchesse to represent M. le Duc de Valois. "To the right was a *perroquet* on its stand, pecking at a cherry, the bird being precious to the Duchesse, and at the left, a blackamoor," Bachaumont noted in his *Mémoires Secrets.*

By 1778, the monster hairdos were taking a nautical turn and heads bearing frigates in full sail were the going fashion; one style, "à la Belle-Poule," was named after a French ship that was victorious in a skirmish with part of the British fleet off the coast of Brittany. In 1783, the Montgolfier brothers and their lighter-than-air ballooning inspired new soaring coiffures. Benjamin Franklin's discovery of atmospheric electricity did not give birth to a new French hairdress, but he was honored with a hat, "*le chapeau paratonnerre,*" with a little metal chain to attract lightning extending from the back of the hatband down to the wearer's heels.

Meanwhile, after the birth of the first Dauphin, Marie-Antoinette's hair began to fall out and Léonard cut it short, inaugurating the style "l'Enfant," the beginning of the end of the super-bouffant hairdos. Soon everything the Queen and the court had taken for granted would come to an *effrayant* finish—but not before one calamitous attempt at escape.

Who knows what course history might have taken if Marie-Antoinette had not entrusted her hairdresser Léonard, of all people, with a key role in the planning for the royal family's flight from France? Insisting that she could not be deprived of his services *"divins,"* in June, 1791, the Queen charged Léonard with the care of the King's *habit de cérémonie* and a great part of the crown jewels, sending the hairdresser in advance on the route to Montmédy. She gave Léonard a letter to the Duc de Choiseul with instructions to order the necessary relays of horses for the royal carriage, and he and the Duc traveled together as far as Bondy, where Choiseul quit his post and canceled the orders for the relays. What Léonard subsequently did at Varennes was catastrophic, for, demanding a fresh relay, he let it be known whom the horses were for and when, later, the royal party arrived, it was recognized, surrounded, and escorted back to Paris. Léonard had continued on his way and is thought to have gone on to Russia, one of hundreds of émigrés who fled from France in the hours of the Revolution, many of them *coiffeurs* like himself, others *valets de chambre*, chefs, and dancing instructors.

"It was by these personages that Europe learned to know us," Èze and Marcel wrote in the eighteen-eighties. "And she came to the conclusion that the French nation was made up of a dizzy and empty-headed lot, composed of dancing masters and hairdressers. The soldiers of the Republic and Napoleon's Empire would later traverse the Continent in every direction over a period long enough to redress these false ideas."

The ultimate fate of the lovely ash-blond locks of Marie-Antoinette is well known. They turned white, most probably on the night of the return from Varennes. On the morning of the day of her death, after she had arranged them carefully under a clean white cap, they were brutally chopped off in her cell at the Conciergerie by her executioner, Henri Samson, who first bound her hands behind her back. Toward the very end, her hair was a sight to rend the heart, as we know from the pitiful picture she makes in the pen-and-ink sketch Louis David did of her from a window on the Rue Saint-Honoré as she was driven by, October 16, 1793, in a cart on her way to the scaffold.

In the gruesome years that followed, hairdressing took on a political significance. On the night of 10 Thermidor An II (the French Revolutionary Calendar date for July 29, 1794), the day that Robespierre was guillotined with his brothers and Saint-Just, a ghoulish party, *le Bal des Victimes*, was hurriedly organized. The women danced in scandalously decolleté and transparent dresses and were seen to have shaved their hair well up the backs of their necks—in homage, it was said, to the victims who had fallen on the Place de la Concorde.

In the First Empire, the Empress Josephine was dressed and coiffed by a Mlle. Despeaux, who was not to the liking of Napoleon. He always had to have his say about his wives' appearance, and he fired her. She was replaced by Leroy, who also designed the clothes and the hair styles for Josephine's successor, Marie-Louise.

It was not until the days of the Empress Eugénie that the hairdresser would again come into his own, and it was Félice Escalier who executed, for Eugénie's marriage to Louis-Napoleon, the coiffure composed of two bandeaux across the front with a center part, the sides raised à la Mary Stuart, and a cascade of ringlets from the top of the head to the nape of the neck.

"The Empress wears this hair style in her portrait by Winterhalter that is at Compiègne," says Alexandre. "But Félice Escalier betrayed her. He did the unforgivable for the hairdresser. For money, he copied the same coiffure for the Emperor's mistress, La Castiglione, and it was then worn by all the courtesans and the demimonde. La Castiglione bribed him. He was stricken off the Empress's list, disgraced, banished. And the Empress found her revenge. La Castiglione appeared at a ball as the Queen of Hearts, with a big heart sewn on the skirt of her gown, and had the gall to ask what the Empress thought of her costume. 'I find,' Eugénie said, 'that Madame wears her heart rather low.'"

The Second Empire was a time when *coiffeurs* dug through old engravings and illustrations in the museum of the Louvre, at Versailles, and in the National Library for new ideas, bringing forth styles like the *byzantin*. The use of peroxide and ammonia and powdered red brick was introduced by ladies of dubious reputation. One of the most notorious, Cora Pearl, made her dramatic appearances in the altogether at dinner parties for men only, when the cover of the huge silver serving dish in which she was carried to the table was removed. She had flaming red hair. Later, hennaed hair became the fashion with ladies of better reputation.

During the Belle Époque, the time of day when the hairdresser brought his curling papers and tongs to his client's house was inclined to be the hour of *l'amour*. The circumstances could hardly have been otherwise, as the historian Eugène Woestyne has noted:

> Admittedly, the *coiffeur à la mode* was usually young, agreeable, well-formed. Happy, in a position of privilege, privy to the mysteries of the dressing room, every day circling about the same woman like the serpent around Eve, awaiting the occasion, caressing the hair with a light hand, flitting here and there as long as he pleased around a charming head; having the right to regard it with love to the measure that he contributed to its enhancement, he must have found the secret of pleasing if he was ingratiating, and he oftentimes was, and always the flatterer, that cannot be denied. *Mon Dieu!* Let us not point the finger at the scandalous history of the times. Think rather of the lightness of the moral standards; consider the abandon of the morning *toilette*, the atmosphere damp and perfumed, the temptations of solitude, and it should not surprise us that the hour of the *coiffeur* was more than once the hour of the shepherd.

Later on, at the turn of the century, as business increased, hairdressers were kept running from client to client on their daily rounds and were in too much of a hurry to engage in such liaisons.

The capillary wonder of the close of the nineteenth century was the invention of the marcel wave by Marcel Grateau, who was thereafter known as *"L'Ondulateur."* The artificial undulation by means of a special curling iron that produced a lasting, natural-looking wave was regarded by Marcel as "one of the sensational revelations in the domain of *la coquetterie*"—as perhaps it was. It led eventually to the invention of the permanent by one of Marcel's neophytes, Karl Ludwig Nessler, the son of a German shoemaker, who plied his hairdressing trade first in Paris and changed his name to Charles Nestle.

By 1912, another shoemaker's son, Antek Cierplikowski of Poland, better known as Antoine, the name he adopted, was bobbing women's hair in his Paris salon where the walls were hung with paintings by his friend Modigliani. Antoine cut hair shorter and shorter until he developed the shingle-back boyish bob, which he first tried out in 1917 on Lady Wimborne, an English social leader. When Antoine came to America in the nineteen-twenties, he was astonished to find that a "battle of the bob"—rather like the more recent controversies over mini and midi skirts and over long hair for men—was in progress. Marshall Field & Co., the Chicago department store, was refusing to employ women with bobbed hair. In Paducah, Kentucky, five nurses were suspended from training school for cutting off their hair. And so it went.

Perhaps the most eccentric of all in the procession of great Paris *coiffeurs*, Antoine, who was also a sculptor, slept in a crystal coffin (to remind himself, he said, of the many things he still had to do "before the door closes on this side of the stage"). He wore dazzling white suits, lacquered his hair in gold or silver, and built a house made almost entirely of glass. He was an accomplished figure skater and when in New York would practice on the ice, in between hairdressing appointments, at Rockefeller Center.

The career of Antoine, whose clientele ranged from Mata Hari (he saw nothing wonderful in her) to all the royals of the day, reached its zenith in the nineteen-thirties when he made so much money that he had two airplanes. One was a French Farman, called *Victory of Samothrace*, and the other, purchased in America, a Stinson he christened *Okay* and took back to France lashed down to the boat deck of the S.S. *Normandie*.

On the day of her marriage to the former King Edward VIII, Antoine did Wallis Simpson's hair. She was then in the habit of having her hair dressed three times a day, which to Antoine did not seem overmuch, as another of his customers, Daisy, the Honourable Mrs. Reginald Fellowes, changed her hair style *ten* times a day. The biggest challenge of Antoine's working life seems to have been his search for the exact wash of color for the white hair of Lady Mendl, a miniature dynamo of the fashionable international coterie who weighed ninety pounds without her jewels. Antoine shut himself up in his atelier and tested every shade of pale blue he could come up with, yet none seemed right. At last he observed that the snow-white coat of his Russian borzoi, Da, could be the proving ground for his experiments. These resulted in the discovery of a tint of mauve, "not an old lady's mauve but the intangible shade of lilacs in shadow," which proved, in the end, to be as becoming to Lady Mendl as to Da.

Antoine, whose Paris operation has passed into other hands, retired to his native Sieradz at the age of eighty-seven, after having, in the words of Alexandre, "created the modern woman."

"We who are the apostles of the religion of *la coiffure* bow before him," Alexandre has said. "He was a prince, a grand prince. He respected the past but he saw that women of this century had need for a new life of beauty. There are so many kinds today: the rich I put in a class by themselves, because they know how to navigate. The chameleons change from one day to the next; the *papillons* rush from one salon to another, never sure of themselves; the *volcans*, who are the eccentrics, can get away with anything. Finally, there are the women who have the wisdom to live within the bounds of their own personalities and daily lives with equilibrium. Yet I find that too many women are still neglecting themselves and I suffer, Madame, I suffer when I see badly coiffed women on the streets. In the twentieth century, there is no reason for a woman to be unpleasing.

"Pride is evil and crushes everything. But vanity, Madame, is like love. We must all have vanity. It is simply a form of respect for oneself, *n'est-ce pas?*"

# An Evening at the de Gaulles'

---·❦·---

*It is ten o'clock, on the evening of October 25th, 1966. General Charles de Gaulle, President of the Republic of France, and Mme. de Gaulle are entertaining at the Élysée Palace. The occasion is a gala reception during the official visit to France of His Majesty Mahendra Bir Bikram Shah Deva, King of Nepal.*

---·❦·---

The procession of limousines turning off the Champs-Élysées into the Avenue de Marigny stops and starts as one of a cluster of police guards, their white raincoats glistening under the street lamp, steps off the curb from behind a barricade which spans the sidewalk and brings each car, in turn, to a halt. The barrier, which stretches across the wide wet pavement to a stone wall, is set up to ward off the curious. But there is no one at all peering past the barricade on this rainy night. The people in the cars have little to look at as they wait unless they happen to notice the spikes—the fence of spears outlined in the hazy darkness above the ledge of the wall against the somber silhouettes of the tall trees in the park inside.

Most of the cars in the line are the black Citroën, the DS Noire Model 21, a beetle-shaped vehicle with a rounded squat front. It is the approved automobile in French government circles. When seen in such mass formation, DS Noires resemble large shiny bugs forming an orderly file as they head for the nest.

As one's driver brakes before the police, one rolls down the back window and shows the head of the guards a white formal invitation—in smart Parisian parlance, *un bristol*.

"*Oui, Madame*," says the chief policeman, with a respectful smile and a courteous tip of the cap. Another of the guards glances toward the end of the insectlike line and speaks quietly into what he calls, as Frenchmen do, his "talkie-walkie." The chief policeman waves the chauffeur on.

The driver speeds up, swings to the right, enters a gate flanked by two mounted French Republican Guards, and whisks through an illuminated covered archway, past a double row of twenty-six Gardes Républicains, helmeted, booted, sabered, the red, white, and blue of their dress uniforms backed by a dark-green forest of topiary laurel trees. Through a second portal at the end of this passage, and the car moves into the Court of Honor.

The chauffeur, having been given a parking number, leaves. The occupant of the car allows a brief moment for an appreciation of the imposing square golden canopy which shields the entrance on ceremonial nights, then goes up the broad, red-carpeted steps which are bordered by ten more Republican guards in full fig. The soldiers hold their swords rigidly, but they permit their eyes to wander unmilitarily.

It is ten o'clock. General Charles de Gaulle, President of the Republic of France, and Mme. de Gaulle are entertaining this evening. Another guest—one of nearly twenty thousand received every year at their residence, the Élysée Palace—has arrived at the door.

The occasion is a gala reception during the official visit to France of His Majesty Mahendra Bir Bikram Shah Deva, King of Nepal, a country which contains the world's highest peak, Mount Everest. On the invitation, which is engraved in the flowing type called *l'Anglaise* favored by diplomats and high society, the name of the guest is painstakingly handwritten in matching script. The President and his wife "beg So-and-So to be so kind as to assist." "*Uniforme, habit* [French terminology for "white tie"], *décorations*" are indicated.

The King, whose nation has an interesting geographical location—it is bordered on the south by the Indian provinces of Uttar Pradesh and Bihar, on the east by West Bengal and the tiny Himalayan kingdom of Sikkim, and on the north for seven hundred miles by Communist China—was invited to France by President de Gaulle in January, 1966. King Mahendra is the thirty-fifth head of state, since the General took office in 1959, to be accorded the ritual of "the Official Visit," which lasts a minimum of three days and follows a customary pattern: greetings, meetings, lunches, dinners, receptions, and galas at the opera.

178

King Mahendra has been preceded on the scene by Prince Rainier of Monaco, the President of Peru, Nikita Khrushchev, the Presidents of Argentina and of Cameroon, the King of Thailand, the Presidents of Madagascar, of Gabon, and of Senegal, the King of the Belgians, the President of the United States of America, the Presidents of the Ivory Coast, of the Federal Republic of Germany, and of Niger, the Shah of Iran, the Presidents of Dahomey, of the Congo, of Chad, of Upper Volta, and of Mauritania, the King of Norway, the Presidents of Finland and of Mexico, the Kings of Sweden and of Morocco, the Grand Duchess of Luxembourg, the Presidents of Italy and of Togo, the Prince of Cambodia, the Kings of Jordan and of Denmark, the President of Lebanon, the King of Afghanistan, and the President of Chile, in the order of their appearance.

Although examples can easily be found in French history of other leaders who have enjoyed entertaining in style powerful or strategically situated national chiefs, President de Gaulle's record for splendorous hospitality is, numerically if not otherwise, clearly impressive. The Official Visits have contributed largely to his image as a lover of pomp and pageantry. Sometime in the course of the second dozen of these fêtes for heads of state, as the General's affection for magnificence and ceremony grew ever more apparent, Foreign Service Officers at the American Embassy in Paris were prompted to remark on the epidemic of "grandeuritis" sweeping the Élysée. Lately, the General has been taking more trips and thus has had less time to entertain at home. The King of Nepal is his first Official Visitor for 1966.

This morning, the day of his arrival, the forty-six-year-old King and his queen, Her Majesty Ratna Rajya Laxmi Devi Shah, thirty-eight, have embarked on a program that is by now a formula all too familiar to the French public. They have been met by the de Gaulles, the French Prime Minister, Minister for Foreign Affairs, and Minister of State at Orly Airport, where a Garde Républicaine band has rendered "La Marseillaise" and the Nepalese national anthem, "May Glory Crown Our Illustrious Sovereign." Following a suitable exchange of honors and compliments (President de Gaulle referred to Nepal as "one of those Himalayan countries, the most elevated in the world, which Nature renders epic," and King Mahendra said that he and his government "are certain that this visit will reinforce the good relations that exist between our two countries"), the party's cavalcade of fourteen DS Noires, a motorcycle escort, and the French Chief of Protocol, Bernard Durand, in the lead has sped from the airport to the Quai d'Orsay on the Left Bank of Paris—making a journey which ordinarily takes from forty minutes to an hour, depending upon the time of day, in exactly twenty minutes. The route from Orly is, of course, blocked off during their ride, and for the better part of the morning the dense traffic in nearby areas of the city comes to a complete standstill, to the exasperation of at least one taxi-driver. "Another *Visite!*" he says, rolling his eyes skyward. "Nepal. Now there's an important country. Who's ever heard of it? Where is it? I'll be here all day." His line of work makes him particularly sensitive to the critical Paris traffic situation, to which the conservative evening paper *Le Monde* has just devoted a full page, under the headline "PARIS, ROULE-T-IL?"—punning on the French title of *Is Paris Burning?*

After honors and introductions at the Foreign Ministry, King Mahendra and Queen Ratna have been installed in the usual apartments reserved for important state guests at the Quai d'Orsay. Later, there is some speculation as to why the de Gaulles have not put them up at the Grand Trianon of Versailles, which was recently restored and refurbished at a cost estimated at $10,000,000 for the express purpose of serving as guest quarters for visiting heads of state. "*Ah, le Roi de Nepal, vous savez . . .*" a member of the government says, with a shrug, when asked about this. It may be assumed that the Élysée is keeping the spectacular setting of Versailles on ice for a bit—perhaps for the next state visits, that of Soviet Premier Aleksei Kosygin in December or of the other Russian leaders, Leonid Brezhnev and Nikolai Podgorny, in April, 1967.

At 12:30 P.M., the King has had a private talk with the General, then had lunch at the Élysée (*déjeuner intime* for forty persons), after which he has been driven up the Champs-Élysées to pay his respects at the Tomb of the Unknown Soldier under the Arc de Triomphe. The avenue is decorated, as are all the government buildings of the city, with the French tricolor and the Nepalese flag, a double pennant in red bordered with blue, with a white quarter-moon on the top peak and a white sun in the center of the lower peak. There are 160 Nepalese banners on the lampposts of the Champs-Élysées, 200 on the Ministries, 45 at Orly Airport, not to mention others at the Place de la Concorde and on various buildings King Mahendra will visit. The flags are made in two sizes. The smaller, four feet long, cost twelve dollars apiece; the larger, three yards in length, thirty dollars each. Flags of nations whose leaders are likely to come for repeat visits are made, as are the French flags, of a long-lasting synthetic fabric that is twice as expensive as the wool bunting used for smaller countries, such as Nepal, whose banners are likely to be hung out only once. No one seems to know what disposition is made of the small nations' flags when the visits are over.

After the observances at the Arc de Triomphe, the visiting monarch has opened an exhibition of Nepalese art at the Guimet Museum, famous for its collection of Oriental sculpture, and has continued the diplomatic round at the formal five-o'clock reception (morning coat or uniform) called the Cercle Diplomatique, held at the Quai d'Orsay for Heads of Missions. The most elaborate event on the calendar for the day, however, is the evening state banquet for 180 at the Presidential Palace followed by a reception for 800, affairs of comparatively moderate size. Some dinners may be for 250 and receptions for 1,500.

The dinner guests have arrived at eight. They sit down in unison at a U-shaped table in the Grande Salle des Fêtes at eight-fifteen. The menu, which has taken the palace staff two days to prepare, is briskly served by footmen dressed *à la française*—white knee breeches, red waistcoat, blue jacket—and begins with Crème Germiny soup. Dishes are likely to be whisked away before the diner is certain he has finished with his course. The General is known not to like to dawdle over his food. The filets de soles Joinville, accompanied by a Riesling '64 wine, and the dindonneau de Bresse Châtelaine, washed down with Château Lafite-Rothschild '59, appear on one of the three great services of Sèvres china that belong to the Élysée—the Capraire, made in 1846. After a green salad, the foie gras des Landes, with Clos Vougeot '59 in the Baccarat crystal, is followed by a parfait Trianon served on the Sèvres Oiseaux plates, a series hand-painted with portraits of birds and created in 1858. If anyone drops a Oiseaux plate, it takes $140 to replace it, but the set is less dear than the third of the Sèvres services, Little Views of France, $160 a plate. In all, the individual dinner guest at the palace has china, silver, vermeil, and crystal worth some $600 set before him during an evening meal. Once in the annals of Élysée entertaining, a diner made off with two silver plates. They were retrieved, with tact. But no such incident is likely to occur tonight in the company of the President of the Assemblée Nationale, the Vice-President of the Sénat, the nineteen Cabinet Ministers, the ten counselors of state, the doyen of the Corps Diplomatique (the Papal Nuncio), and other high representatives of officialdom.

De Gaulle and Mahendra rise to make their respective toasts (with Veuve Cliquot Ponsardin '61 champagne). The General takes this opportunity to speak of "the external intervention in Southeast Asia and the odious conflict this intervention involves." The King, whose languages are English, Urdu, Hindi, and Sanskrit, responds in English through an interpreter with reference to his country's situation "between two friendly nations, India and China," and with emphasis on Nepal's pride in her traditions of "sovereign independence and territorial integrity."

As the dinner comes to an end, the people invited for the reception begin to drive into the Court of Honor. Many are Hindus wearing, like the King, a black topi on their heads and a black Western jacket over their white tunics and jodhpur trousers. Women gather their long skirts above their ankles before mounting the red-carpeted steps. All are momentarily dazzled by the flashes of prismatic light from the massive crystal chandelier that shine through the solid glass wall of the entrance hall that faces the court. Eighty lighting fixtures of similar proportions hang from the high ceilings of the Élysée and it takes two men eight days to clean each chandelier.

The transparent doors open. *Bristol* at the ready, the guest crosses the threshold. One of an efficient-looking team of officers in full dress, swags of red cord looped to the shoulders of their navy-blue uniforms and rows of multicolored medals across their chests, springs forward.

He says, *"Bonsoir, Madame,"* or *"Bonsoir, Monsieur,"* and scans the invitation to see whether or not there is a blue triangular mark at the top left corner. The guest with a blue-marked *bristol* is motioned to the right, for he is among the seven hundred persons invited who will not be introduced to the host or hostess or the guests of honor. The hundred bearers of unmarked invitations are sent to the left, the route to the receiving line. (Restricting the number of handshakes at Élysée functions is a relatively new practice which a French news magazine has seen as an indication that the seventy-six-year-old General now tries to conserve his energy.) Leaving their coats at a checkpoint behind the grand staircase where wraps are sent downstairs in a special dumbwaiter, guests tapped for presentation are directed to the corridor at the left of the stairs.

All the semipublic social events at the Élysée are held in the rooms on the ground floor, a chain of salons that continue along the back façade of the palace and face an enormous park. As the reception progresses,

182

the stream of traffic moves to the right through these salons and is prodded along by a crew of palace factotums. It is in the first of these rooms, the Salon of the Portraits, a mélange of eighteenth-century and First and Second Empire décor, that guests who will be formally received take their places in line. While waiting, they have a view through the massive French windows of the arbored rose garden to the left and the swans on the lake at the foot of the park, floodlit for the evening's festivities. Every day, the President and Mme. de Gaulle take a turn in the park, where they are observed only by a patrol of police inspectors (there are twenty-five on the palace grounds) or, on occasion, the telephoto lens of an enterprising photographer from *Paris-Match* who has managed to find a perch on a neighboring rooftop.

On the approach to the receiving line, guests next enter the Hémicycle Salon—Savonnerie rug, gold-and-white carved paneled walls. The Marquise de Pompadour, a mistress of Louis XV, slept here. She was one of the historic figures who have occupied the palace, which dates to 1718, when it was constructed by a courtier of Louis XV, Henri de la Tour d'Auvergne, the Comte d'Évreux, who had a rich wife. Napoleon I lost his throne at the Élysée. He signed the order of abdication in the palace the day after the Battle of Waterloo. Earlier, Josephine lost Napoleon and is supposed to have cried a lot in one of the rooms on the floor above, the Salon d'Argent. Most of the large "N" monograms in the corners of the ceilings of the *rez-de-chaussée* salons were put there, however, by Louis-Napoleon Bonaparte, who pulled off his coup d'état at the Élysée and who, with the Empress Eugénie, gave brilliant palace parties in the latter part of the nineteenth century. De Gaulle is the seventeenth of a succession of French Presidents since Napoleon III to have used the building as a residence.

When the guest arrives at the door leading to the Salon des Ambassadeurs, he surrenders his invitation. The noise of conversation in the crowded Hémicycle is considerable. A person may fail to recognize his own name when it is called out by the announcing usher, whose title, "Aboyeur-Huissier," means "Barker-Usher" and who takes his cues from M. Durand, the Chief of Protocol. An imperious man resplendent in the traditional ambassadorial uniform (black, covered with scrolls of golden embroidery) of Ministre Plénipotentiaire which is conserved for his office, M. Durand is posted at the right of the door.

As he steps into the relative quiet of the Salon des Ambassadeurs the guest is suddenly alone with President de Gaulle, King Mahendra, Queen Ratna, Mme. de Gaulle, the announcing usher, the Chief of Protocol, two interpreters, and, at a discreet distance, a few bodyguards. Benign and genial, the General, garbed in his midnight-blue Army dress uniform with pearl-gray waistcoat, is bathed in rays of golden light from the monumental chandelier overhead. His responses are cordial. They range from the terse *"Monsieur,"* to the "Ah! *Untel!* Delighted to see you!" to a quick exchange of phrases with a notable de Gaulle already knows. Compliments to pretty women may begin with the simple, *"Mes hommages, Madame,"* and flower into "Your grace honors this ancient house, Madame." At an intimate Élysée dinner for forty, a beautiful woman recalls, de Gaulle reached into his pocket, put on his powerful spectacles, and looked her up and down when she was introduced to him, but she was exceptionally striking and the circumstances relatively informal.

King Mahendra, whose 10,000,000 subjects regard him as an incarnation of the Hindu god Vishnu, rarely asks for the services of the interpreter behind him and speaks to the guests with agreeable restraint. Men go through the motions of hand-kissing without actually kissing the hands of Queen Ratna and Mme. de Gaulle. Many of the women curtsey to both ladies. The Queen, like her husband, wears sober black-rimmed glasses, but her smile is warm and her native dress (a rose-red sari embroidered in silver) and royal jewels (a pearl-drop diamond necklace and matching earrings) far from severe.

Mme. de Gaulle, who often used to frown in public, looks radiant and gracious in the dark-green moiré dress designed by her couturier Jacques Heim. Her graying brown hair is closely cut at the back of the neck and dressed in set waves. The freshness of her complexion is extraordinarily youthful for a woman of sixty-six years. By nature of a character typical of many French middle-class women who are frugal, who have an unshakable respect for tradition, a strong sense of order and organization, and who uphold the old established moral virtues, Mme. de Gaulle is deeply religious. She has the reputation of being the regime's Mrs. Grundy and is widely considered to be the unofficial censor who has brought about the banning of certain books, plays, and films in France. She is thus blamed for having taken much of the fun out of life in a city once known as Gay Paree. An Army wife for forty-five years, she runs the palace staff of a hundred and sixty with dispatch. The turnover in pastry cooks is supposed to be rather high. Much of the personnel is recruited from the military. The chef comes from the merchant marine. Mme. de Gaulle has never granted an interview or posed for an official photograph. She is an accomplished knitter. She once said that her ideal wardrobe was two black dresses: "One on my back and one in the closet." Those days are over. She has tweezed her eyebrows and learned to use lipstick. Since she is above all what an acquaintance describes as "a woman of duty," she now does her best to act the part of the First Lady of France by being well-dressed and by overcoming her innate shyness. She is an extremely dignified person but has none of the regal comportment of her husband.

An assistant Chief of Protocol overseeing the exit from the receiving line hurries the guests out with sweeping gestures toward the adjacent antichamber, the Salon des Aides de Camp. Hastening past, a guest is poked in the eye by a flower piece bristling with gladioli. Seated near the door in rapt conversation with a lady is the stout, sixty-seven-year-old playwright Marcel Achard, one of the members of the venerated Académie Française who are present; he is wearing the ornate attire in which Academicians appear for ceremonies—a swallow-tail coat embellished with elaborate designs of green, gold, and white silk. The colors match the medal of Officer of the Légion d'Honneur which hangs from a red ribbon on his chest. The protocol man notices him and tells him to get up, saying, "The passage must be kept clear." Dissembling their annoyance, Achard and his companion move on. The young footmen in their tricolor livery are passing silver trays of American, English, and French cigarettes. Mme. Hervé Alphand, wife of the former Ambassador at Washington, who herself works as *directrice* of the *haute couture* house of Paris designer Pierre Cardin, a proponent of miniskirts and futuristic men's wear, chats smoothly with a functionary in a corner. There are few women of fashion at this gathering, and Mme. Alphand—however subdued she may be in elegant, unobtrusive black, with only one shoulder bared—stands out.

Her carefully groomed husband, now Secretary-General of the Ministry of Foreign Affairs, is decorated with the large badge of Commander of the Légion d'Honneur. It is worn on a wide red ribbon around the neck. "Virtually obligatory at the Élysée," notes a palace aide, pointing out that two-thirds of the men in the room wear the same decoration. "But the Cross of the Liberation—bronze with black Cross of Lorraine, green and black ribbon—is also, of course, most acceptable."

In the next room—the lovely gold-and-white Salon Murat, which has wall paintings of Rome and of a château in Alsace—a black-garbed *huissier*, the long silver chain of his office strung around his neck, urges the company ahead into the vast Salons des Fêtes. He gives directional signals by waving his white-gloved hand in swooping motions, in the manner of a courtier on the stage at the Comédie-Française. Celebrities, who ignore his efforts to keep the traffic circulating, pause for minutes of conversation, while other guests amuse themselves by identifying the celebrities and by counting decorations.

The great historian, biographer, and *Académicien* André Maurois is remarked upon because he has chosen to wear merely a broad red sash across his chest, attaching his Grand Cross of the Legion of Honor to a large red bow on his hip, and has left his other medals at home. The devout Gaullist writer and Nobel Prize winner François Mauriac, writer Joseph Kessel, playwright Marcel Pagnol, film director René Clair and the Nobel Prize–winning physicist Louis, Duc de Broglie, are other Académie Française members invited. Among the best-decorated men present, Prince Guy de Polignac is given high marks for distinction, for, although only an Officer of the Legion of Honor, he holds four different Great Crosses, even if they are not French, and is the only man in the assembly who has the Grand Cross of the Order of Malta hanging from his neck.

Those well versed in medals are stumped when Foreign Minister Maurice Couve de Murville comes in wearing a wine-colored ribbon about his neck with an unfamiliar order hanging from it. He retires to the end of the salon to confer with a *député* next to a priceless table fashioned entirely of Sèvres porcelain and ormolu. It is a prize piece among many antiques in the palace. All Élysée furniture belongs to the French people and is administered and cared for by the nation's storage warehouse, the Mobilier National. However, the majority of French people do not see these Élysée treasures. There are no public tours of the palace. Prime Minister Georges Pompidou, exuding health and well-being, passes through, his white shirt front crossed with a huge sash of vivid blue with green borders. "Nepalese orders," explains the palace aide. "They got those this afternoon and naturally they put them on this evening. Couve de Murville is now a Commander of the Right Hand of the Gurkha. Pompidou has the Great Cross of the Three Divine Powers, but please do not ask me what they are."

The black-clad usher is intensifying his efforts to get the crowd to move ahead and the rhythm of his arm movements is gaining speed. "If you want to have a good look at the main event," says the aide's wife, "the best spot is near the potted plants on the edge of the winter garden."

The Salons des Fêtes, an ensemble of three barn-sized halls and connected galleries, are an appendage of the Élysée built in 1888, and they reflect the flamboyant taste of that period. The big state dinners are given here, and when they are over the palace staff stacks the precious plates, crystal, and silverware, strips off the Porthault linens, and wheels the lot away with well-oiled precision in seventeen minutes flat. After that, another crew moves in and sets up three huge buffets for the reception. Some of the help are "*les extras*" hired from outside. *Un extra* gets around a great deal in the *haut monde* and is usually a terrible snob. He always carries his dress suit, gloves, and his own knife and ice pick in a valise. He does not necessarily relish being assigned to the Presidential palace, where the pace is fast. "Also," one of them has said, "it offends our dignity. They search our bags."

A third of the floor space of the immense winter garden of the Salons des Fêtes is taken up with a sixty-piece orchestra of the Garde Républicain, manfully playing Rossini's Overture to "*La Pie Voleuse*" (*The Thieving Magpie*), but only a note or two can be heard over the chatter of a thousand voices. The walls are draped with twenty-four of the seventy-one splendid Gobelins tapestries housed in the Élysée. Three of the Gobelins in the Salons des Fêtes depict the story of Esther and are thought by experts to be particularly fine. The Gobelins that hangs in de Gaulle's office, the Salon Doré, located directly above the Salon des Ambassadeurs and much the handsomest room in the house, belongs to another series of tapestries and shows "Don Quixote Being Cured of His Madness by Wisdom."

The passage into the Salons des Fêtes is cleared. The nine hundred and eighty guests break apart instinctively, leaving a broad lane in the center of the gray carpet. From the rustle of activity in the rooms beyond the Salon Murat, it is evident that the dramatic peak of the soirée is about to be reached.

With stately tread, through the portals of the winter garden, come four ushers, two by two, solemn-faced, their silver chains glinting against their black uniforms. Following them, solo, walks the Chief of Protocol, his looks forbidding, his gait measured, the intricate gold braid curlicues of his uniform redolent of another century. He carries a flattened bicorne edged with white feathers in his left hand and appears to use a staff with his right. Behind him, the two chiefs of state, King Mahendra to de Gaulle's right, are somewhat more relaxed. Across the General's chest is a wide yellow ribbon, also worn by Queen Ratna, who is paired off in the procession with Mme. de Gaulle. "The Great Cross of Ojaswirajanya," murmurs the palace aide. "Reserved for Heads of State. Please do not ask me what Ojaswirajanya means."

Since the retinue does all but cry, "Make way . . ." as the party continues its march down the length of the Grande Salle des Fêtes where the company breaks ranks at the buffet, it is difficult not to be reminded of La Gloire and stirring moments in France's monarchal past. The General's likeness to certain caricatures of himself is amazingly accurate. Seeing him on display automatically brings to mind the drawings which show him as "the Sun King"—Louis XIV—and which appear in the French satirical weekly *Le Canard Enchaîné*, with a column, written in the eighteenth-century manner, by André Ribaud. At the beginning of the de Gaulle regime, there were a number of humorous stories and anecdotes about the President and his wife, who is popularly known as Tante Yvonne. M. Ribaud was even invited, after the publication of his two books *The Court* and *The King*, which travestied the administration, to a cocktail reception at the Élysée where he was introduced to the General. As the government settled in, the atmosphere changed. Now, as more than one Frenchman has put it, "The joke is over." Entertainers who do topical monologues in Paris nightspots hardly ever allude to de Gaulle. Many are aware that since the President has been in power, Article No. 26 of an appendix of the legal code, which makes it a penal offense to insult the Chief of State and which was rarely put into effect before 1959, has been the infraction cited in some three hundred arrests.

On this particular occasion, the General is charming and seems almost approachable as he stands at ease in the Grande Salle under the eight mammoth crystal and bronze *doré* chandeliers, each of which has fifty-six lights. The guests who have never seen him before at close range form a circle a few yards back from his party, where they stand and stare in open curiosity. The form for anyone who wishes to speak to him is, first, to be already acquainted with him and, second, to make the request for an audience to the Chief of Protocol. When he terminates an interview, de Gaulle sometimes pats a man's shoulder in grandfatherly fashion even if the man is almost the same age as himself.

The Queen and Mme. de Gaulle do not eat or drink anything from the buffet. Only one woman in the congregation rushes up to speak to the President's wife and she is affably received. A lady in the crowd nearby, who is identified on the guest list as a *"personnalité diverse,"* mentions to a British friend that the de Gaulles have been married since 1921 and that Mme. de Gaulle is her husband's constant companion. "You know the story Cecil Beaton tells about Lady Churchill sitting next to the General at luncheon," says the Englishman in an undertone. "There were frequent long silences during which she was thinking about the kind of life Mme. de Gaulle must lead. Suddenly the General said to her, *'Vous savez, Madame,* it must be very difficult, being the wife of Mr. Churchill.'"

The hour is 11:25 P.M. The King tells the Chief of Protocol that he wishes to leave. Once again, the crowd divides into two parts to make a passageway as the official party falls into formation. The musicians sound the opening notes of Liszt's Hungarian Rhapsody No. 2. Many of the guests strain for a final view as the procession leaves the halls. Others do not bother to look up, too engrossed in their own conversations.

There is a last movement toward the buffets, where few of the three thousand sandwiches and canapés are left but most of the five thousand petits fours remain uneaten, arranged in tidy pink pyramids on a lesser service of Sèvres china with a deep blue-and-gold border. "No caviar," says a visiting journalist from Moscow, accepting a glass of champagne. "No Scotch," notes the Englishman, choosing a brandy-and-soda instead. "Only French drinks served here. House rule," says an editor of *Paris-Match.*

Foreign Minister Couve de Murville is seated on a banquette against the wall, still talking animatedly with the same *député,* but most of the rest of the top-echelon of the hierarchy have already said good night. The orchestra begins to play *Eine Kleine Nachtmusik.* The rooms of the Salons des Fêtes empty and the guests converge in the main entrance hall where a radiophone operator signals their chauffeurs and another guard announces the numbers of the cars as they drive up to the red-carpeted steps. The hundred and ten clocks of the Palais de l'Élysée strike midnight. Another grand performance is over.

# Longchamp, the Bois, and the Arc de Triomphe

---

"By its conformation, its dimensions, its décor of greenery, and its vista of hills, Longchamp, even in the opinion of strangers, is the most beautiful racecourse in the entire world."

---

Since the time when the Romans came down the river Seine and established on its banks a community called Lutetia, Paris has had many troubadours, who have grown lyrical over most, if not quite all, of its celebrated aspects: its churches, its architecture, its rooftops, its rabble (so memorably etched by the truly unforgettable voice of Edith Piaf), its soft light—an ideal setting, it seems, for young lovers—even its bookstalls on the Seine. But not one minnesinger, to my knowledge, has yet limned the praises of one of the city's most noteworthy topographical features—the Bois de Boulogne, a remarkable area unequaled, in its size and variety of activities, by any similar tract in a national capital anywhere in the world.

The Bois, which lies on the western edge of Paris, comprises an expanse of 865 hectares (2,137.415 acres) in its present dimensions and includes within its boundaries such diverse attractions as the Pavillon de Bagatelle, built by the Comte d'Artois in sixty-four days to win a bet with Marie-Antoinette that he could have it constructed in that time; nine sizable *maisons* devoted to dining or banqueting, plus a tenth which includes a restaurant along with its bowling facilities; a zoo; two covered riding rings; a number of private clubs; a flower garden featuring championship roses; a miniature railroad, which accommodates adult passengers as well as children; and the picturesque hippodromes of Longchamp and Auteuil.

The Bois is a magnificent, impeccably ordered, litter-free park on the edge of a crowded metropolis of nearly three million. There one may enjoy the spectacle of Parisians jogging, riding horseback on its many trails, rowing on its lakes, playing *pétanque* (a wide-open game related to *boule*) or bowling on the green, playing football (soccer), tennis, and volleyball, shooting clay pigeons, fishing in its several lakes, swimming in its *piscines*, or simply lying in the sun.

Napoleon III recognized the need for such a playground and had the land set aside for that purpose in 1852, when it officially became part of the capital. Parisians rich and poor have been everlastingly grateful.

Before it became the citizens' favored place for relaxing, the Bois had been a royal domain, a regal forest preserve dedicated to the royal hunt, where bear, deer, wolves, and wild boar were the quarry. Today, even the last of the deer have disappeared, coincident with the increase in the number of avenues for automobilists—totaling 70 kilometers in length —that crisscross the Bois; only 600 pheasants, an undetermined number of ducks, 24 swans, and some small four-footed animals remain, impervious to the traffic noise, which penetrates the otherwise sedate calm of this Parisian retreat.

Keeping the birds company, the only other inhabitants of the Bois are a few zoo attendants, 25 *gardiens* (20 *gardes des promenades*, and 5 *forestiers*, who care for the birds, animals, and the many varieties of trees) living with their dogs in small gatehouses, and—along its northern border but inside the Bois—a handful of private residents, including the Duchess of Windsor, a confirmed Bois-lover.

The earliest written record relating to the area that is now the Bois de Boulogne is a charter signed by Chilpéric II at Compiègne in 717, whereby he gave to the abbey of Saint-Denis the forest of Rouvray, situated in "le Parisis, au bord de la Seine."

There, along the river in a clearing called *longus campus* (later Longchamp), Isabelle, sister of Saint Louis, founded, in 1255, a "monastery for women"; the earliest nuns were called the Minor Sisters Enclosed by the Humility of Our Lady, which subsequently became shortened to the Order of Sainte Claire. Isabelle retired to the institution she founded and died, in 1269, without a hint of the scandals that were to hang over the

194

convent like the November morning mist that settles over the Bois. References to the state of morals among the nuns were made more and more openly; finally, in 1652, Saint Vincent de Paul wrote to Cardinal Mazarin: "It is certain that, in the last two hundred years, this monastery has moved toward the total ruin of discipline and the depravity of morals; its parlors are open to anyone, even young people without parents; the nuns wear immodest clothing." While no contemporary fashion writer was ever on hand to describe the nuns' outfits or their origins, it is possible that the abandoned atmosphere may have dated back to the time when Superior Catherine of Verdun, a young nun of twenty-two, became the mistress of Henri IV. In 1727, when an accomplished opera singer, Mlle. Le Maure, retired to the convent, many came to hear her sing, especially during Holy Week; one visitor commented on the talking and laughing, and remarked, "A girl taking up a collection was seen there in an attire hardly intended to stir up devotion."

"*L'amour*," as M. Jean Rives, *ingénieur de travaux de la ville de Paris*, put it recently, "has always been a part of the Bois." After the goings-on at the "monastery," there was the Comte d'Artois and his bagatelle, a monument to the art of love and the craft of debauchery. (Though the Comte d'Artois won his bet of 100,000 livres, it cost him 1,200,000 to do it, thanks to the employment of nine hundred workers laboring day and night to meet his deadline.) La Folie d'Artois, as it came to be called, was also the scene of a series of elaborate fêtes, often given by the aristocratic mistresses who were installed there from time to time.

The Bois, with its expanse of wooded terrain and cozy secluded open patches tucked away in its interior, was an ideal location for *l'amour*, as well as for the conduct of duels, which often involved personalities prominent in the worlds of the court, diplomacy, finance, and the arts—all usually concerned in one way or another with love, in its various guises. One match, performed with épées, featured two elegant adversaries, a Frenchwoman and a Polish lady, both in love with an opera singer. Another, with pistols as weapons, paired a Mme. Théodore, a dancer, and a Mlle. Beaumesnil, a singer at the Opéra, intent on resolving their annoyance with each other. The duel was interrupted by the arrival of the Opéra's *chef d'orchestre*, who threw himself between the combatants and put an end to the argument. (The Paris Opéra of that time was a breeding ground of seething emotions.) The Comte d'Artois also had his hostile moments in the Bois, and the Duc de Bourbon was a regular at the dueling grounds, with a reputation for overdoing things a bit.

Though the duelists, like the deer, have disappeared, the Bois still seems to induce thoughts of love in its partisans. But M. Rives, who serves as a kind of overseer of the domain, has other matters of more immediate concern than the current state of *l'amour* in his district. For one thing, a section of a new Boulevard Périphérique, which will encircle Paris without resorting to the employment of one traffic light, is being constructed near its eastern extremity, passing under the paddock of the Auteuil racecourse and through fifteen hectares of the Bois's territory, necessitating the felling of six thousand trees. (However, the Bois has a self-renewal program involving a number of nurseries: all types of trees in the Bois are grown on a graduated basis, with each cycle geared for a twenty-year span.) For another, a minority group is demanding permission for the use of water pedal boats on the Lac Inférieur, and this has already caused a storm of protests from traditionalists, who believe in the inviolability of rowboats.

Security in the Bois has been controlled by Parisian police since 1929—four years after it was incorporated into the capital's fashionable 16th *arrondissement*; otherwise, for all practical purposes the Bois is virtually an autonomous preserve, with its own special rules and regulations. Even responsibility for the operation of the Stade Roland Garros, where championship tennis matches are held, lies with the administration of the Bois, in spite of the fact that the stadium is actually situated just outside the Bois.

For most Parisians, the Bois is a center for the sportive—for those who prefer to indulge actively in games like football or tennis—as well as for the spectator type. For the former, the favorite club in the Bois—or, for that matter, in Paris—is the Racing, which provides numerous tennis courts and an Olympic-size pool. For both participant and spectator there are Le Polo Paris, where international matches are sometimes held, and Le Cercle Hippique du Touring Club et Le Cercle Hippique de Paris, and Le Cercle de l'Étrier—show rings for jumping horses and their riders.

For those who elect to find their sport in watching horses competing in races on the flat and over obstacles, the Bois is really the hub of the universe. The very best events in Europe of both types are contested in two of the most attractive hippodromes in the world—Longchamp and Auteuil, both situated in the Bois, where the first equine test of speed, on

May 15, 1651, matched horses ridden by the Prince d'Harcourt on his own steed and by Le Plessis du Vernet, master of a riding academy, for the Duc de Joyeuse, before a group of spectators including a number of persons from the court, for a stake of a thousand écus.

Most French authorities on the subject consider the first horse race in their country the one that pitted horses representing King Charles VI and his brother, the Duc de Touraine, in 1389. Some feel the honor of the first such contest should go to the much earlier race won by the legendary Bayard, an event arranged by Charlemagne. But the first really organized racing in France dates from the reign of Louis XIV, and it was not until the days of Louis XVI's rule that serious attempts were made to bring French racing to the level of the British, where thoroughbred racing was already an established sport.

With the enthusiastic support of the Comte d'Artois, brother of the King and himself the future Charles X, and the Duc de Chartres, later to become the Duc d'Orléans and still later Louis-Philippe, French horsemen of the day imported English thoroughbreds, English training techniques, and in fact a number of English trainers themselves. A proper course was created on the plain of the Sablons, near what is now the northern extremity of the Bois; another was constructed at Fontainebleau; and a third at Vincennes, on the eastern edge of Paris.

The Revolution did not succeed in damping the spirits of the French racing addicts: in the Champ-de-Mars, which today stretches like a lush green carpet between the Tour Eiffel and the École Militaire, three concentric tracks were arranged—one in the center for foot races featuring human runners, another for horse racing, and an outer *piste* for chariot races, all events taking place simultaneously.

In some quarters, credit for the inauguration of French horse racing is given not to Charlemagne or Louis XVI but to Napoleon, who issued a series of decrees regulating the sport similar to his dicta on every imaginable subject relating to life in France. During the Restoration, a French Stud Book was begun, and all thoroughbreds imported from England or born in France were registered; many were descended from the three venerated stallions who founded, in large measure, the thoroughbred line: Byerly Turk, Darley Arabian, and Godolphin Arabian.

The definition of a French thoroughbred adopted by the Société d'Encouragement pour l'Amélioration des Races de Chevaux en France, which was formed in 1833 to administer French horse racing, refers to horses and mares born and raised in France "and born of a mare and stallion whose genealogy is recorded in the English Stud Book or who would be themselves the products of ancestors whose names would be found there." Another definition, in the Règlement of 1832, admits also horses and mares descending in a straight line and without mixture of sire and dam from Arab, Berber, Turk, or Persian breeds.

The president of the committee which founded the Société d'Encouragement was Lord Henry Seymour, a French-born Englishman, who provided the impetus for the start of classic French thoroughbred horse racing in Chantilly, north of Paris, where the Prix du Jockey Club (known as the French Derby) and the Prix de Diane were first contested, the former in 1836 and the latter, a classic race for three-year-old fillies, seven years later. Lord Seymour, along with the Comte de Cambis and Messieurs de Normandie, Fasquel, and Charles Laffitte, was responsible for the selection of the terrain at Chantilly and for the planning of the tracks and the hippodrome itself. It is he who is most often referred to as the actual father of French horse racing.

When, a score of years later, it became evident that French horse racing could no longer be confined to its Cantilien heath, it was the Duc de Morny, half brother and strong right hand of the Emperor Napoleon III and soon to be the founder of the elegant resort of Deauville, who moved firmly forward with the plan for a hippodrome in the Bois de Boulogne. A fifteen-member committee, including Morny and the Barons de la Rochette and Nathaniel de Rothschild, the Comte Henri Greffulhe, and M. Laffitte, worked unremittingly in securing the necessary permissions and finance, and on April 26, 1857, the first race at the new hippodrome called Longchamp was run.

It was a comfortable period dedicated to luxury for those with the means to enjoy life as *le gratin bien lavé* of the mid-nineteenth century believed it should be lived. It was a time when many Parisians and Parisiennes, both in the Bois and in the city proper, were *à cheval*; a great many more of the capital's populace, while not mounted, were horse-drawn.

In the Bois, especially in the morning, there were more equestrians than pedestrians. And the etiquette that prevailed was just as inflexible as that of a formal dinner party. The talented chronicler Crafty, in his definitive work of text and drawings, *Paris à Cheval*, published in Paris in 1884, describes the scene—a typical *matin* in the Bois: "*Voici, comme*

198

*toujours, au nombre des premières arrivées madame la duchesse d'——
. . . aussi complètement chez elle sur sa selle que dans son salon; elle
fait aux cavaliers qui la croisent les honneurs du Bois, en leur laissant le
passage libre par une volte ou un changement de main aussi facilement
exécutés que le geste par lequel une maîtresse de maison indique un
siège à un visiteur.*" ("Here, as always, among the first arrivals, is Madame
la Duchesse d'—— . . . as completely at home in her saddle as in her
salon; she accords to the horsemen who cross her path the courtesies
of the Bois, leaving them a free passage by a change of course or a wave
of the hand as easily executed as the gesture by which a mistress of the
house indicates a chair to a visitor.")

On an important race day, the parade through the Bois included a
wide assortment of vehicles. "*Toutes les voitures connues,*" wrote Crafty,
"*sont représentées dans ce défilé précipité. Il y a de tout: des fiacres, des
omnibus à quatre et à cinq chevaux, des mails, des coupés, des carts, des
ducs, des poneys-chaises, et des vélocipèdes.*" ("All known carriages are
represented in this headlong parade. There are all types: hackney carriages,
coaches with four and five horses, mail coaches, coupés, carts, pony carts,
and velocipedes.")

It had not been too long, Crafty observes, since one had said of a man
who passed most of his time following the races, "He does nothing."
But at the time of writing his book the position had changed; then one
said, "He is one of the busiest men you will find. He doesn't miss a single
race." For, he adds, to follow the races conscientiously one must forgo
vacations, and not pass one day in idleness.

The leading historian of French thoroughbred racing of the day,
Henry Lee, of English origin but resident in France and writing in the
language of his adopted country, stated flatly that the period beginning
with the opening of Longchamp in 1857 and extending to the start of
the Franco-Prussian War in 1870 was incontestably the most brilliant
in the history of French racing. This opinion was made from the vantage
point of 1913, as he finished his masterwork, for publication the following
year in Paris, *Historique des Courses de Chevaux de l'Antiquité à Ce
Jour.*

"An enormous crowd of the curious," he wrote, of the opening day,
"invaded the Bois de Boulogne in inclement weather attracted by the
desire to see the new 'promenade' which was being offered to Parisians."
Seven hundred *voitures,* including eleven with four horses, two hundred

and fifty cavaliers, and some twelve thousand spectators on foot turned out for the inauguration ceremonies and for the five-race program.

Lee found the scene quite intoxicating: *"Par sa conformation, ses dimensions, son décor de verdure et son horizon de coteaux, Longchamp, de l'avis même des étrangers, est le plus beau champ de courses du monde entier. Il n'en est aucun qui soit plus grandiose et plus plaisant, tout à la fois; aucun, où le spectateur puisse mieux suivre toutes les péripéties d'une course.*

*"La piste fût jugée des plus élastiques, les tribunes des plus confortables et l'installation générale parfaite. . . ."*

("By its conformation, its dimensions, its décor of greenery, and its vista of hills, Longchamp, even in the opinion of strangers, is the most beautiful racecourse in the entire world. There is no other that is grander or more pleasant, at the same time; none, where the spectator can better follow the complete progress of a race.

"The track has been judged the most resilient, the stand the most comfortable, and the total installation in general perfect. . . .")

Among the notable spectators on that red-letter day whose names Lee jotted down for his account of the inauguration were: Jérôme Bonaparte, King of Westphalia, and his son the Prince Napoleon, representing the Emperor (Napoleon III) and Empress (Eugénie)—accompanied by the Prince of Nassau and escorted by the Prince Murat; Maréchal Magnan; the Duc de Morny, then president of the legislative corps; Achille Fould, Minister of Finance; M. Rouher, Minister of Agriculture and Commerce; M. Baroche, president of the Council of State; and the Prefects of the *département* of the Seine, and of the Police. In a five-horse field, Éclaireur, a four-year-old owned by M. Auguste Lupin, beat out Miss Gladiator, a five-year-old mare, collecting the winner's prize of 1,000 francs in La Bourse, and a new era in French thoroughbred racing was begun.

In the early years, Longchamp flirted with the idea of punctuating its programs with hurdles races, but this romance lasted only a few seasons.

During those memorable years before the start of the war in 1870, a series of classic races for three-year-olds was instituted—among them the Prix Greffulhe, Hocquart, Daru, Noailles, and the Grand Prix de Paris, all contested today as high spots in Longchamp's spring meeting. (In addition, a Grand Prix de l'Empereur and a Grand Prix de l'Impératrice, both for four-year-olds and up, were organized in honor of Longchamp's royal supporters.)

This radiant span of years was capped by the Exposition Universelle in 1867, the "most brilliant year of the Second Empire," according to Lee. Kings and sovereigns were present in the glittering crowds that attended Longchamp's *réunions*, including the Emperor of Russia, who attended the Grand Prix de Paris of that year.

The change was swift. Late in 1870, the hippodromes were closed and French horses of any promise were sent abroad, chiefly to England; the following year Longchamp was sacked and destroyed by the invading Germans. The burgeoning sport of thoroughbred racing was abruptly nipped, and the Société d'Encouragement took over the administration of breeding in the beleaguered nation.

Following the end of the war, the sport of kings slowly recovered; some unforgettable names were inscribed on the growing list of truly great horses, after Gladiateur: Boïard, Flageolet, and Franc-Tireur among them.

The founding members of the Société d'Encouragement died in the latter years of the century, but Longchamp continued to hold its place as the *premier hippodrome* in France. In 1898, its *tribunes* were heightened, its homestretch widened, and its grandstand area beautified.

The hippodrome and its partisans flourished until another, nearly fatal shock occasioned by the onset of the First World War. French racing and breeding did not recover from this second serious blow until well after the Armistice, when the directors of the Société d'Encouragement organized a new important weight-for-age race called the Prix de l'Arc de Triomphe. It was felt by French racing authorities that such a race was needed to help re-establish the prestige of French breeding, which had suffered badly during World War I.

The Arc, as it came to be known, has won its acceptance as the world's top thoroughbred test in a comparatively short time, having been run for the first time in its present incarnation in 1920, when it carried a modest purse of 200,425 francs, or $13,091. (The title of the race was appropriated from a pre-World War I claiming race of that name, with a winner's prize of 5,000 francs.) An English horse, Comrade, bearing the French silks of M. Évremond de Saint-Alary, won the first edition of this new international weight-for-age race.

Through the years that followed, the equine élite of Europe, and subsequently of the United States as well, were drawn more and more frequently to this popular race, whose conditions gave each entrant a fair chance to prove its worth. (All three-year-old colts carry 55½ kilograms, three-year-old fillies 54, older horses 60, mares 58½.)

In its fifty runnings to date, six fillies have led the way to the finish, one—Corrida—repeating her victory the following year. The names of some of the world's greatest thoroughbreds are listed on the Arc's roster of winners: Ribot (two victories), Tantième (two), Ballymoss, St. Crespin, Exbury, Sea Bird, Vaguely Noble, and Sassafras, among recent winners. The victory assured their value at stud, and many in the fraternity of Arc winners became celebrated as stallions. It need hardly be added that a foal sired by an Arc champion will bring top money in the sales ring.

The annual classic, run on the first Sunday of October, was canceled twice, in 1939 and '40, at the outset of World War II in Europe. It was resumed in 1941, but in 1943 and '44, Longchamp having been closed by the Germans, it was transferred to Le Tremblay racecourse, just east of Paris.

The German occupation provided a new setback to the steady advances in the quality of French thoroughbred stock and supplied a few unexpected problems for the keepers of the French Stud Book. Since the Germans are themselves enthusiastic horsemen, it was no surprise when they began to look into the operation of French racing, and more particularly into the state of the French studs. Many of the world's outstanding sires and dams were still in residence—some had been sent out of the country before the arrival of the German armies—and the opportunity to employ these prized bloodlines to improve the native stock in Germany was irresistible.

In most cases, German breeders and thoroughbred enthusiasts were quite correct with their conquered French counterparts, although Jewish proprietors fared badly—there are unconfirmed stories about changing registrations to disguise the identities of the best horses. There were those who were not so correct, notably a certain Dr. Joseph Pulte, an officer who was intent on establishing a stud of grandiose proportions at Altefeld for the German Army. After carefully studying French breeding records, he took to paying unannounced visits to various prominent French *haras* and demanding that the best stallions and mares be sold to him for ridiculously low prices (often no more than 600,000 anciens francs— $1,200—for stallions and 60,000 for mares). When he was refused by some courageous French breeders, he invariably seized the desired animals anyway, using his German Army connection as authority.

Perhaps the most notorious case was that of the stallion Pharis, winner of the Prix Noailles, Prix du Jockey Club, and the Grand Prix de Paris before his career was cut short by the fortunes of war, and subsequently a sire who became a legend. Dr. Pulte paid one of his calls on Marcel Boussac, a French textile industrialist and proprietor of the Haras de Fresnay-le-Buffard in Normandy and today the president of the Société d'Encouragement pour l'Amélioration des Races de Chevaux en France. Offered a price so minimal that he couldn't believe he was hearing properly, M. Boussac refused Dr. Pulte with, perhaps, a hint of scorn, whereupon the German officer seized the horse anyway and shipped him off to Germany. Boussac was so furious at the theft of his champion stallion that he adamantly declined to sign, as the stallion's owner, any certificates for foals sired in Germany. These foals are listed in the French Stud Book as sired by "X" and have no standing with relation to Pharis's "legitimate" (pre- and post-German) progeny. (Pharis was recovered by M. Boussac and returned to Normandy after the war.)

According to the most knowledgeable sources—including J. H. Ranson, author of *Who's Who in Horsedom*—Dr. Pulte appropriated with his subordinates two hundred and one French horses and shipped them off to Germany and Hungary during the occupation of France. Even today, more than twenty-seven years after the last German soldier had quit French soil, the name of Dr. Pulte still produces reddening faces and protruding veins among members of the French racing community.

Another German who "acquired" a considerable number of thoroughbreds during the occupation was Herr Christian Weber, president of the Munich racecourse and a close friend of *der Führer*. Weber, who announced that he was working for von Ribbentrop, expressed interest in buying some of the best of the Baron Édouard de Rothschild's stock, and—when informed that his choices were not for sale—he made a quick trip to Berlin and returned armed with a special order; almost at once the horses were put on a train to Munich.

Weber made a personal haul of 118 French thoroughbreds; in all, 664 representatives of prime French bloodstock were sent to Germany and Hungary during the years 1940–44. All were not stolen, notes Monsieur N. E. Marot (an anagram for M. Jean Romanet, *directeur-général* of the Société d'Encouragement today)—in a paper recording the desecration, written after the Liberation of France—but for the most part the consent of the owner was obtained under threat.

Thus, in 1939, just as French breeding had reached the top level vis-à-vis international competition, after a fresh start following the end of World War I, it received another major reverse. (In 1939, four hundred French products won races abroad, and French stallions and mares were in great demand—in fact were fought over—by breeders in all countries of the thoroughbred world.)

Understandably, with the onset of the war, the racing itself also suffered, but the fervor of the racing fraternity remained undiminished. Soon after Paris was occupied the Germans installed batteries of anti-aircraft guns at Longchamp, and one afternoon a formation of Allied planes appeared during a race meeting and bombed the hippodrome, killing several paying spectators and more outside the grounds. The track itself was not hit by any bombs, and the next race was run only slightly behind schedule. The possibility of a return of the bombers did not deter the bettors in the crowd from queueing up at the windows in totally exposed positions.

Nevertheless Longchamp was closed, over the protests of the racegoers, and its programs transferred to other tracks outside the capital. It remained closed until well after the Americans had taken Paris and had appropriated the hippodrome for their own military purposes. As the retreating Germans were driven farther and farther from Paris, the racing public clamored for the reopening of the "pearl" of French hippodromes. It remained for a U.S. liaison officer, Lieutenant (s.g.) Frank Vogel, of the U.S. Navy—attached to the Army—concerned with the state of the French people's morale, to convince his commanding officer, General Lord, to change his mind and agree to the resumption of racing at Longchamp.

Vogel, now one of about a dozen and a half American proprietors who race their charges in France, still receives the gratitude of the Société d'Encouragement and has taken his place in the racing milieu.

Driving through the Bois to Longchamp after an absence of three and a half years, I was reminded of the many agreeable days I had spent in thrall to French thoroughbred racing, a very special sport conducted in a magnificent manner. I had forgot how green the Bois is in October, and what subtle shades of green and yellow the leaves and grasses reflect in

204

the autumnal sun. One could picture the scene reproduced in a Cézanne or a Seurat, with precisely the same interplay of light and color.

The parents playing ball with their young in the open stretches of the park presented a vision that had a certain dreamlike quality; I was transported backward not merely four years in time but into a quite different world. Longchamp came into view just ahead, and as we drove between the site of the ancient *abbaye* on the right and—opposite—the landmark windmill (the Moulin de l'Abbaye de Longchamp) within the grounds of the hippodrome itself, I felt as though I had never really been away.

Going racing at Longchamp on an ordinary race day generates excitement enough, but this was a very special occasion, featuring the fiftieth running of the Prix de l'Arc de Triomphe, which in the last half-dozen years has come to be regarded by just about everyone as the most important horse race in the world. It is also the richest thoroughbred event, with a purse this time of 2,479,150 francs, or $450,755. (There is a quarter-horse race at Ruidoso Downs, New Mexico, each year with a slightly larger purse.)

In France, attendance figures are not announced, but estimates ranged from a conservative 60,000 to 100,000 persons who had come from all over France, and from England, Ireland, Sweden, Germany, Denmark, Italy, Japan, and the United States, among other places, to see this most respected contest.

The grand circle formed by the junction of four Bois *allées*, before the imposing iron-grille gates of Longchamp, was choked with cars—Rolls-Royces, Bentleys, and Mercedes-Benzes, as well as Volkswagens and Citroën Deux Chevaux. I have visited racecourses on four continents, but nowhere are the racegoers as atypical of race-track crowds as at Longchamp: they are well-dressed, orderly, soft-spoken—some titled persons, many businessmen, social and government leaders, plus a large number of merchants, shopkeepers, and weekday-working men and women, with only a sprinkling of those universal types who seem to spend most of their lives at race tracks, usually in the betting queues. Nor is the feeling of excitement quite as intense anywhere, in my experience, as at Longchamp on the day of the Arc.

Inside the hippodrome, one is greeted by a black life-sized bronze statue of Gladiateur, the French-bred champion (by Monarque out of Miss Gladiator) who won the Epsom Derby, Grand Prix de Paris, Two Thousand Guineas, and St. Leger in 1865, on his way to a memorable racing career. To the right is the extensive *enceinte privée*, a privileged sanctuary which includes an administration building, with its committee room, stewards' rooms, jockeys' dressing quarters, film projection room, a glass-enclosed weigh-in room, and an overhead glass corridor enabling the riders to reach the interior of the picturesque paddock without passing among the viewers circulating in the enclosure.

Six years ago, the "new" Longchamp was put on display; all the buildings save two still have the appearance of having been just completed, in a splendid modern, unpretentious style. In fact, the entire hippodrome has a crisp, shipshape look, with everything in place, all services (betting windows, cashiers, bars, restaurant, telephones, telegraph) readily available, and the grounds beautifully landscaped. The many blooms are supplemented along the sweep of walking space in the grandstand area by window boxes of geraniums, which match the reddish-pink uniforms of the solicitous hostesses who outdo the most dedicated air stewardesses in their attentiveness to the spectators' requests. Gray-and-white awnings shield the benches on the first deck, overlooking the paddock, which is itself set within an amphitheatre where—in the enclosure as well as outside in the grandstand area—racegoers have an unobstructed view, from several levels, of the horses circling the paddock and the owners and trainers discussing the coming event in the bower that is the interior of the large oval.

The escalator that connects the *enceinte privée* with various reserved sections on the first floor (above the ground level) and with the proprietors' boxes at the top of the four-story *tribunes* was already in use. (Through the glass at the back of the *tribunes,* proprietors who don't care to ride the elevators and escalators all afternoon have a good view, aided by their binoculars, of the paddock.) The fences on both sides of the approach to the escalator, separating the *enceinte* from the grandstand area, were already lined with those who were willing to take a chance on losing their places in the stands in order to have a close-up look at the Aga Khan IV, the Baron Guy de Rothschild, and the assorted counts and countesses, barons and baronesses who compose the upper stratum of Longchamp's population.

This would be the sixth Arc to be run at the "new" Longchamp: during 1965 the shining new stands were constructed some 200 meters from the old *tribunes,* and when the season had ended the old were demolished and the new rolled into position on a set of rails, in time for the opening of the spring season of 1966. The new stand gives a perfect view of the entire course from any part of its four tiers; the whole has a feeling of openness that did not exist before. Traditionalists who mourned the end of the charming old *tribunes* for a time soon came to appreciate the modern replacement with its conveniences—escalators, elevators, glass-enclosed areas, a full complement of bars and buffets, and a rooftop restaurant whose cuisine compares favorably with some of the capital's better middle-rank epicurean establishments. Inside the infield, a parking space for three thousand cars is accessible by a tunnel under the track.

The racing area spread out before the viewers in the *tribunes* stretches to a width of about a thousand meters and a depth, from the stands, of more than five hundred. Beyond the backstretch and the avenue adjoining it, one of the many wooded areas in the Bois provides a restful background for those following the field through their binoculars along the outer limits of the hippodrome.

The racing strips themselves, in various combinations, permit a variety of courses of assorted distances for what are euphemistically called flat-racing events. Perhaps the most notable feature of Longchamp is its long uphill backstretch; the principal course, the Grande Piste, starts to the spectator's far left, in one corner of the terrain, hard by the windmill, proceeds gradually but relentlessly up a formidable hill, with the horses passing out of the viewers' sight for a few moments behind a small stand of chestnut trees known as the *petit bois* (the *montée* covers 600 meters and in that span rises 9.36 meters), turns to the right at the far turn, and descends to the turn for home, again to the right, for the final two-and-a-half-furlong stretch run before the *pavillon* and the *tribunes* to the finish, a total distance of 2,400 meters (about a mile and a half). It takes a horse with both speed and staying power to succeed on the Grande Piste, the course on which the Arc de Triomphe is run.

As M. Pierre Arnoult, Inspecteur Général des Finances Honoraire, put it, in his paperbound accolade titled *Les Courses de Chevaux:* "*En définitive, il n'est pas exagéré de prétendre que la France possède maintenant le plus rationnel et le plus bel hippodrome du monde.*" ("Finally, it is no exaggeration to claim that France now possesses the most sensibly laid out and the most beautiful racing establishment in the world.")

Today, the old *pavillon* still stands along the homestretch, between the grandstand and the final turn into the stretch—eventually to be replaced by a new structure matching the style of the new *tribunes*. The Tribune

Présidentielle, a thin building perched on the finish line, and enveloped by the new stand, has been allowed to remain intact.

The 1971 running of the Arc, which promised to be one of the most strongly contested races in the series, was graced by the presence of the President of the Republic and Mme. Georges Pompidou, who arrived with suitable fanfare shortly before the main event and passed along a path through the crowd arranged for them by the colorfully outfitted Gardes Républicains, helmeted and plumed, to a rolling cascade of cheers. This was the first visit of the French *chef de l'état* since the rebuilt, refurbished Longchamp opened its gates.

The ceremonial arrival of President and Mme. Pompidou distracted attention from the running of the third race on the card, which ended just as they arrived. Dark Baby was posted as the winner of the race—the Critérium des Pouliches, for two-year-old fillies. I was one of a goodly part of the crowd who missed the race entirely.

As the horses strode onto the track for the *défilé* before the start of the main event on the card, a low murmur, just beginning, rose gradually in intensity, as though someone were gently tuning up the background sound, reaching a peak as the eighteen entrants burst out of the gates. From that point, it continued at a high volume until the head of the stretch, when it exploded into a crescendo, with a hundred thousand voices at full cry.

The race itself was run true to form. Ossian, a leader for Ramsin, both from the stables of the Baron Thierry de Zuylen de Nyevelt, moved smartly to the front and set a fast pace. Mill Reef, the favorite, an English-trained U.S.-bred colt (by Never Bend out of Milan Mill), owned by American Paul Mellon, was tucked neatly into fifth position up the famous hill in the backstretch. At the bottom of the *descente*, Hallez, a four-year-old bay owned by Mme. Guy Weisweiller and ridden by Lester Piggott, moved briefly into the lead, with Mill Reef along the rail ready to make his move if an opening presented itself. To the accompaniment of a strong surge in the volume of sound, Mill Reef shot through along the rail and at the head of the stretch had a slight lead over Hallez, the three-year-old filly Pistol Packer, and four-year-old Caro. With an acceleration reminiscent of Sea Bird, the 1965 Arc winner whom some call the greatest runner of modern times, Mill Reef increased his advantage, finishing a good three lengths ahead of Pistol Packer at the *poteau,* with Cambrizzia, another filly, a length and a half farther back in third place.

The crowd roared its approval of the well-earned victory—in the record time for the event of 2 minutes 28³⁄₁₀ths seconds. The horsemen in the audience were equally pleased with the confirmation of Mill Reef's merits as a classic runner.

The victory brought Mr. Mellon 1,399,150 francs ($254,391); second place was worth 480,000 francs ($87,273) to French trainer Alec Head, who had bought Pistol Packer for his wife at the Saratoga yearling sales for $14,000. Both M. and Mme. Head were well satisfied with the place. In all, with her Arc winnings, Pistol Packer has collected more than half a million dollars in her nine starts on French tracks, never finishing out of the first three, in her first two years at the races. In her two-year-old year (1970), she began competing late in the season, in two modest events, scoring one victory and one second place. In 1971, as a three-year-old, she registered five winning efforts in seven stakes races, with one second-place and one third-place finish.

It was a memorable day for Americans in the audience—with the first victory ever in the Arc by a U.S.-bred horse, and with the first two to finish bringing added prestige to U.S. East Coast breeding. (Mill Reef was born in Virginia, Pistol Packer in Pennsylvania.)

Later in the month, over an excellent dinner with Alec and Ghislaine Head at their Villa Vimy in Chantilly, the conversation turned to Longchamp. "Yes, it is a difficult course," he said. "For a horse to win at Longchamp, in races from a mile and a half up, he must be well bred, well trained, and in top form.

"Longchamp has often been compared with Epsom," he added. "But at Epsom the run to the finish is downhill, and a good mile-and-a-quarter horse has a chance to win a mile-and-a-half race there. But that's not the case at Longchamp." (At Epsom, the very last sixteenth is uphill.)

Both Longchamp and Auteuil, the two hippodromes in the Bois, were designed to provide the stiffest but also the fairest tests possible for thoroughbreds at various stages of their development. Auteuil, with its twenty-eight obstacles, including high rail fences, stone walls, hedges, and water jumps, sometimes combined, is considered the toughest steeplechase course in the world—even surpassing Aintree, the site of the Grand National at Liverpool, England.

At Longchamp, the spring three-year-old season is capped by the Grand Prix de Paris, on the last Sunday of June, at 3,100 meters (just under two miles). In the fall, after the Arc, the most demanding test of endurance for older horses is the Prix Gladiateur, at 4,800 meters (three miles). It was once run at 6,200 meters (one furlong short of four miles). (In the United States, by comparison, a mile-and-a-half race—2,400 meters—is considered a distance event.)

The 1971 Gladiateur, on the penultimate of Longchamp's thirty-five days of racing, attracted a field of ten stayers, including a representative from England and one from Ireland. Coming into the stretch, the second time around the long course, it looked as though the 1970 winner, Faux Monnayeur, might repeat, but Barado, a chesty four-year-old bay who had been bred in France by the Société d'Élevage et d'Exploitation Agricoles, came on strong to win by a length and a half. The course, which called for the field to race up the long incline on the backstretch twice, was run in 5 minutes 28½ seconds by Barado, whose sire, the Italian Molvedo, scored a memorable victory on the same track in the 1961 Arc, in a race just half as long.

The respected position that French thoroughbreds have achieved in the international world of racing is due partly to selective French breeding (the French Derby and sometimes the Arc are won, some say, on the rolling fields of Normandy), partly to French training methods—not forgetting the admirable facilities provided for that training at Chantilly. But not least of the reasons is the experience gained by two-year-olds, in their first months at the races, on the challenging *pistes* of Longchamp. Many an international champion developed a canny feel for racing in its early appearances there.

"It's a true test for a thoroughbred," said Jean Romanet, *directeur-général* of the Société d'Encouragement, as we looked out over the elongated teardrop-shaped course at the end of the day. The late-afternoon sun cast long shadows across the track, and Romanet checked with his assistants to make certain that all would be made secure.

Of the new structures, he said: "We wanted to make it a comfortable place—comfortable for the horse, as in England, and comfortable for people, as in the United States." He smiled engagingly.

On the main *piste,* before the *tribunes,* a workman walked over to the rail and lowered the wooden arm topped by a red circle that marks—for the oncoming jockeys—the *poteau.*

"The Société purposely chose this difficult terrain, more than a century ago," he said as we walked beneath the *tribunes.* "At Bagatelle, for example, the ground is perfectly flat. Uninteresting . . . This course was created as a test."

210

The almost unbelievably beautiful Parisian autumn was finally turning chilly as November approached. The horses were walking back to the barns adjoining the paddock for the last time in 1971.

As we prepared to leave, Romanet concluded, a note of pride in his voice, "A winner at Longchamp must be a first-class horse." That conviction is confirmed about two hundred fifty times each year.

# And on the Seventh Day, They Play the Tiercé

---

*The tiercé, in its simplest form, calls for the selection of the first three horses to finish in a specified race. There are 6,840 possible combinations, if the field includes twenty horses, and the Sunday morning habitués of the PMU cafés usually play them all.*

---

The pattern of life on a Sunday in France was, they say, laid down—like everything else in this country—by Napoleon, who worked out the modern French legal, judicial, educational, financial, and social structures during time left over from plotting his grand strategy for the conquest of Europe and the world. (In spite of much talk of educational reforms, the students at the French *lycées* still learn by rote; their lessons are crammed into them in much the same manner as the forced feeding of the Strasbourg geese.)

But the traditional Gallic Sunday—morning Mass, elaborate picnic lunch in the country or a grand repast at an inn, a little football with the *gosses* —all that came to an end as a way of life in 1954, when a perspicacious citizen of the Republic named André Carrus introduced an idea that was to prove irresistibly fascinating to six million Frenchmen. Each Sunday morning, on fifteen holidays, and on about a dozen ordinary working days during the year, Frenchmen of all persuasions sit shoulder to shoulder in some 5,000 cafés bearing the designation PMU (Pari-Mutuel Urbain) throughout the nation, hard at work on their solution to that particular day's puzzle.

The *tiercé,* in its simplest form, calls for the selection of the first three horses to finish in a specified race, usually at one of the Paris tracks. For three francs (about sixty cents) one has a chance at a return as high as $70,000, depending, of course, on the winning combination. Even if the three horses picked finish in a different order, but are still the first three, the bettor still wins—usually about one fifth or one sixth of the amount for the correct order.

The French love to make things complicated, and there are seemingly endless variations on playing the *tiercé*. The six million *citoyens* who participate in the Sunday morning ritual each week at their local PMU cafés are equipped with their own book of tickets (ten for twenty centimes) and their own *pince*, a small clipping instrument the size of a miniature nail scissors. Over an apéritif or two, the form sheets must be studied; every detail of the horses' past performances and workouts is considered in scrupulous detail, as well as the digestion and state of mind of the jockeys, and even the position of the stars. Finally the selection is made: a *joueur* with more money to spend may pick four horses (for twelve francs), five (thirty francs), six (sixty francs), seven (105 francs), and so on; he may even pick every horse in the field, which ranges from eleven to more than thirty, but of course in almost all cases he wouldn't win in that situation.

If the first three finishers are included in his list in order (even if not necessarily consecutively), he wins the top award; if out of order (and not necessarily consecutively) the lesser amount. Thus, if our Sunday *tiercé* player chooses, let us say, horses numbered 4, 17, 12, and 3 in that order (for twelve francs) and the actual order of finish is 4, 12, and 3, our man wins in order.

But that, says Pierre Carrus, son of the originator of the *tiercé* and currently the general manager of the PMU, which handles all offtrack betting in France, is the *combinaison simplifié* (CS). "The specialists tend to play the *combinaison complète* (CC), which requires them to bet six times the CS amount; in return they will win—if they have the first three horses— once in order and five times in *désordre*."

The aficionado may also pick two horses and have all the remaining horses in the field for the third horse—for a stiff price: fifty-four francs if it is a field of twenty horses.

There are 6,840 possible combinations, if the field includes twenty horses, and the Sunday morning habitués of the PMU cafés usually play them all. Each *tiercé* day some 70,000,000 francs ($14,000,000) is bet on the *tiercé* alone, not including other bets.

"My father never imagined how successful his idea would become," Pierre Carrus recalls thoughtfully. "We had had quite a bit of interest in the *couplé*, a bet on two horses, so he thought to increase the payoff one must complicate the problem.

"The Frenchman is attracted to the *tiercé* because it's not just a game of chance like the *loterie*: his judgment comes into play. When he wins the *tiercé*, he proudly shows his ticket to all his friends before cashing it."

The system of sorting out the tickets—an ingenious one involving the use of knitting needles, which hold up the tickets punched with the wrong combinations and allow the winners to drop—makes it possible to announce the exact amounts of the winning payoffs, in order and out of order, by eight o'clock on the evening of the race, run at about four-thirty that afternoon. Of the total pot, the winners share 68 percent; 8.5 percent goes to the race tracks, which support the PMU, a nonprofit-making operation employing 2,500 workers; and the French government collects 23.5 percent. (The cafés, which pay their own *tiercé* ticket takers and cashiers, take—off the top—one percent of the amount bet at their establishments.)

On a certain Thursday during the reign of the late President Charles de Gaulle, one surprised customer at a PMU bar asked what was the reason for a *tiercé* on a midweek business day. "This is the one," he was told, that pays for General de Gaulle's state visit to South America."

In sum, M. Carrus's game has kept the French occupied, amused, and reasonably content with their lot in life, and sometimes rewarded for their Sunday morning labors; brought an average of 17,000,000 francs ($3,400,000) into the government's coffers seventy-eight times a year; helped make French horse racing the best-regulated sport of its kind in the most stunning surroundings anywhere in the world; brought the café owner a considerable increase in his Sunday morning bar business; and, finally, brought home to all the fact that a majority of six million Frenchmen can indeed be wrong.

# Index

72 73 74 75 10 9 8 7 6 5 4 3 2 1